William Howard Taft

The Travails of a Progressive Conservative

In this new biographical study of the only American ever to have been both president and chief justice of the United States, Jonathan Lurie reassesses William Howard Taft's multiple careers, which culminated in Taft's election to the presidency in 1908 as the chosen successor to Theodore Roosevelt. By 1912, however, the relationship between Taft and Roosevelt had ruptured. Lurie reexamines the Taft–Roosevelt friendship and concludes that it rested on flimsy ground. He also places Taft in a progressive context, taking Taft's own self-description as "a believer in progressive conservatism" as the starting point. At the end of his biography, Lurie concludes that this label is accurate when applied to Taft.

A professor of history emeritus and now Academic Integrity Facilitator at Rutgers University, Newark, Jonathan Lurie has been a member of the Rutgers history department since 1969. His books include *The Chicago Board of Trade*, *Law and the Nation*, *Arming Military Justice*, *Pursuing Military Justice*, *The Slaughterhouse Cases* (co-authored with Ronald Labbe), *Military Justice in America*, and *The Chase Court*. Lurie's fields of interest include legal history, military justice, constitutional law and history, and the eras of the Civil War and Reconstruction. The book on the Slaughterhouse cases received the Scribes award in 2003 as the best book written on law for that year. Lurie served as a Fulbright Lecturer at Uppsala University Law School in Sweden in 2005, was the Visiting Professor of Law at West Point in 1994–1995, and has lectured on several occasions at the United States Supreme Court.

William Howard Taft

The Travails of a Progressive Conservative

JONATHAN LURIE

Rutgers University, Newark

CAMBRIDGE UNIVERSITY PRESS
Cambridge, New York, Melbourne, Madrid, Cape Town,
Singapore, São Paulo, Delhi, Mexico City

Cambridge University Press
32 Avenue of the Americas, New York, NY 10013-2473, USA

www.cambridge.org
Information on this title: www.cambridge.org/9780521514217

First published 2012
Reprinted 2012 (twice)

A catalog record for this publication is available from the British Library.

Library of Congress Cataloging in Publication Data

Lurie, Jonathan, 1939–
    William Howard Taft: the travails of a progressive conservative / Jonathan Lurie.
        p.   cm.
    Includes bibliographical references and index.
    ISBN 978-0-521-51421-7 (hardback)
    1. Taft, William H. (William Howard), 1857–1930. 2. Taft,
    William H. (William Howard), 1857–1930 – Political and social views.
    3. United States – Politics and government – 1909–1913. 4. United States –
    Politics and government – 1865–1933. 5. Roosevelt, Theodore, 1858–1919.
    6. Presidents – United States – Biography.   I. Title.
    E762.L87   2011
    973.91´2092–dc22   2011007926

ISBN 978-0-521-51421-7 Hardback

As always, for Mac and our Family:
David and Hikari, Debbie and Jason
Dan and Katherine and our five grandchildren

"The defeat is by no means altogether disappointing, and I hope for a different verdict when history is written."

W. H. Taft, November 9, 1912

"The longer I live, the more certain I am that history is greatly helped by correspondence."

W. H. Taft, November 29, 1924

"...when one looks back upon the record and weighs it as a whole, one is brought to the conclusion that [Taft] was a President both with constructive ideas and with some real liberality of outlook...."

Rochester Times-Union, March 10, 1930

"The law was his mistress, and he adored her."

John Welsh, March 11, 1930

Contents

Illustrations

Preface

The idea for this book came as I studied a letter from William Howard Taft decrying Woodrow Wilson's nomination of Louis Brandeis to the High Court in 1916. In the letter, Taft described himself as "a believer in progressive conservatism."[1]

The term intrigued me because I had never seen Taft categorized in such a manner, least of all by himself. What did he mean? Was not "progressive conservatism" a contradiction in terms? During the several years in which I researched and wrote these chapters, it became clear to me that Taft's career confirmed the accuracy of his description, and if there is one theme that ties my chapters together, it is the way in which this contention can be demonstrated.

In this book, then, I reexamine the commonly accepted view of William Howard Taft as a hide-bound traditionalist. It might be noted that in 1916, *after* his internecine battle with his former best friend, Theodore Roosevelt, and *after* he had left the presidency – greatly relieved even as he was grievously repudiated – he described himself as noted in the opening paragraph of this Preface. The following chapters examine the relevance of such a description for a number of experiences in Taft's life and career. It is obvious that Taft did not see himself as we do today. Why is this the case?

The usual assessment of Taft is that he was a one-term loser; a conservative of narrow viewpoint; a chief executive lacking initiative, leadership, and popular appeal. It would seem that such a description invariably results when we compare Taft with both his immediate predecessor, Theodore Roosevelt, and his immediate successor, Woodrow Wilson. His era seems frozen in time on one side by the dynamism of TR, hunting, fighting, expounding, and exploring, and on the other side by the eloquence and moral imperatives (sometimes accompanied by effective leadership) of Wilson. In between them is William Howard Taft.

[1] William Howard Taft to Gustave Karger, January 31, 1916, Taft–Karger Correspondence, Mss qT1241k, Box 1, Folder 30, Cincinnati Museum Center.

But when one explores and evaluates Taft's career on its own, eschewing comparisons at least to some extent, a different picture emerges. His record as president is complex and varied to be sure, yet one that should discourage the use of negative adjectives that merely oversimplify. Indeed, it may be quite reasonable to view Taft as he saw himself. I propose to do just that here, and in so doing, we may be able to restore some historical relevance toward understanding our past, and in particular the Progressive Era. If ever a historical portrait needed a variety of colors, shadings, and conclusions to give it relevance, it would be one of William Howard Taft.

In the first two decades of the twentieth century, three Americans occupied the White House: Theodore Roosevelt, William Howard Taft, and Woodrow Wilson. Each of them had been brought up in an environment of material comfort, if not wealth, and paternal affection. Each had attended Ivy League schools: Harvard, Yale, and Princeton, respectively. All three went on to law school, but Roosevelt never finished, and Wilson abandoned the law early in his career, opting instead to attend graduate school. Indeed, both Roosevelt and Wilson willingly embraced politics over careers in law and academe. In contrast, as either an administrator or a jurist, Taft lived happily within the law, loved its constraints and sense of order, and relinquished it with deep regret to enter what he regarded a maelstrom of politics. To him, this represented an alien world. Finding total fulfillment as a judge, content as an administrator, and willing to serve as a competent and devoted subordinate to one he respected and admired, Taft had no interest or aptitude for politics, and characteristically, as will be seen, conceded that fact.

These three contemporaries were born in consecutive years – 1856, 1857, and 1858 – and their careers intersected at various times throughout their lives with a fascinating mixture of hubris, envy, affection, respect, regret, and even bitter hatred. Each left lasting imprints on his country – Roosevelt as a dynamic president; Taft as both an innovator in executive administration, and possibly more as chief justice of the United States than as president (he remains the *only* American in history to have been both president and chief justice); Wilson, the college president (he remains the *only* president with an earned Ph.D.) as a reform governor, progressive president, and ultimate architect of the dual tragedies concerning education reform at Princeton and American participation in the League of Nations. Interest in Roosevelt and Wilson, long regarded by historians as two of our more distinguished presidents, has eclipsed that in Taft. Indeed, these two remain the subjects of a vast and ongoing body of scholarship.

Objective analysis and evaluation of Taft's career, however, have not been as frequent. Serving only a single term, sandwiched between Roosevelt and Wilson, Taft has invariably been dismissed as the stale filling separating two fresh and energetic chief executives. An example is the comment of Mark Carnes, who wrote that "Taft will never be regarded as a great president or even a good one, but perhaps some day his obesity may cease to be his legacy."[2] Such an assessment, while understandable, is both unwarranted and lacking in historical perception. Unfortunately, in the wake of a generation of progressive historiography, it has been the norm. Perhaps, however, a different view of Taft is emerging. See, for example, two recent books.[3]

Seen in the context of his adult life, which began at the height of the Gilded Age and ended on the eve of the New Deal, Taft's years included the American triumphs and tensions of industrial expansion; imperialism; cycles of growth and recession; the conflicts out of which emerged the Progressive Era; American involvement in World War I; currents of legal reform; and expansion of the modern administrative state. Sometimes as a participant, sometimes as a critic, always as an observer, Taft lived through it all. The scope of his numerous "careers" remains remarkable: trial judge, solicitor general, circuit judge, president of the Philippine Commission, secretary of war, president of the United States, professor of law at Yale (he disclaimed interest in the presidency of the university), and chief justice of the United States. Many of the issues that interested Taft continue to trouble us today, and a study of how he conceived and confronted some of them can be of value as we continue to do the same.

There is another reason why Taft as president warrants attention. In large measure, he owed his presidency to TR. No other Chief Executive labored so much in the shadow of his predecessor as did Taft, and no president has ever been the subject of such strenuous efforts by his predecessor to reclaim his office. Indeed, Taft is unique in this regard, and American history can furnish no similar examples. It is true that some presidents have cast large shadows over their successors. Andrew Jackson and Martin Van Buren immediately come to mind. But Jackson retired to Tennessee, and unlike Taft, Van Buren was a masterful politician.

Harry Truman succeeded to the presidency barely three months into Franklin Roosevelt's fourth term. Yet, in 1945, there was little left of FDR's influence in Congress, and Truman was very much at home in domestic politics. For Taft, the image of TR – whether away hunting big game in Africa or welcoming Republican malcontents to his home in Oyster Bay, New York – was a constant, looming presence in his presidency from beginning to end. By 1911, the presence seemed to portend travail and conflict.[4]

---

[2] James McPherson, ed., *To the Best of My Ability* (New York: DK Publishing Co., 2004), 194.

[3] Morton Keller's analysis of political history, *America's Three Regimes* (New York: Oxford University Press, 2007), 182. "Taft in his way was a Progressive president, surpassing TR in antitrust suits and subscribing to an administrative more than political model of the presidency." I agree more with Keller than with Carnes. See also Lewis Gould, *The William Howard Taft Presidency* (Lawrence: University Press of Kansas, 2009), xiii. "...Taft was a competent chief executive who...had kept the nation out of war, presided over a prosperous economy, and observed the constitutional limits of his office."

[4] One interested observer of Taft's administration was young Felix Frankfurter, working as an assistant to Henry Stimson, Taft's secretary of war. Writing in 1911 that an acquaintance had called Taft "the Van Buren of his party," Frankfurter found this "a most memorable comparison." "Like Van Buren he was the choice and nominee of his predecessor and hardly any man can

Widely admired in his day for his integrity and strong sense of morality, Taft seems to have set a standard for personal conduct that later presidents have had, to put it mildly, some difficulty in attaining. It is all the more surprising therefore, that in our era, wherein conservative and conservatism are now considered common concepts widely used, Taft is a neglected figure. Somehow, the "progressive conservatism" of his day no longer resonates with conservatives in our time. Perhaps this is because what was called conservatism in 1910 might not be so labeled in 2012. In these chapters, I explain why this might be so. Yet I do not try to rejuvenate as much as to reconsider certain aspects of Taft's career. Though not intended as a vindication, in several instances this is a revisionist study.

First, I reexamine the relationship between Taft and Theodore Roosevelt with some care, and I shed fresh light on the rupture between them, so significant after 1910. I look anew at this relationship, which started in the late 1880s, and argue that while it was an association built on real respect and friendship, it was always replete with viable and palpable family tensions. Further, contrary to more traditional accounts, it posits that this break was inevitable, with the seeds of conflict and misunderstanding sown during Roosevelt's second term in office, well before Taft occupied the White House. Traditional accounts place the origins of the rupture somewhere in the first half of Taft's term as Chief Executive. Understanding how Taft worked with TR between 1901 and 1909 makes it easier to comprehend the collapse of the relationship after 1910. Further, in this study I explain the subtle but still fundamental incompatibility between the two friends as politicians, observers, and in Taft's case, a loyal subordinate.[5] At bottom, the two were so different in outlook that each failed to see it in the other until it was too late. Similarities in viewpoint abounded between 1904 and 1911, but there is, as both men would discover, a big difference between loyal implementation and execution of policy as a cabinet member, and the articulation of proposals as a Chief Executive.

Second, I view Taft both in his presidential years and thereafter as separate from Roosevelt, whom he followed, and Wilson, who defeated Taft for reelection four years later. Invariably, in any comparison between the dynamic, ebullient, politically astute TR and the phlegmatic, deliberative, methodical, judicious Taft, the latter suffers because of the nature of the comparison. Especially when compared with earlier presidents such as McKinley or Cleveland, Roosevelt is regarded as our first "progressive" president. And, in fact, he made effective use of a "bully pulpit" as had no other president before him. But progressivism remains a difficult topic to understand, a movement

---

satisfy such a role – on the one hand either avoid slavish devotion and thus loss of self- respect[,] or condemnation through departure from his predecessor's policy." Joseph P. Lash, *From the Diaries of Felix Frankfurter* (New York: W. W. Norton & Co., 1975), 104–105.

[5] It might be noted that one reason why the TR–Taft friendship ruptured was that it had never been as deep as both men liked to claim. When, in 1912, the break between Taft and TR became open and bitter, Taft stated almost in tears that "Roosevelt was my closest friend." In reality, such had never been the case. Nostalgia colored Taft's recollection.

replete with contradictions and inconsistencies. While no single definition of it has emerged, certain key progressive values in vogue by Taft's election in 1908 can be identified:

1. Belief in the continuing relevance of the public interest, as well as the necessity for and the legitimacy of increased governmental activity beyond traditional laissez-faire limitations.
2. Rethinking and reducing the protective tariff.
3. Expanding the size and strength of federal antitrust litigation.
4. Emphasis on efficiency and modernization concerning the growth of the federal establishment.
5. Concern with issues of conservation.

By every standard measure of progressive regulation, Taft appears to have exceeded the record set by his predecessors. Indeed, in terms of the traditional measures of progressive reform just noted, Taft topped the accomplishments of Roosevelt. Thus the question arises as to why Taft, whose progressive record is clear, is dismissed as one whose participation in progressivism supposedly reflected failure rather than success. Why, in other words, when twentieth-century historiography has been dominated by muckraking and the progressive tradition, is one of the seemingly progressive presidents ignored as irrelevant? The answer may lie in our historical disinclination to consider the relevance of Taft's "progressive conservatism" for his career.

Finally, although intended neither as a new biography nor as a detailed study of Taft's presidency, this book reexamines certain events in his tenure that can explain his self-description, emphasized earlier. I will argue that Taft brought administrative expertise to the position, sorely lacking in his predecessors. Like other progressives, he respected expertise, especially when it came from the university, and more than any other Chief Executive before him, Taft modernized the presidency. But at a time when the Republican Party was split in an internecine struggle that, as it turned out, neither Roosevelt nor Taft was capable of solving, his efforts were unappreciated and, depending on one's viewpoint, unwelcome. In politics, timing is essential, and it may well be that Taft was at the wrong place in the wrong time. Certainly he never sought the office he won, nor did he find fulfillment in it, as had Roosevelt. The reasons for these facts may explain how not only the public but also Taft himself perceived his presidency.

The leading biography of Taft is that by Henry Pringle, published in 1939, and authorized by Taft's heirs. Pringle's book was the first based on virtually unrestricted access to Taft's papers. His two volumes reveal a subtle bias against Taft, which did not go unnoticed by his children. An unabashed supporter of Franklin Roosevelt's, Pringle wrote and researched his study between 1933 and 1939, and thus he observed the remnants of Taft's Supreme Court in action against the New Deal. He had no difficulty in labeling Taft as a militant conservative, one who died before the New Deal came to life.

In many essentials, Pringle's volumes remain the starting point for assessing and understanding Taft. It is in this sense that they have been used here. In addition to Pringle's copied excerpts from the Taft Papers, a number of manuscript sources – some not available to him – have been very significant for this book. Most important is the Morison and Blum edition of the Roosevelt Letters, which contains a great many excerpts from TR to Taft. Further, they include many significant references to Taft, especially after 1910. The letters to Taft reveal Roosevelt as a young, nervous office-seeker; Roosevelt as a frustrated governor and vice president, convinced that there is little in the future for him; Roosevelt suddenly catapulted into the presidency as the youngest chief executive thus far in our history; and Roosevelt's offering Taft appointments, encouragement, fulsome praise, and advice (sometimes critical), as well as numerous instructions. After 1910, TR's letters about Taft reflect regret, disdain, and increasing contempt.

I have consulted the correspondence between Taft and his three children, as well as the large number of letters from and about Taft in the Mabel Boardman Papers. Boardman, an old Taft family friend, remained an important member of the Republican establishment in Washington throughout the Roosevelt and Taft eras. I have also examined a series of extremely candid letters between a newspaper correspondent, Gustave Karger, whom Taft had hoped would write his "authorized" biography, and the former president. Finally, I have looked anew at various papers of Taft's contemporaries.

These sources, as well as several recent analyses of Taft that have been published since Pringle's day, make it possible to reconsider Taft's career. My chapters freely draw on his own observations and insights, faulty though some turned out to be. But they do not form a biography of the man as much as they seek to explore the reasons for his successes as well as his failures. Taft was often candid, sometimes too candid – and this coming from a very prolific correspondent. Frequently I have let Taft speak for himself, and if these chapters tend in some measure to be critical of him, nevertheless I have acquired a lasting sense of sympathy for his failures – all the more so as they seem to have eclipsed his real accomplishments. In spite of them, a sense of hubris hangs over his single term. Because the presidency is a political institution, and our greatest presidents have understood this, sound political instincts are the sine qua non for success in the office. Taft totally lacked such instincts, having succeeded so well as an administrator or jurist precisely because in these fields – to a great extent – they were unnecessary. In reality, however, the cards were stacked against him well before he occupied the White House. One suspects that he may have sensed this truth, and these chapters seek to explain why this is so.

ACKNOWLEDGMENTS

I wish to acknowledge, first, the kindness of Melvin Urofsky, who from the early origins of this study provided counsel, criticism, and encouragement. He read every chapter, some more than once, and while he may still disagree with a few of my conclusions, I know the book is much improved because of his efforts. Professor Lewis Gould, the most distinguished expert on the Taft era, kindly permitted me to read two of his manuscripts prior to publication. Yale Law School Dean Robert Post, himself at work on what will be the definitive study of the Taft Court, visited with me in the early stages of my research. Jeff Flannery and Gerard Gawalt, both of the Library of Congress Manuscripts Division, went out of their way – as they do so often for so many researchers – to assist me, and Dr. Gawalt alerted me to the small trove of letters from Taft to his daughter Helen.

Cameron J. Wood, History Curator of the Ohio Historical Society, kindly sent me some important material on the Superior Court of Ohio. Lewis J. Paper permitted me to examine his papers, housed in the Special Collections Department at Harvard Law School. In its original form, my study was intended as a volume in the Library of American Biography Series, but when it had expanded in scope far beyond the appropriate length for such a book, General Editor Michael Boezi generously released me from my contractual obligations so that I could work with Lew Bateman, Senior Political Science and History Editor at Cambridge University Press.

In addition to Lew Bateman, who gave me consistent encouragement throughout the project, others at Cambridge have been more than helpful. I am very grateful to Anne Lovering Rounds and Marc Anderson for their guidance concerning illustrations and permissions. A special word of acknowledgment goes to Ronald Cohen, a superb editor whose counsel and suggestions have helped me construct the book I hoped I could write.

I am especially indebted to Harvard University Press for its kindness concerning citations from the Roosevelt Letters. All excerpts cited and quoted therefrom are reprinted by permission of the Press from *The Letters of Theodore Roosevelt*; Volumes II–VIII, selected and edited by Elting E. Morison, Cambridge, MA: Harvard University Press, copyright 1951, 1952, 1954 by the President and Fellows of Harvard College, copyright renewed 1979, 1980, 1982 by Elting Elmore Morison. I am grateful to Christine Engels, Archives Manager of the Cincinnati Museum Center, for permitting me to examine, cite, and quote from the Taft–Karger Correspondence, as well as from multiple copies of Taft's letters to his wife. I would also like to thank The H. F. Woods Camp Trustees and HarpWeek LLC for kindly granting me permission to use the following material: H. F. Woods Camp Trustees for Figures 2 and 3 and HarpWeek LLC for Figures 4, 5, and 8.

While my deep gratitude goes to all these individuals, all responsibility for any remaining errors is mine. Finally, a special word of affectionate gratitude must be said to Mac, who for forty-two years has read, critiqued, and improved every piece I have produced. Her constructive influence can be seen on every page of this book.

PART ONE

THE ROAD TO THE PRESIDENCY

I

The Early Years, 1857–1887

Chartered as a village in 1802 and incorporated as a city in 1819, Cincinnati by 1843 had become a typical Midwestern urban center. Already the city featured macadamized roads, a canal and railroad system, and a bustling waterfront replete with daily arrivals of cargo and passengers. In mid-century, it was home to meat packers, brewers, dry goods merchants, book sellers, printers and publishers, physicians, and above all, lawyers, who easily outnumbered all the other occupations. Names such as Wurlitzer, Proctor, and Gamble attested to the city's success as a magnet for new commercial enterprise, while, increasingly, well-known politicians such as Salmon P. Chase affirmed its relevance as a community replete with significant discussions/meetings on national political issues such as the tariff, internal improvements, temperance, abolition, and the looming threat of civil war. By the 1870s, its population had reached more than 200,000.[1] Numerous houses of worship dotted the greater Cincinnati area, and the city even boasted of a growing line of suburbs that had sprung up among the seven hills that surrounded the downtown area.[2]

One of these suburbs was known as Mt. Auburn, where late in 1853 a young lawyer and widower, Alphonso Taft, resided. His first wife had died in 1852, leaving him with two young sons. Barely eighteen months later, Taft remarried. The resulting family included five more children, of whom four survived. The oldest son, William Howard Taft, was born in 1857. Throughout their lives, the five Taft brothers – Peter and Charles (from their father's first marriage), William, Henry, and Horace – formed with their wives the nucleus of a surprisingly close family network. As will be seen, the influence of his family upon William (the subject of these chapters, and familiarly known as Will) should not be underestimated.

[1] Ishbel Ross, *An American Family: The Tafts, 1678 to 1964* (Cleveland: World Publishing Co., 1964), 8–9; hereafter cited as Ross.
[2] Henry F. Pringle, *The Life and Times of William Howard Taft*, 2 volumes (New York: Hoet, Rinehart and Winston, 1939), 6–7; hereafter cited as Pringle; Ross, 58–59.

The Taft boys grew up in a home that was comfortable, with financial means ample but not excessive. It revolved around Alphonso and Louisa Taft, who apparently were devoted but demanding parents. Louisa has been described as "enormously energetic, aggressively intellectual, and decidedly ambitious."[3] One of his sons later remembered Alphonso as a father with "a rare combination of strength, gentleness, simplicity and tolerance."[4] To these might be added the skills of an able attorney with what appears to have been a well-deserved reputation for honesty and integrity.

A graduate of Yale, Taft, like many of his generation, gravitated from the Whig party to the newly established Republicans. Indeed, he ran for Congress as a Republican in 1856 and, as will be seen, unsuccessfully sought the gubernatorial nomination in 1875 and again in 1879. Elected a trustee of both Yale and the University of Cincinnati, he also served on the Cincinnati city council. As the second administration of President Grant became mired in corruption, Grant turned to his fellow Ohioan, Alphonso Taft, and appointed him first as his secretary of war, and then as attorney general, a position he held for the last eight months of Grant's term.

Three characteristics of Taft's career should be noted. He graduated from Yale, studied law, and from 1854 until his death thirty-seven years later, consistently identified himself as a Republican. All the sons of Alphonso Taft followed the same road. All went to Yale, all studied law, and all considered themselves (with a few occasional and temporary exceptions) as Republicans, seeking with varying degrees of success to serve the public interest. In the late nineteenth century, political independence did not mean what it means today. Once party affiliation had been determined, one rarely changed it. One might criticize from within, participate in what sometimes could be very bitter factionalism, and even call for stringent reforms – but always as a member of the party. It is one of the many ironies associated with William Howard Taft's life and career that he would be involved in the greatest internal crisis of the Republican Party since its founding.

Until his death in 1891, the elder Taft watched his sons with a sense of patriarchal pride, attended with lasting expectations of excellence. In 1865, the Ohio legislature appointed him to the superior court, the same bench on which his son would sit at the start of his own judicial career. Four years later, possibly in tribute to his reputation for integrity, both Republicans and Democrats nominated Taft for a second term. He served until 1872. His most famous case concerned bible reading in the Cincinnati public schools, a controversy that for a short time attracted national attention.

---

[3] Judith Anderson, *William Howard Taft: An Intimate History* (New York: W. W. Norton & Co., 1981), 39.

[4] Ross, 51. Will Taft's wife, Helen (Nellie), described her father-in-law as "one of the most lovable men that ever lived because he had a wide tolerance and a strangely understanding sympathy for everybody." Carl Sferrazza Anthony, *Nellie Taft: The Unconventional First Lady of the Ragtime Era* (New York: William Morrow, 2005), 86.

Responding to the potential divisiveness of this issue within an environment of many different faiths, the school board in 1869 had barred any "religious instruction and the reading of religious books," including the Holy Bible. Its action received nationwide publicity and, not surprisingly, a case questioning the board's authority to enact such a ban soon reached the Ohio Superior Court. In 1870, by a vote of 2–1, that tribunal rejected the board's new regulations. The lone dissenter was Alphonso Taft. Because his actions were widely criticized in some quarters, and because his son William later received similar negative attention for *his* religious views, his father's dissent merits a brief discussion here.

Taft argued that far from having a constitutional right to mandate bible reading, the school board in reality was obligated to end the practice. In fact, it represented "an unconstitutional preference of one religion over another." Bible-reading from the King James version actually was an effort to enshrine Protestantism as the religion of the Cincinnati School District, something neither the court nor the school board had any authority to undertake. Further, Taft did not want his dissent equated with a plea for religious toleration. An inherent right was not to be equated with a generous offer of acceptance. Rather, he spoke of the "natural indefeasible rights of conscience which, in the language of the [Ohio] Constitution, are beyond the control or interference of any human authority."[5] In 1872, the Ohio Supreme Court unanimously reversed the lower Court's decision, and closely followed Taft's analysis.[6]

The negative fallout from Taft's dissent may well have killed his chances for statewide political office, even though he remained proud of it. Seeking the Republican nomination for governor in 1875 (he lost to Rutherford Hayes) and again in 1879, he was passed over each time, with his position in the Bible Reading Case cited as a key reason for his perceived "inelectability." Yet another drawback also applied to Alphonso. The elder Taft seemed to have "no driving ambition to rise in the political sphere."[7] With the exception of his brief cabinet stint for Grant, his failed attempts at statewide office in Ohio, and his ambassadorial services to Austria-Hungary and Russia from 1881 to 1885, he did not seek much beyond the law. As will be seen, this lack of interest in the warp and woof of politics was also noteworthy in William Howard Taft, who loved and lived in the law and had no desire to play the political game. This reluctance – perhaps revulsion is not too strong a word to describe it – would have major consequences later in his life. These consequences would be all the more important because of Alphonso's oft-stated conviction that "the parents' accomplishments were measured" not by their own deeds, but "largely by the honor and prosperity of their children."[8] Will

---

[5] Ross, 54. Taft noted that plaintiffs in the case "have a constitutional right to object to" bible reading "as a legal preference given by the state to the Protestant sects, which is forbidden by the Constitution."

[6] *Board of Education of the City of Cincinnati v. John D. Minor*, 23 Ohio St. 211, 240 (1872).

[7] Anderson, 41.

[8] Ibid.

Taft did not disappoint them, although his father occasionally pointed to a few missteps in his path toward this goal.

Thus the Taft boys matured, nurtured in a tranquil, loving atmosphere, but nourished by high expectation. Outwardly austere in manner, Alphonso to his family reflected "a gentleness and sweetness far more familiar to the children." When they were away, he found the house too quiet. "There is no noise and no mischief ... and on the whole it is not satisfactory to have no mischief about the house."[9] The boys all attended public school, and soon Will began to demonstrate some tendencies that would characterize his entire career.

An attractive young man, quite agile for one with a heavy build, Will Taft appears not to have possessed a particularly precocious mind. He compensated for this by an unusual "ability to concentrate," balanced by a tendency to procrastinate. On the other hand, if attracted to a topic or assignment, he worked at it with single-minded determination. For the most part, the result was excellent grades, earned by an extremely good-natured lad who "took few things, particularly his own gifts, very seriously."[10] In one class, his performance was less than outstanding, resulting in a statement from Alphonso that "mediocrity will not do for Will."[11]

These traits were reaffirmed when the thirteen-year-old Taft entered Woodward High School in 1870, located in the downtown area, more than a mile from his house. Thus he had a two-mile round-trip every school day, climaxed by a steep climb up the hill to the family home in Mt. Auburn. Again, Alphonso had chosen a public high school, even though by 1870, he could well have afforded a private school for his children had he so desired. According to one of Taft's biographers, Woodward High School "resembled a grim looking building ... with an iron fence suggestive of the Bastille."[12] Apparently, academic standards were high, and on one occasion the headmaster did not hesitate to dismiss 40 percent of a class when it did not measure up to his standards.

Taft enrolled in what today might be called college prep courses. As in elementary school, so also in high school, Will did very well, but not that well. One of his instructors told Alphonso Taft, who of course relayed the conversation to Will, that "you had the best head of any of my boys and if you [were] not too lazy you would have great success."[13] Judith Anderson notes that Will's parents "openly debated the question of [his] alleged laziness, since they felt that the high grades he earned" came as a "result of their prodding."[14] She further argues that from an early age, young Taft concluded that academic diligence and "exemplary behavior" would result in affection and approval from his family. Thus, she writes, "doing his duty became a special obligation,

[9] Pringle, 15.
[10] Pringle, 22–23.
[11] Ibid.
[12] Ross, 52.
[13] Pringle, 21.
[14] Anderson, 42.

and yet he often delayed," resulting in "guilt and, in turn, anxiety." Therefore he felt he had to "work doubly hard" in order to compensate "for his prior neglect."[15] Finally, Anderson posits that demanding parents tend to withhold fulsome praise from their children, resulting in an "over concern for accomplishment," frequently accompanied by a feeling of inadequacy and dissatisfaction with what has been accomplished.[16] She believes that this analysis accurately described the young Will Taft.

While not necessarily agreeing with all of Anderson's analysis, there is no doubt that throughout his career, as will be seen, Taft would downplay his successes and "belittle his own abilities," even predicting failure on his part.[17] Further, he apparently had a deep-seated need for external sources to continually urge him forward – roles taken first by his parents, then his brothers, and later by his wife, Helen, best known as Nellie. From an early age, Taft also demonstrated a healthy respect for what today might be called feminine rights. Before he graduated from high school, he wrote an essay extolling both coeducation and the suffrage for women. Coeducation, insisted Taft – soon to be a freshman at Yale – "shows clearly that there is no mental inferiority on the part of the girls...." Taft confidently predicted that "in the natural course of events, universal suffrage must prevail throughout the world."[18]

YALE AND LAW SCHOOL

All the Taft boys followed their father to Yale, which had changed somewhat from the days when Alphonso had been a student there in the early 1830s. Tuition had been $33 a year, and the students were required to attend religious services on a daily basis. Daily classes started at 6:00 A.M. How much Yale had changed or not changed by 1874 when Will arrived may be surmised from the comments of one biographer that Taft "found the chapel seats unduly hard, the sermons dull, and Livy difficult."[19] About chapel, he added in one letter to Alphonso, "the Fickle Goddess sleep wouldn't come worth a cent and I was doomed to listen to one of the driest sermons I ever heard." A week later, Will asked "why don't they try to make religion a little more attractive?"[20]

Handsome, heavy, already equipped with a jovial laugh that would in time become one of his most famous and endearing characteristics, Will – as a classmate later recalled – "stood high, but that was because he was a plodder and not because he was particularly bright." His academic credentials were very good, but his reputation for integrity was supreme. "He towered above us all as a moral force," and, consequently, was the most admired and respected

---

[15] Anderson, 43.

[16] Ibid., 46–47.

[17] He wrote to his father in 1874 that "You expect great things of me, but you mustn't be disappointed if I don't come up to your expectations." Pringle, 35.

[18] Pringle, 30.

[19] Ross, 60–61.

[20] Pringle, 40.

man ... in my class...."[21] As usual, Alphonso was less than impressed with Will's potential for popularity. "I doubt," he wrote to his two youngest sons, "that such popularity is consistent with high scholarship."[22] Medals Will received, and he served as the salutatorian for his class at commencement; but unlike his older brother Peter, Will failed to win the Woolsey [Yale amard] for the highest rank in the class. His parents had to settle for his standing second in a class of 132. They were disappointed, but young Taft probably thought it was just fine.

Of special interest was the senior oration he delivered in June 1878. Taft noted and faulted the evils currently afflicting the country. He commented on "political corruption, the growth of unsound radical thought," and above all "the too great centralization of government." As for the Republican Party – to which he would soon form a lifelong affiliation – in truth it "has lost its grip on the affections of people," largely because of the "irresponsible position of power to which [it] had been elevated" because of the Civil War. Finally, he predicted of his generation that it would be part of an age "when there are no political giants because of the absence of emergencies to create them."[23] Within only three decades, Will Taft would succeed his closest friend at the time to become president of the United States.

Meanwhile, the study of law beckoned Will, for Alphonso had already decided that such "is his destiny and he should be in it."[24] Although he did not know what his immediate future held in 1878, Will Taft in time would happily embrace a career in law and the judiciary. Indeed, he would yearn for nothing else. Other members of his family, however, had different goals for him. While bitterness and frustration were not to be absent from his career, in fact the most meaningful years of his life would begin and end with judicial appointment to a court.

The decision for Will Taft to undertake the study of law was easy. After all, he was Alphonso's son, and every one of the Taft boys had attended or would go to law school. Taft the elder had studied law at Yale, while two of Will's brothers selected Columbia. Yet Will chose to return to Cincinnati, and enrolled in its school of law in the fall of 1878. His choice was understandable and in some ways typical. His social life had always revolved around his home city rather than New Haven. Moreover, the choice of law school was not that important a matter in 1878. Legal education had not yet been captured by the full-time law school reforms of Christopher Langdell at Harvard Law School.[25] In 1878, it was still very easy to pass the bar and never attend law school at all.

[21] Pringle, 35.
[22] Ibid.
[23] Ibid., 44.
[24] Ibid., 32.
[25] An outstanding analysis of legal education and its transformation in the late nineteenth century is found in William P. LaPiana, *Logic and Experience: The Origin of Modern American Legal Education* (New York: Oxford University Press, 1994).

Compared with that of his undergraduate years at Yale, the pace for Will Taft dramatically lessened in intensity while he was at law school. His average class time was barely two hours a day. Even so, the young law student "disliked the drudgery of his courses."²⁶ He soon started part-time work as a legal reporter for a local newspaper, the Cincinnati *Commercial*, and began the actual process of "reading law" in his father's office. Under Alphonso's tutelage within a working office – as contrasted with the leisurely pace of the classroom downtown – Taft participated in a process that "has the effect of making me absorb some of the practical workings of the law."²⁷ But Alphonso, who apparently found the art of relaxation impossible to master, soon had several gripes with the recent Yale graduate.

Within the year, while Will was enjoying himself on some sort of summer trip, Alphonso reminded him that "you ought to be at home for the business you have to attend to." He followed this complaint with a longer exposition of what he expected from his son. Had he been at the office, Will might have "earned a nice little fee for yourself.... This gratifying your fondness for society is fruitless or nearly so. I like to have you enjoy yourself, so far as it can be consistent with your success in life...." Indeed, before the year ended, Alphonso informed the future president that "I do not think you have accomplished this past year as much as you ought with your opportunities. You must not feel that you have time enough to while away with every friend who comes."²⁸ Reflecting his underlying concern, Will's father reminded him that "our anxiety for your success is very great[,] and I know that there is but one way to attain it, & that is by self-denial and enthusiastic hard work in the profession."²⁹

During mid-1879, Will continued his desultory work as a reporter, even as he assisted Alphonso in a vain attempt to gain the Republican nomination for governor. The news job was easy, and it had a fringe benefit in that he visited the county and federal courts on a regular basis and had ample opportunity to become more familiar with their legal environments. By 1880, he was ready to take the Ohio bar exam, even though he had not yet finished law school. Henry Pringle, Taft's leading biographer, observed that while automatic bar admission was no longer the rule, "only obvious idiots or persons of demonstrable depravity" had cause for concern. Obviously Taft had none. Together with a group of law-school acquaintances, he spent the night before the exam drinking and singing songs about Yale. The entire group passed.³⁰

²⁶ Ross, 66.
²⁷ Pringle, 48.
²⁸ Ibid., 48–49.
²⁹ Ross, 67.
³⁰ Pringle, 52–53.

EARLY PATRONAGE FOR WILL

Yet the twenty-three-year-old lawyer still hesitated to start out on his own, even though Alphonso was headed to Europe as Minister, first to Austria-Hungary, then to Russia. Instead, he accepted an appointment as an assistant to the Cincinnati prosecutor, with whom he had become acquainted while making his reporter's rounds. He served for barely one year, and did a competent job. Will failed, however, to demonstrate any desire to tap public interest or concern or to use the public as an aid in his court cases. At such an early age, while he gained good experience in the courtroom, he declined to seek publicity, and disclaimed any interest in politics.

Taft later recalled to William Allen White that from 1882 to 1892, any political benefits he had received came from the confluence of two factors. "I got my political pull, first, through father's prominence, and second, through the fact that I was hail-fellow-well-met with all the political people...." Like "every well trained Ohio man I always had my plate the right side up when offices were falling."[31] Taft's description was especially apt in describing Ohio politics during 1881 and 1882. Congressman Benjamin Butterworth apparently called President Chester Arthur's attention to Will Taft as a "popular young man in Hamilton County, showing power and good spirit." Further, "Will Taft had no enemies."[32] Arthur, a veteran of the rough "stalwarts" school of politics, welcomed an opportunity to make a change in Ohio patronage even as he was about to appoint Will's father Minister to Austria-Hungary. In January 1882, President Arthur formally offered Will the post of collector of internal revenue in a federal district with headquarters in Cincinnati.

One should not be surprised to note that Alphonso, reflecting once again a candid honesty uncommon in Gilded Age politics, if not in our own, did not welcome news of Will's selection. He was too young, believed his father. And how, with his own ambassadorial appointment imminent, could his son's new post be seen as anything but "favoritism?" Indeed, Alphonso went so far as to point out that in his judgment, Arthur's action would not constitute "a sound political appointment."[33] Further, Ohio Senator John Sherman – no great admirer of Arthur's – approved of Will's nomination, although he doubted that "so inexperienced a person" would succeed in such a post.[34] Yet the elder Taft realized that the time was past when he would or could order the actions of his five sons. Will accepted Arthur's offer and took office in March 1881, just a few months before his parents sailed off to Europe.

Taft's brief career as tax collector – he lasted barely one year – provides some insights as to why he did not find it rewarding or satisfying. It further helps us understand why he was never very effective in the political arena. There are

[31] Pringle, 57–58.
[32] Ross, 70.
[33] Ibid.
[34] Pringle, 61.

at least two possible reasons why he accepted an appointment as revenue collector – a job far distant from his training as a lawyer. In the first place, he may have viewed the position as affording an opportunity to "repay some of the political debts incurred by his father."[35] Further, he may have found it impossible as a young attorney all of twenty-four-years old to decline a nomination from the president of the United States to a position, it might be noted, that once had been filled by William Henry Harrison, who was elected president in 1840, only to serve the shortest presidential term in American history.

Will could not have been under any illusions about the real nature of the job he now held. The son of a major figure in Ohio Republican politics, he was well aware of the role that patronage played in the process. In his position as the tax collector in a large district, the currents of patronage flowed all around him. Pringle seems to have been quite accurate when he described the IRS of 1882 as "a refuge for politically deserving veterans of the G.A.R. [Grand Army of the Republic] and other hacks."[36] Civil Service reform had not yet happened, although the first major federal step in that direction was about to be undertaken with passage of the Pendleton Act in 1883. Early in his tenure, Taft was informed that he was expected to replace current employees with Republicans "of the right sort." These instructions came from a former Ohio governor who supported Arthur's efforts – ultimately unsuccessful – to gain renomination in 1884.

Will was "advised" that some of the employees in his office "should be removed at once." Thomas Young further informed Taft that President Arthur "thinks you are shrewd enough and have sufficient knowledge of the politics of Hamilton County to know who these men are.... He depends on you as his friend." Will balked at such a request, and reported to Alphonso in Vienna that the targeted employees "are perhaps the best men in the service for reliability, [and] knowledge of duty." Indeed, "if they are removed ... it will cause a very big stink in the district and I do not want to have any hand in it. I would much rather resign and let some one else do Tom Young's service and dirty work ... ."[37] Taft refused to follow the suggested course of action put forth by Young, and took some criticism for being "disloyal." Will felt it appropriate to send President Arthur "renewed assurances of my appreciation and obligation to you and of my fidelity to your interests...."[38] Nevertheless, after the 1882 elections, which resulted in some major losses for the Republicans, Will resigned his post, effective in March 1883.

He had found the work uncongenial and, as in the instance just described, sometimes demeaning as well. At an early age, Will had become acquainted with the seamy side of politics. He experienced firsthand what Ishbel Ross calls "the corruption that could cloak federal office holding."[39] As he continued

---

[35] Ibid.
[36] Ibid.
[37] Pringle, 62.
[38] Pringle Papers, LOC, Box 28, Taft to President Arthur, July 29, 1882.
[39] Ross, 70.

along the path that ultimately would take him to the White House, he accepted as a matter of course machine politics and what went with it as undesirable and unfortunate. They probably represented, he believed, inevitable traits of a system that despite all this, offered much good. But Taft himself would have no part of any corrupt dealings. If this is the way the game was played, he might overlook it in others, but not in himself. Moreover, the interval as tax collector confirmed to Taft that he had no liking for politics itself. Corrupt or clean, whatever the motives, the process involved tasks and practices to which he objected more and more as he matured.

It is no coincidence that, with one minor exception, until he attained the presidency Taft had never found it necessary to submit himself to the exigencies of the electorate for approval. A closely contested race meant nothing to him as a participant, but only occasionally as a campaigner for someone else. Indeed, the visceral sense of combat so typical of Theodore Roosevelt, with whom Taft would become well acquainted, seemed foreign to his nature. Much more deliberative than dogmatic in character, perhaps one reason he was such a poor campaigner was because he had so little interest in it, and rarely for self-gain. Every major office he held was offered to him. Again, his comment to White remains both candid and accurate. Taft somehow "always had my plate the right side up when offices were falling."

From Vienna, Alphonso wanted Will's resignation to occur "without censure and without loss of popularity." Indeed, one newspaper had hailed his appointment "as the personal choice of the President," and welcomed "the youngest collector in the United States ... , large, handsome and fair, with the build of a Hercules and the sunny disposition of an innocent child."[40] Somehow, Will convinced President Arthur of his real desire to begin the "active practice of law," and his resignation was accepted without rancor. However, his stint as an actual partner in a law firm turned out to be very brief. Within two years, Will had his "plate right side up," once again.

Relieved of and removed from his position as tax collector, Will Taft happily spent part of the summer of 1883 traveling in Europe and visiting his parents. All too soon, he had to return to Cincinnati, where Alphonso expected him to be "working with uninterrupted constancy." Looking back at Ohio, Will's father wondered if Will might suffer political reprisals for leaving the country while Ohio was in the midst of a bitter campaign for the governorship. The Republican candidate was Joseph Foraker, a seemingly perennial figure in Ohio politics, with whom Will was to maintain friendship, but more often enmity, for the next thirty years.[41] The Democratic candidate was Taft's former law professor, George Hoadley. As a "good Republican," Taft would have been expected to support Foraker, yet the fact that Hoadley defeated Foraker probably did not disturb the homeward-bound Will unduly.

[40] Pringle, 61.
[41] Pringle, 65–66.

In 1884, national politics reached either the heights or the nadir (depending upon one's viewpoint) of partisanship. President Arthur hoped for renomination, only to see his party's choice fall to Congressman James G. Blaine, known according to the Democrats as "the continental liar from the state of Maine."[42] A national political triumph had been a longtime coming for the Democrats; they had not won a presidential election since 1856, and could claim, with a minimum of plausibility, that their 1876 victory had been stolen. However, their chosen candidate, Grover Cleveland, had recently been revealed as the possible father of an illegitimate child. Thus the Republicans responded with chants of "Ma, Ma. Where' my Pa? Gone to the White House. Ha ha ha."

Back working in Cincinnati as an attorney, but not with outstanding success, Taft would have preferred Arthur. From as far away as Vienna, however, his mother warned Will that such a choice represented "a forlorn hope." While Alphonso regarded Blaine's nomination "as a disappointment," he insisted that Will campaign on Blaine's behalf. "We have but one course," noted the elder Taft, "and that is to support the ticket."[43] Will did just that. In 1912, he would echo his father's strictures and apply them to his own candidacy, but as in 1884, to no avail. For the first time since 1856, a Democrat occupied the White House.

Now in the twilight of his governmental service, and transferred to St. Petersburg as Minister to Russia, Alphonso acknowledged the efforts of his sons with some pride, even as his youngest son Horace lamented "the disgrace of having a Democrat for president again."[44] For his part, Will had not enjoyed stumping for the Republican ticket. Of much greater interest to him was the opportunity to become involved in the disbarment of a notorious Cincinnati criminal lawyer, one Thomas Campbell. Taft had already tilted against him, and with no success. Here was an opportunity far more attractive than Ohio politics, "and if I can assist to get rid of Campbell I think I shall have accomplished a much greater good than by yelling myself hoarse for Blaine."[45] Working (unsuccessfully as it turned out) to win the Campbell case, however, was not Will Taft's main concern in 1884 and 1885. By then, a young woman had entered his life, and until Taft's death early in 1930, Nellie Herron would remain a dominant focus in his world.

FALLING FOR NELLIE

It is not clear exactly when Will Taft first became acquainted with Nellie. The Herron family moved in the same social circles as the Tafts. John Herron had been a law partner of Rutherford Hayes's, and would later serve as a

---

[42] Matthew Josephson, *The Politicos* (New York: Harcourt, Brace & World, Inc., 1938), 368.
[43] Pringle, 66.
[44] Pringle 68.
[45] Ibid.

United States attorney during Benjamin Harrison's administration. Indeed, as a youngster – she was the oldest girl in a family with eleven children – Nellie had been a guest of the Hayes's during his presidency, and apparently recorded in her diary that "she would like to be First Lady."[46] As Will's older brother Charlie had married and now resided in a home very near the Herrons, it was to be expected that the younger members of these two families especially would have ample opportunity for social contacts.

By 1880, Nellie could write that she had received an invitation to a party from Will. "Why he asked me I have wondered ever since," all the more as "I know him very slightly though I like him very much."[47] Their relationship took a few years to develop, but by 1884, they were seeing a great deal of each other. Taft, constantly referring to Nellie as "My dear Miss Heron," placed her upon a pedestal of quality, which he consistently emphasized was higher than his own. He referred to her "clear-cut intellect and well-informed mind." Speaking to her of marriage, which he did sometime in the spring of 1885, Will reiterated anew that his regard for her was "founded on a respect and admiration for your high character ... and your intellectual superiority."[48] He assumed that Nellie would be "his senior partner," an accurate assumption on his part.

Whether because of inner uncertainty or because such was the accepted custom of the times, Nellie turned Will down flat. In response, he now focused on his own shortcomings. These could be overcome "with your ... sweet sympathetic nature ... you would strengthen me where I falter...."[49] By June 1885, Nellie had accepted him in what seems to have been a somewhat lukewarm manner, provoking in turn even more vigorous expressions of devotion from Taft. "Oh Nellie, you must love me. I rely on time to help me.... The consciousness of having made me a much better and truer man which you can not fail to have when you shall have become my wife will make you happy...."[50] In due course, Nellie came around, and in turn reminded Will of her own shortcomings as a housewife. She could not even, she noted, "thread a worm on a fishing hook." With some accuracy, Will replied that "without a wriggle she had hooked one gasping fish weighing 240 pounds."[51]

With Nellie's somewhat grudging acquiescence, Taft was finally able to inform his parents of his impending marriage, but it was not to take place until June 1886. Alphonso welcomed the match, writing to Will of his children that "my sands are so nearly run that I can only hope to live to see them

---

[46] Ross, 82.
[47] Pringle, 73.
[48] Pringle Papers, LOC, Box 28, June 17, 1885.
[49] Pringle, 78.
[50] Ross, 91. Taft emphasized to Nellie that "I love you for your noble consistent character, for [your] sweet womanly disposition, for all that you are, for all that you hope to be." Robert Taft Papers, LOC, Box 15, May 10, 1885.
[51] Ibid., 92.

start and make some estimate of what is to be the complexion of their future lives."[52] In July 1885, Nellie and her parents went on vacation, leaving Taft truly miserable. "I find no pleasure in going anywhere," he wrote. His loneliness was only exacerbated by the fact that Nelllie was a poor correspondent. "When I don't get a letter I read all the old ones over again." Will mentioned an older couple sitting on their porch. "He was reading something and she sat ... behind him doing nothing, reading nothing and certainly thinking nothing. A horror of such a match seized me at first, and then a deep sense of joy and relief at the thought of how different my married life was to be. I may do Mrs. Skinner an injustice, but it strikes me that [she] would hardly recognize an idea if she met one on the street."[53]

Until his death almost forty-four years after their marriage, Taft never wavered in his total devotion to Nellie or his total need for her encouragement and support. Yet her reserved manner contrasted with Will's "fun loving personality." Will noted of a reply from Nellie that "there was no word of endearment or affection from one end to the other, and the tone of it sounded to me so hard and complaining."[54] Ambitious for herself as well as for Will, she could be quite free with candid criticism of his actions. As his parents had pushed and prodded him to accomplish much, Taft now saw this role pass to Nellie, who was more than willing to "take command of him, to drive him, to counsel and reassure him at each step of the way."[55] In 1911, Will wrote to his oldest son, Robert, that "your mother is in good condition, and especially able to boss me, which indicates a healthy state...."[56] On the other hand, Nellie's goals were not always those of her husband's, and the resulting conflict between what Taft desired, and what his wife determined that he desired, would lead to unhappiness and turmoil later in Taft's career.

In the meantime, after a honeymoon abroad, Will and his new bride settled into their new home in Cincinnati, where he resumed his law practice. He also had been appointed an assistant county solicitor. In this capacity, he represented Hamilton County in civil litigation. Aside from the "infamous" Campbell case, Taft's practice seems not to have been very exciting. To be sure, in going after Campbell, the young attorney had found fulfillment rather than any sort of fee as compensation for the many hours of work involved in preparation for the trial.

He accused the veteran trial lawyer Campbell of "corruptly obtaining jurors, and of corruptly and improperly influencing their verdicts." In a four-hour summation, Will insisted that the legal "profession must be kept pure." We "deny nothing" to the defendant, Taft added, "except integrity," exactly what Campbell lacked.[57]

[52] Ross, 95.
[53] Pringle Papers, LOC, Box 28, July 16, 1885.
[54] Anderson, 54.
[55] Ibid., 55.
[56] WHT to RT, Robert Taft Papers, LOC, Box 15, August 27, 1911.
[57] Pringle, 90–91.

Alphonso Taft observed his son's efforts with sympathetic detachment. "I suspect," he had predicted (accurately as it turned out) that "you will be disappointed and lose all your labor." Seen in the cold, hard light of day, Campbell's tactics might not be "such as you would approve," yet "he is not as bad as you have taken him to be."[58] The elder Taft indirectly pointed to what Pringle lists as two difficulties with Will as an attorney. His idea of legal ethics was "far more rigid than that of the majority" of lawyers around him. Moreover, "Taft was handicapped, as he always would be, by using intellect to combat emotion."[59] The court acquitted Campbell of all but a minor charge, and even remitted the penalty imposed for it. While ultimately winning his quest for Nellie Herron, Will had lost what he considered to be a most important case.

As a young attorney, Taft absorbed certain values and assumptions that characterized legal thought in the Gilded Age. Although those values may have appeared to him as fixed and unchanging principles, in fact they resulted more from what William Wiecek has well described as a fearful and frightened reaction by the legal order to very rapid change.[60] In particular, these changes were reflected in four areas, all very familiar to Will Taft – urban expansion, the growth of labor unions, corporate and industrial enterprise, and expanding corruption, which all too easily seemed to attach itself to the other changes. In Cincinnati, Taft had seen them all, and concluded that they represented very real threats to the trilogy of values on which he had been nurtured: preservation of the social order, individual liberty, and Republican government. He never abandoned either his faith in their validity or his perennial fear of their endangerment.

On the other hand, especially in his younger years, Taft was not blind to the discrepancies between what Wiecek calls "classical legal thought" and the reality of industrial America. In theory, for example, contractual agreements were based on the presumption that each individual party to a contract was equal in freedom to agree, to consider, accept, and/or reject the offer. In the Gilded Age, such freedom was more fictional than factual. Of course, the government's primary obligation was to ensure that individual liberty received consistent and effective protection. But Taft worried that government, especially urban government manipulated by political machines, could endanger such liberty. He saw the late nineteenth century as a period of real tension between the power of government, especially state government, and the liberty of the individual.

It was the function of the court to stand between these two forces – to control political power in order to secure individual freedom. The politicians might kowtow to the mob, and the legislature might not be immune

---

[58] Ibid., 88.

[59] Pringle, 90. Pringle's point has special relevance for Taft in the 1912 presidential campaign, where his two major opponents were TR and Wilson, both much more adept at inspirational speech making than Taft.

[60] See William Wiecek's outstanding analysis, *The Lost World of Classical Legal Thought: Law and Ideology in America, 1886–1937* (New York: Oxford University Press. 1998).

to its pressures, but the courts were to serve as a permanent barrier against such mischief. In their independence and integrity, something Taft glorified throughout his life, he saw the salvation for America as it struggled with the forces of modernization and industrialism. He did not exaggerate his feelings when he noted that "I love judges and I love courts. They are my ideals, that typify on earth what we shall meet hereafter in heaven under a just God."[61]

Evidence concerning the intensity of this struggle was very clear to Taft. While still an undergraduate at Yale in 1877, the bloodiest railroad strike thus far in American history had occurred, leading President Hayes to take the unprecedented step of ordering federal troops to restore order during a work stoppage. Barely a decade later, even as Will and Nellie settled in to social life in Cincinnati, the Haymarket riot inflamed issues and emotions in Chicago. Strife between labor and capital seemed ongoing, as was the growing discrepancy between wage earners and capitalists. Furthermore, Taft could recall the senseless assassination of another Ohio Republican, President James Garfield, in 1881.

To what extent these symptoms of unrest troubled Taft is not clear. There is no doubt, however, that he accepted the underlying assumptions of classical legal thought just mentioned. On the other hand, the young lawyer also understood that the corrosive effects of force were not confined only to labor violence. To a greater extent than might be supposed, he knew that the conduct of the greedy, the wealthy, the powerful industrial and financial "interests" of the day had contributed in large measure to the condition of America in the late nineteenth century. Between 1887 and 1900, much of Taft's career would be spent trying to accommodate – if not reconcile – the conflicting characteristics of industrial expansion, handicapped though he was by the values of his class.

By 1887, Taft had lost some interest in partisan politics. Always a devoted Republican, he had done his share of campaigning for local candidates in Ohio, including Joseph Foraker, defeated in 1883 as the Republican gubernatorial candidate. Occasionally over the next two years, their paths had crossed, usually as opposing counsel. Foraker had represented the notorious Tom Campbell in 1884. Foraker and Taft had another confrontation in 1885, resulting, as Will informed Nellie, in Taft's conclusion that "I do not like Foraker.... He is a double-faced Campbell man and when a man bears such a brand, I will have none of him."[62] In 1885, however, Foraker joined forces with another notorious Ohio politician, the Republican boss in Cincinnati, George Cox. An effective and expedient alliance resulted not only in Foraker's election as governor for two consecutive terms, from 1885 to 1889, but also in two terms as U.S. senator, from 1896 to 1908. What became of Taft's insistence that "I will have none of him"?

---

[61] Anderson, 259.
[62] Pringle, 94.

As a sixteen-year-old, Foraker had enlisted in the Union Army, from which he emerged as a captain and a participant in Sherman's famous march through Georgia. By 1869, he had graduated in Cornell University's first class, and gravitated toward law and politics in Cincinnati. One year after Taft graduated from Yale, Foraker was elected to the superior court, the same court on which Alphonso Taft had sat. Among his colleagues was Judson Harmon, an acquaintance of the elder Taft's. By 1885, Foraker had been elected governor of Ohio, and was reelected two years later. In 1887, Harmon resigned to go back into private practice, and appears to have suggested to Foraker that Will Taft be his replacement. In 1887, Foraker had long since put aside his personal hostility to Taft. With a shrewd sense of the practical as well as the practicable, he may well have seen much to gain in making the appointment. Pringle notes correctly that naming Alphonso's son to his old court would reflect well on Foraker's "high regard for the judiciary," as well as his awareness that Taft's gratitude might be of some benefit to Foraker as he planned his campaign for a U.S. Senate seat.[63]

The court on which Taft would serve as a replacement was the Superior Court of Cincinnati, a tribunal that had been established by the Ohio legislature in 1854. An earlier court with the same name had been created in 1838, to be superceded by the newer version under the Ohio constitution of 1851. In its wisdom, the Ohio legislature opted not to establish an intermediate trial court of general jurisdiction. Rather it created three additional superior courts in Cleveland, as well as in Montgomery and Franklin counties. The jurisdiction of the courts was limited to civil matters, subject to appeal to the Ohio Supreme Court.

With few exceptions, such as the famous bible-reading case mentioned earlier, what seems significant about the Superior Court of Cincinnati is not so much its cases as its judges, a number of whom went on to noteworthy if not distinguished careers. Indeed, service on its bench frequently led to advancement. Beside both Tafts, Governor Joseph Foraker would become a U.S. senator, while Judson Harmon would become Ohio's governor and serve as attorney general under President Cleveland. Stanley Matthews sat briefly in the U.S. Senate, and in 1881 became a justice of the United States Supreme Court.[64]

Early in January 1887, Foraker appointed Taft to an unexpired term of fourteen months to the Ohio Superior Court. Later in his career, Taft always insisted that his appointment had been totally unsolicited on his part. Be that as it may, Taft realized how much he owed to the man about whom – only two years before – he had emphasized that "I will have none of him." He quickly expressed his new-found gratitude. "Considering the opportunity, so

---

[63] Ibid., 94–95.

[64] Carrington T. Marshall, ed., *A History of the Courts and Lawyers of Ohio* (New York: American Historical Society, 1934), vol. 2, 467–469.

honorable a position offers to a man of my age and circumstances, my debt to you is very great. The responsibility you assume for me ... will always be a strong incentive to an industrious and conscientious discharge of my duties."[65] It would not be the last instance where Taft sought and gratefully acknowledged Foraker's support.

Only twenty-nine-years old, Taft assumed his judicial duties in March 1887. He won election on his own to a full term in April 1888, but as will be seen, did not complete it. Reelection to the superior court was not a real challenge for the young judge. Judicial elections in Cincinnati in general were rarely controversial, and much less so for the son of Alphonso Taft. Not until his successful run for the presidency twenty years later would Will Taft ever again have to face the exigencies of the electorate. He described his new judicial responsibilities as a "pleasant harbor." Indeed, his words represented an apt description. Yet it seemed to Nellie Taft that her husband might well become becalmed there, and she had more ambitious plans for herself as well as for him. For the moment, however, Taft had become one of the youngest judges to sit on the Ohio Superior Court.

[65] Taft to Joseph Foraker, Foraker Papers, Cincinnati Historical Society, Box 24, Folder 1, January 31, 1887.

2

Judges and Justice, 1887–1900

Will Taft never wrote his memoirs, and the man he had counted on to write an "authorized" biography, his friend and confidante Gus Karger, died in 1924. Had he been so disposed to write of his past, however, there is no doubt that he would have placed positive emphasis on his years as a judge, and especially later as chief justice. Mention has already been made of Taft's tendency to need prodding and pushing for his career and his self-doubt concerning his own qualities for success, On the bench, he found a welcomed respite from all of this. In his courtroom, he was master, handing down decisions in an unhurried atmosphere far removed from the rough world of Ohio politics. There, his word was law, even as he held in his hands the fate of defendants who came before him. His three years on the superior court convinced him that a judicial career would be the most rewarding goal he could attain. And while he would suffer much travail and endure humiliating disappointments in later life, his final judicial career (his third) proved him absolutely correct.

Taft's major biographer, Henry Pringle, has commented on the remarkable frequency with which Taft wrote about his various activities.[1] But if Taft was facile with the pen, he was less than fluent in his writing style. Both as a jurist and as Chief Executive, his prose was solid, ponderous, and all too often overly extensive. One need only compare his inaugural address in 1909 with that of his successor Woodrow Wilson in 1913 to understand this point. Although, as will be seen, there are a few exceptions to this generalization, Taft could not find elegance in his writing, be it either in judicial decisions or in affairs of state. The occasional eloquence of Louis Brandeis and the epigrammatic wit of Oliver Wendell Holmes, two of Taft's future colleagues on the High Court, will not be seen in Taft's written work. On the other hand, even as early as his superior court tenure, his opinions were carefully crafted, thoroughly researched, well grounded in precedent, and to a very great extent upheld by the Ohio Supreme Court. Moreover, they reflect some values that Taft held for the remainder of his life, as an examination of two

[1] Pringle, 99–100.

early Taft decisions will demonstrate. They may serve as typical examples of his approach toward juridprudence.

JUDGE TAFT

In 1887, shortly after he became a judge, Taft undertook to resolve an intriguing question concerning the secrecy of a manufacturing process for the casting of bells. The plaintiff claimed that he had recently bought both the business and the secret process, and that the defendants – one of whom had once worked as a foreman for the company under its previous owners – had somehow acquired knowledge of the casting process in spite of the agreed secrecy that had been part of the sale. Defendants further were prepared to make "the bells according to the secret process belonging to the plaintiff," even as they claimed that there was no secret involved, and that the plaintiff's process "is well known to the trade."[2] Here, Taft had to weigh the issue of free competition in the marketplace against agreements that, if enforced, would limit market access to the defendants.

Taft conceded that "property in a secret process is the power to make use of it to the exclusion of the world. If the world knows the process, than the property disappears." There can be no protection for a process "if knowledge of it is common to the world." But the new jurist explored the "secrecy" involved here. He noted that the original bell manufacturer had not changed the form, weight, or volume of his bells since 1866. Taft further found that no other bell manufacturers were making similar bells in the same way. This, he concluded, demonstrated that for twenty years, "the process does not seem to have been successfully reproduced because of the effective trade secret protection."

As to the previously mentioned foreman, he had to know from the nature of his role what the process was, and "I am inclined to think that his obligation to preserve such secret as the property of his employer must be implied."[3] Finally, Taft also enjoined the defendants from implying in their brochures that they and not the plaintiffs were the legitimate successors to the older company. His opinion explored in some depth not only the process of bell casting, but also current law dealing with issues of trademarks and advertising. Moreover, it reflected Taft's thoroughness and even-handed approach to the case. On the other hand, this litigation was less a matter of public interest than an arcane legal issue. How would Taft respond to a more notorious case that was to provoke major public awareness, an incident arising from the industrial conflict so characteristic of the time?

Shortly after the birth of his first child, Robert, in September 1889, Taft handed down what may have been his most significant opinion as a member

---

[2] *Cincinnati Bell Foundry Co. v. John B Dodds et al.*, 1887 Ohio Misc. Lexis 181: 10 Ohio Dec, reprint 84.

[3] Pringle, 4–5.

of the Ohio Superior Court. Certainly it was notorious in terms of the criticism offered against the decision by his political opponents later in his career. Because the case involved a work stoppage at a time of national tension between labor and industry, his decision did not go unnoticed, even though at that time, the decisions of the Ohio Superior Court officially were neither printed nor published. Although Taft would later go on to write a number of labor decisions, what seems to have been his first such opinion – in *Moores & Co. v. Bricklayers' Union No. 1* – was significant in that it apparently revealed Taft to be both sympathetic and at the same time hostile to organized labor.[4] In several later cases, as a federal judge, he would again demonstrate this irreconcilable dualism, even as he tried to reconcile it himself.

The facts in *Moores* were not complicated. A large Cincinnati union of bricklayers that apparently included "ninety five percent of the trade in this city" was unable to resolve a dispute with a major building contractor. In response, the union called for a boycott against this firm, Parker Brothers, and designated one employee from its rank to coordinate the boycott. Requests were distributed to all involved in the building trades that they not do business with Parker Brothers. Any building materials company that declined or "ignores this request is hereby notified that we will not work his material upon any building, nor for any contractors by whom we are employed." One such firm was Moores & Co., which soon felt the effect of the union's action. The Company took the union to court, charging "a wrongful and malicious conspiracy," and won a verdict of $2,250. The union moved for a new trial, and speaking for a unanimous three-judge panel, Taft denied the motion.

Early in his opinion, Taft made the point that the right to join a union was *not* at issue in the case. Similarly, the inherent legitimacy of Union No. 1 was not questioned. Every man, he wrote, "is entitled to invest his capital, to carry on his business, to bestow his labor, or to exercise his calling, if within the law, according to his pleasure." Any resulting competition which harmed some of the participants was "*damnum absque injuria*," damage without injury – and thus not recoverable at law. A brick layer had the right to refuse to work with materials "not satisfactory" to him, and "he may lawfully notify his employers of his objection and refuse to work it." Any resulting loss "is not a legal injury.... And so it may be said that ... what one workman may do, many may do, and many may combine to do without giving the sufferer any right of action against those who cause his loss."[5]

One might reasonably have concluded from these words that in this case, the conduct of the union was beyond the reach of the law. But Taft reached a very different conclusion. It was one thing when everyone is competing in the marketplace; it was quite another when their conduct is based upon simple motives of malice. Citing a number of British precedents, he held that where

---

[4] *Moores & Co. v. Bricklayers' Union et al.*, 1889 Ohio Misc. Lexis 119; 10 Ohio Dec. Reprint 48.

[5] Ibid., 2–3.

there is mutual interference and loss, not at all uncommon in business ventures, "such loss is a legal injury, or not, according to the intent with which it has been caused, and the presence or absence of malice in the person causing it." In this light, the conduct of the union against Moores & Co. was unlawful and inappropriate.[6]

That conduct was based neither on an issue of wages, nor on a demand for better working conditions. Rather, the union had deliberately tried to bully Moores' customers into declining to do business with him, thereby getting back at Parker Brothers. Such conduct "is without just cause, and is, therefore, malicious. The immediate motive of defendants here was to show to the building world what punishment and disaster necessarily followed a defiance of their demands," whether legitimate or not. An individual union member acting alone might avoid legal action, but not when the group acted as a combination of individuals. At such a point " it is clear that the terrorizing of a community by threats of exclusive dealing in order to deprive one obnoxious member of means of sustenance will become both dangerous and oppressive."[7]

Taft's decision bristled with precedents and analysis explaining both the principles behind his decision and the negative effects of the secondary boycott that had been utilized against Moores & Co. Taft reiterated once again his firm rejection of the claim "that in this state or country a combination by working men to raise their wages or to obtain any mutual advantage is contrary to law," provided, he insisted, "that they do not use such indirect means as obscure their original intent, and make their combinations one merely malicious to oppress and injure individuals."[8] Taft held to this distinction throughout his career, and remained proud of his 1889 decision. As he saw it, the outcome epitomized the ideal and proper relationship between the rights of labor and the rights of capital. At least in theory, he envisioned both having rights that were enforceable at law. As will be seen, however, his vision was clouded by the harsh realities of urban industrialism.

Taft greatly enjoyed his years on the superior court. But if he was happy and content, Nellie was not. Ambitious not only for her husband but also for herself, and occupied as "a teacher, wife, mother and housekeeper," Nellie found Cincinnati too confining. Carl Anthony comments that while she "wanted a larger life[, …] her husband was content as a judge." She feared what she described as "the narrowing effects of the Bench," seeking rather to move beyond her respectable but humdrum existence at home. [9] The most appropriate vehicle for such a move was, of course, her husband.

With the uncanny luck that sometimes comes to those who don't work for it, Will had by 1888 won reelection for a full term on the superior court.

---

[6] Ibid., 5.

[7] Ibid., 6.

[8] Ibid., 6.

[9] Anthony, 93. The influence of Nellie Taft during her lengthy and loving marriage to Will was of crucial importance to his career. With a candor that some might have considered excessive, she consistently served as his counselor, confidante, and critic.

Less than a year later, one of his now-retired colleagues, as well as Governor Foraker (shortly to be defeated for reelection), called newly elected President Benjamin Harrison's attention to the young jurist, and urged his appointment to the United States Supreme Court. Whatever Taft's later recollection might have been concerning his claim that he never solicited his own advancement, his letter to Foraker in September 1889 suggests that his memory was somewhat faulty.[10] Taft had heard, he wrote to Foraker, that "the President has my name under serious consideration for the vacancy." He "was somewhat excited" upon such news, although "I considered the mere mention a high compliment and nothing else."[11]

Yet Taft yearned for appointment to the High Court with lasting consistency: "But if there is a chance[,] I think that the prize is so great that I ought to improve it if by [any] honorable and dignified means I can." He went on to solicit in no uncertain terms a letter from Foraker to Harrison on his behalf.[12] As a Judge of the superior court, "to be even mentioned for such a high place, as that which, with more ambition than modesty perhaps I have my thoughts on." Foraker did indeed communicate with Harrison, whereupon Taft wrote him once again. "If anything could make a success of what, in the nature of things, is only a very remote chance, I am sure your support given in such an emphatic way will do it."[13] Earlier, Will had written to Alphonso, now in California and in failing health, that because Harrison apparently still remained very uncertain of his selection, some observers considered "that the chances are excellent. This is a very roseate view to take but of course it doesn't disturb my equanimity for I know the chance is only one in a million, but still the chance is something at so great a prize."[14] In fact, he added in a later letter, "my chances of going to the moon and of donning a silk gown at the hands of President Harrison are about equal."[15]

Possibly because of his youth – he was just over thirty years old – possibly because of his limited judicial experience, Taft did not receive the appointment. Again, he was under no illusions, in spite of his hopes. He wrote of Harrison that "I am quite sure if I were he[,] I would not appoint a man of my age and position to that bench."[16] But there would be other opportunities, and although he did not know it, Taft would in fact later receive a number of offers

---

[10] It will be recalled that earlier, Taft had written to then Governor Foraker that "my debt to you is very great. The responsibility you assume for me in making this appointment will always be a strong incentive to an industrious and conscientious discharge of my duties."

[11] Ibid., September 17, 1889.

[12] Ibid. " ... to ask you whether you can conscientiously add another letter to the many obligations I am under to you by writing a letter to the President recommending me for the vacancy on the Supreme Bench."

[13] Ibid., September 25, 1889.

[14] WHT to Alphonso Taft, August 10, 1889, Pringle Papers, Box 28. Taft added that "Mother and Nellie will sc[off?] at this and probably they are right."

[15] Ross, 105.

[16] Pringle, 107.

of nomination to the High Court. He would turn down at least two of them. Harrison, however, was not yet done with Will Taft.

SOLICITOR GENERAL

Well aware of the young judge, thanks to the efforts of Foraker and other Ohio Republicans, the president had decided that if the United States Supreme Court was not appropriate, a lesser post dealing with judiciary might well be more suitable for Taft. In the fall of 1889, Harrison offered him an appointment as the solicitor general of the United States. One of two significant moves by Congress to improve the federal judicial system during the late nineteenth century (the other being creation of the circuit appellate courts in 1891), the post of solicitor general had been established in 1870. Although a prime function of the SG was to represent the United States in cases before the Supreme Court, the SG also was on call to advise the attorney general, as well as the president himself. The SG had to be familiar not only with federal statute law but also with the rules of federal practice and the decisions of the High Court – all areas in which Taft previously had not needed nor acquired any expertise.

It is not surprising that Taft's first instinct was to decline Harrison's offer, nor that Nellie Taft – eager as ever to leave Cincinnati for a larger and more lively environment – strongly encouraged him to accept it. So, too, did Will's father. The challenges Will faced represented a "Herculean task," but his son should "go ahead and fear not."[17] Further, both Alphonso and Nellie may well have realized that Taft's new position placed him very close to the entire executive branch of the federal government. More important, as Foraker had indicated, Taft should consider "the other position to which I can clearly see that it leads ... the bench of the Supreme Court."[18] In fact, no SG had ever been or would be appointed to the High Court in Taft's lifetime – except himself. In a scenario that would be repeated more than once later in his career, Taft allowed himself to be persuaded to accept a position he did not really desire.

Another reason for his willingness to accept was that his half brother, Charles Phelps Taft, had offered to augment Will's salary by several thousand dollars a year. The oldest and wealthiest of the four Taft brothers, Charlie had graduated from Yale (of course) and Columbia Law School. For a short time, he practiced law in Cincinnati. He married into wealth and gained further income on his own as the successful publisher and editor of the Cincinnati *Times-Star*. The oldest Taft brother also served one term in Congress, but chose not to seek reelection. Throughout his pre-presidential career, Will Taft benefited from his brother's consistent generosity. It further extended into his two presidential campaigns

[17] Pringle, 108.
[18] Pringle, 109.

Taft served as SG for two years, and he had mixed reactions to the experience. The Tafts found social life in Washington congenial. He and Nellie became acquainted with a number of individuals, both active in or observant of Washington politics. They included Henry Adams, already known for his caustic wit and cynical outlook; Henry Cabot Lodge, already regarded as the quintessential Boston Brahmin; and Lodge's close friend Theodore Roosevelt, at the time a member of the Civil Service Commission and already displaying a mercurial temperament, an incredible intellect, and unconcealed political ambition. Taft got to know them all, especially Theodore Roosevelt, who, or so it seemed, would become one of Taft's closest friends. While Nellie enjoyed the hubbub and hobnobbing in the nation's capitol, her husband was less inclined to participate.

Will found his job demanding and varied. With impressive diligence, he mastered both federal precedents and procedures, provided advice when requested by President Harrison, served for a time as acting attorney general, and argued a total of eighteen cases before the High Court – winning sixteen of them. In terms of public reaction, his most significant brief and argument concerned the Bering Sea and a continuing dispute with Great Britain. With its purchase of Alaska from Russia in 1867, the United States claimed jurisdiction over fishing rights "in the entire Bering Sea." By 1887, federal revenue cutters had initiated seizure of fishing vessels, some of them more than sixty miles offshore and thus far beyond the traditional three-mile territorial limit.

Such conduct inspired vigorous opposition from Great Britain in the form of numerous diplomatic complaints. The dispute reached a sort of climax in 1891 with the United States' seizure of yet another fishing vessel from Canada. Without waiting for condemnation proceedings, the British government applied to the United States Supreme Court for a writ of prohibition, which would have blocked action from a lower federal court. In a brief of more than 300 pages, plus a well-delivered oral presentation, Taft argued against the British request. He had, so he wrote to his father, prepared most of it and revised all of it. The High Court accepted Taft's claim that it was inappropriate for the justices to take up the merits of an issue while it was under diplomatic negotiation within the executive branch. And ultimately this dispute was resolved not by the courts but through international arbitration.[19]

Yet Taft had tended to doubt the qualities of his oral arguments. Reporting to Alphonso early in his tenure as SG that "I do not find myself at all easy or fluent on my feet," he alluded to his apparent inability to attract the sustained attention of "a lot of mummies." The justices, he added, "seem to think when I begin to talk that that is a good chance to read all the letters that have been waiting for some time, to eat lunch [sic], and devote their attention to … other matters.…" But he would gain "experience in not being overcome by circumstances."[20] His mother also urged him not to be "disappointed at

[19] Pringle, 117–119.
[20] Pringle, 115.

FIGURE 1. The United States Supreme Court in 1890. The Court was described by Taft as "a lot of mummies." Reproduced by permission of the Curator's Office, Supreme Court of the United States.

the indifference of the old fogies of the Supreme Court. It is a new experience which you will get used to."[21] And so he did. After he had left the presidency, Taft in 1913 recalled with nostalgia and humor his two years as solicitor general.

He wrote that the Supreme Court "is a great court. They hear you state the case, ... and after that when you go on to make your argument, if they are with you they don't pay much attention to you. For the first six months, I had good causes for the Government, and I would present the cases and then attempt to make an argument – and really it was just like talking to nine tombstones! In fact, it was a little worse than that, because they would be affirmative in their disregard of your argument.... Well in about six months after that, I got a lot of cases in which I didn't have a good cause, and then I found that their attention was altogether too minute."[22] Eight years later, Taft would become Chief Justice among the "tombstones" (Figure 1).

[21] Ross, 107.
[22] Mabel T. Boardman Papers, Folder 1913. Quote is from a speech given by Taft on December 21, 1913.

In the spring of 1891, President Harrison had the opportunity to name nine new circuit judges, one for each circuit. Taft's friends in Cincinnati lost no time in pushing his candidacy. Two different circumstances from their previous attempt in 1890 to get him on to the Supreme Court may be noted. In the first place, Harrison was much better acquainted with Taft by 1891, and this appointment on top of Taft's successful term as solicitor general might have seemed much more appropriate to the president. Moreover, despite Taft's oft-stated recollection that he never sought any of the numerous offices that came to him, again there is no doubt that Taft pulled every string he could to obtain this one. Ohio Senators and Congressmen, as well as a select committee of lawyers from Cincinnati, all came forward.

But Nellie still retained her concerns. She warned Will that "if you get your heart's desire ... it will put an and to all the opportunities you now have of being ... with the bigwigs."[23] Possibly with herself as well as with Will in mind, Nellie later recalled that she feared "the narrowing effects of the bench and prefer[red] for him a diverse experience which would give him an all-round professional development." Her husband, however, had no such fears. "I like judicial life," he wrote in a letter to Alphonso. "Federal judgeships like that don't lie around loose, and if you don't get them when you can, you will not get them when you would. It would be in the line of promotion to the Supreme Court, and I am sure would be a fine position to hold. It would keep me poor all my life if I were to get it....[24]

Alphonso Taft did not live to see his son receive formal appointment as a circuit judge. But he advised Will to accept the offer if it came his way, and he noted a comment made by his friend and physician concerning Will Taft. " ... [T]here will always be something good for you in your line.... [T]he presidency will be for assignment and ... there is no special trouble in your being prepared for it."[25] As early as 1891, then, Will Taft was considered presidential material, even if he had little interest in such an office. Indeed, as will be shown, Taft never had any great desire for the presidency, even when it was virtually forced upon him.

CIRCUIT JUDGE

His father died on May 21, 1891. With the new judicial appointment informally promised but not yet proffered, Will sensed an uncertain future as he mourned Alphonso's passing. He wrote to Nellie that "I have a kind of presentiment that Father has been a kind of guardian angel to me in that his wishes for my success have been so strong and intense as to bring it." As his life ended, now "I shall cease to have the luck which has followed me thus far."[26] Taft need not

[23] Carl S. Anthony, *Nellie Taft: The Unconventional First Lady of the Ragtime Era* (New York: William Morrow. 2005), 105.
[24] Ross, 109.
[25] Pringle, 121.
[26] Ross, 110.

have worried. In March 1892, he happily resigned as solicitor general to take up his new appointment as U.S. Circuit Judge for the 6th Circuit. In Taft's view, an ideal career as a very young federal appellate jurist, life tenure, and a salary generously augmented by his brother Charlie awaited him. Will anticipated permanence, prominence, and professional and personal fulfillment at last. Or so he thought.

Thus the Tafts returned to Cincinnati, where Will ordered a new judicial robe and prepared to work within a circuit that covered the states of Ohio, Kentucky, Michigan, and Tennessee. As a circuit judge, he did not feel that a robe was necessary, but when he sat with Supreme Court Justice John Harlan on the Court of Appeals, more formality seemed appropriate. For the next eight years, Taft found satisfaction and challenge in his work. While Nellie probably preferred Washington to Cincinnati, she soon found a project that brought her both satisfaction and challenge. She was the guiding spirit behind the establishment of the Cincinnati Orchestra. She "supervised the workings" of the new ensemble, selected the musicians, and negotiated their contracts. In 1900, the Orchestra Association did not exaggerate when it labeled her as "the creator of this organization."[27]

Her husband adjusted readily and happily to his new position. The cases interested him. His responsibilities involved hearing motions, issuing orders, and deciding both civil and criminal cases. He was required to travel with some frequency, and especially enjoyed "in particular the dinners given by his legal associates in the cities" within his circuit. He wrote enough opinions to provide indications of his judicial values. Before we explore some of them, it should be noted that in Taft's case, applying traditional labels such as liberal or conservative to a jurist of marked integrity is somewhat difficult.

The most famous and controversial decisions rendered by Taft involved three areas: rights and responsibilities of labor, negligence and corporate conduct, and the emergence of antitrust law. This is understandable as the last decade of the nineteenth century witnessed labor violence in the context of the Pullman strike of 1893 and 1894, passage of the Sherman Antitrust Act in 1890, and changing judicial standards toward the traditional rules of negligence. Taft handed down important rulings in all of these fields, and appears to have gained considerable contemporary stature as a distinguished federal jurist during his time on the circuit bench.

Early in his term as a judge, Taft considered issues of industrial accidents and liability. Existing case law reflected two well-established doctrines, both unusually unfavorable to workers. The "fellow-servant" rule simply meant that a worker in a factory or on a railroad could not sue the owner for on-the-job injuries caused by another employee. It was based on the notion, increasingly outdated by the 1890s, that an owner (manager) and laborer all stood on equal terms in respect to making a contract. Thus, upon agreeing to work for

[27] See Lewis L. Gould, *Helen Taft: Our Musical First Lady*, (Lawrence: University Press of Kansas), 2010, 12–13.

the company, the worker assumed the risks of such injury. In addition to the fellow-servant rule, the doctrine of contributory negligence severely limited the laborer's right to recover.

Taft began his circuit duties late in 1892, and while he usually affirmed the general validity of both rules, it was not necessary for him to do so in one of his first labor decisions. The case involved an injury to a railroad worker "who admits that, with the knowledge that an engine was approaching, on a very dark night, lay down with his arm over the rail and went to sleep. Grosser negligence, more certain to result in injury, can hardly be suggested."[28] Taft conceded that an engineer faced a much more rigorous standard to safeguard passengers and travelers on a train, but he emphasized that the engineer had a right to rely on the presumption that "no one would be so grossly negligent in courting death." Because an engineer would not expect to find a sleeping man on the tracks, "there was no negligence in his failing to see [plaintiff.]"[29]

As a judge, Taft was not uniformly hostile to labor. Indeed, the case just cited demonstrates this fact, based as it was on an issue of common sense rather than on railroad negligence. Further, it involved labor, but not organized labor, and this distinction was of major significance for the judge. Although, as will be seen, he never abandoned his objection to what he termed the secondary boycott, he was capable of an even-handed approach to issues between labor and management. Thus, in one case decided in 1894, he reversed a lower-court decision that had gone against an injured plaintiff. The railroad worker claimed that the railroad was negligent in failing to repair the floor of a shed on which he had been working, and that the company should have known of its dangerous condition. Taft agreed, noting that the shed had been "in bad repair for several years," and that the company "must be presumed to have had knowledge of this...." Manifestly, he added, "plaintiff had the right to submit to the jury the issue of whether he was negligent or not."[30] Taft ordered a new trial.

But if Taft was objective concerning some aspects of the never-ending issues between capital and labor, and if he consistently affirmed labor's right to strike, he deplored any resulting violence, especially when he saw it as a result of a secondary boycott initiated by a union. Toward the end of his tenure on the Ohio Superior Court, he had already ruled against this practice in the Moores & Co. case. In 1894, as the Pullman strike convulsed Chicago, it again attracted his attention. Taft prided himself on his ability to separate his own viewpoint from issues coming before him as a judge. However, by nature conservative and believing in ordered legal processes, on occasion he may well have been unable to do this. Of course, the violence that characterized the American Railway Union (ARU) strike affected his perspective.

---

[28] *Newport News & M.V. Co., v. Howe.* 52 F. 362, 367 (1892).
[29] Ibid., 369.
[30] *Norman v. Wabash R. Co.* 62 F. 727, 729 (1894).

By 1894, the United States was in the midst of the worst depression thus far in its history. The industrialist George Pullman reacted by increasing the rents and rates paid by workers in his famous company town of Pullman, even as he reduced their wages. No less a figure than Mark Hanna, the Ohio businessman who would successfully orchestrate the nomination and election of William McKinley as president barely two years later, considered Pullman's move callous and uncalled for. As the workers went out on strike, Hanna reacted with candor. "Oh hell," he supposedly said. " ... [F]ind out how much Pullman gets selling city water and gas ten percent higher to those poor fools. A man who won't meet his men half way is a God-damn fool!"[31]

The strike by the Pullman workers took on an added dimension in June, when the ARU announced that it would not operate any train to which a Pullman car was attached. Within a month, the railroad network was in chaos. Against the wishes of Illinois Governor John Peter Altgeld, but on the advice of his attorney general, President Grover Cleveland sent federal troops into Chicago, claiming that the strikers were preventing the U.S. mail from prompt delivery. The claim rang hollow if only because the ARU had supposedly agreed to operate trains with mail cars attached, but not the Pullman cars. By early July, battles, bloodshed, and violence characterized Chicago's railroad yards. Circuit Judge Will Taft watched with consternation, and his letters to Nellie reflected anger at the strikers, rather than any sympathy for their cause.

On July 6, 1894, he informed Nellie that "it will be necessary for the military to kill some of the mob before the trouble can be stayed." One day later, he reported that "thirty men have been killed by the federal troops. Though it is bloody business, everybody hopes that it is true." On July 8, he considered "that the Chicago situation is not much improved. They have only killed six of the mob as yet. This is hardly enough to make an impression." Only three days after he had pointed to the necessity of killing "some of the mob," Taft concluded that "the most demagogic and insane [labor] leaders ... are determined to provoke a civil war."[32]

Private correspondence is not necessarily incompatible with a public posture of impartiality, but the Pullman strike, especially its aftermath, gave Taft an opportunity to practice publicly what he had pronounced privately. As the goal of the ARU was to shut down as much of the nation's railroad traffic as possible, it is not surprising that its leadership turned to Cincinnati, which functioned as an important junction of several major railroad lines. One of them, long since out of business – as is true of virtually every privately owned American railroad – had been in federal receivership for more than a year. Early in July 1894, the receiver sought an injunction against one F. W. Phelan, an associate of ARU president Eugene V. Debs's. The receiver accused Phelan of seeking to incite his railroad workers to strike, in an effort "to prevent the

[31] Pringle, 127–128.
[32] Pringle, 128–129.

receiver of this court ... from using Pullman cars ... though [he] is under contract to do so." Apparently a sort of union organizer working closely with Debs, Phelan had made a number of speeches supposedly urging all the workers to quit the railroads, thus "to tie them all up, and to prevent others from taking their places, by persuasion if possible, by clubbing if necessary."[33] Taft enjoined Phelan from any further such obstruction, but only two days later on July 5, agreed to hear a motion that Phelan be punished for disobeying the injunction Taft had issued.

After a week of argument and rebuttal, Taft handed down what would become known as his most notorious antilabor opinion. Like so many of his opinions, the decision was thorough and carefully researched, and although phrased in cold unemotional language, in fact it bristled with indignation over Phelan's conduct. He emphasized that the rights of labor both to form a union and to go out on strike were not at issue. Phelan had come to Cincinnati to incite local railway workers to go out on strike in order to compel Pullman to negotiate with the ARU. But Pullman's wages to his workers were not a legitimate concern to Cincinnati's railway employees. Rather, Phelan had sought "a paralysis of all railway traffic of every kind throughout that vast territory traversed by lines using Pullman cars."[34] In short, he had organized a secondary boycott, something that Taft had already denounced as a superior court judge.

Local railroad workers, insisted Taft, had no contractual relationship with Pullman. "He paid them no wages. He did not regulate their hours, or in any way determine their services."[35] Striking workers of the ARU had every right to strike the Pullman factory. But they had no right to injure him by compelling other railroad companies under threat of a boycott to refuse to transport trains that also carried Pullman cars. Such action made "the injury inflicted unlawful, and the combination by which it is effected, an unlawful conspiracy."[36] Taft relied heavily on his earlier opinion in the Moores case, although he omitted the fact that he had authored that opinion.

But Taft went much further in his denunciation of the railway union, insisting that "the gigantic character of the American Railway Union staggers the imagination." Phelan, he concluded, had sought to "paralyze utterly all the [railroad] traffic by which the people live." His intent was to "starve the railroad companies and the public into compelling Pullman to do something which they had no lawful right to compel him to do."[37] Finally, Taft pointed to Phelan's continued defiance of the injunction Taft had imposed, and quoted Phelan in a speech as stating that "I don't care if I am violating injunctions.

[33] *Thomas v. Cincinnati, N.O. & T.P. Ry. Co; in re Phelan,* 62 F. 803, 805 (1894).

[34] Ibid., 807.

[35] Ibid., 817. "Phelan came to Cincinnati to carry out the purpose of a combination ... [,] and his act in inciting the employees of all Cincinnati [rail]roads to quit service was part of that combination."

[36] Ibid., 818.

[37] Ibid., 821.

No matter what the result may be tomorrow, if I go to jail for sixteen generations, I want you to do as you have done. Stand pat to a man." For Taft, such blatant defiance of a judicial edict represented the nadir of individual responsibility. It could not be tolerated, and in response, Phelan was ordered to serve a six-month term in prison.

Given Taft's previous decisions, the Phelan case is not surprising even though it affirmed the rights both to organize unions as well as to strike. But, again, especially when considering his years as a circuit judge, one should be wary of calling Taft a reactionary jurist. Three cases decided toward the end of his tenure as a circuit court judge well illustrate the point. In each case, Taft moved the law forward from its current position. If his opinions can be described as conservative, they represent a dynamic if not progressive conservatism, reconciling changing industrial conditions with long-held expectations of due process, precisely the goals of the Progressive Era.

In 1897, Taft considered a complaint filed by an injured railroad worker against a railroad.[38] Employed as a messenger for an express company, the worker had earlier signed an agreement waiving his rights to sue the railroad for any and all injuries he might receive while riding on its lines. He rode in a special car provided by the railroad for the use of the express company employees. When confronted with his written agreement not to sue, plaintiff responded with a demurrer, and argued that his previous pledge had nothing to do with the expected obligations of a railroad carrying passengers for hire. Taft not only sustained the demurrer, but awarded the plaintiff $6,000 plus costs.

When the railroad carried passengers, Taft held, it "is discharging its function as a common carrier of persons." By the late nineteenth century, railroads had long been held to a strict level of care concerning their passengers, as contrasted with that of their employees. In this instance, however, an employee rode as a passenger, and Taft found "no such difference in the risk of carrying the express messenger and the ordinary passenger in the same train." The railroad cannot claim to be a private carrier in order "to escape the rule of public policy which forbids the common carrier from stipulating against liability for its own negligence."[39] In expanding the scope of liability on the railroad, however, Taft ran afoul of the contemporary doctrine of liberty of contract, and the U.S. Supreme Court had no difficulty in reversing his finding.

Justice George Shiras Jr. noted that "the right of private contract is no small part of the liberty of the citizen.... Further, the "most important function of courts of justice is rather to maintain and enforce contracts than to enable parties ... to escape from their obligation on the pretext of public policy...."[40] Unlike Judge Taft, the High Court concluded that Voight's status resembled "that of an employee, [rather] than that of a passenger." Thus he could not

---

[38] *Voight v. Baltimore and Ohio Southerwestern Railway Co.*, 79 F. 561 (1897).
[39] Ibid., 565.
[40] *Baltimore & Ohio Southwestern Railway Co., v. William Voight*, 176 U.S. 498 (1900).

recover for injuries caused by the negligence of fellow employees. Voight had entered into a contract "freely and voluntarily" to be a messenger for the railroad. As part of his work, he rode not as a passenger but as an employee. Therefore the obligations owed to him by the railroad were much lower than had he been a paying passenger.[41] In a lone dissent, Justice Harlan insisted "that the [fact that] the person transported is not technically a passenger and does not ride in a car ordinarily used for passengers is immaterial."[42]

A second instance of Taft's position that was ahead of current legal doctrine is seen in what is perhaps his best-known opinion in the area of antitrust law. Handed down toward the end of his tenure as a circuit judge, Taft's opinion on appeal in *United States v. Addyston Pipe and Steel Co.* received unanimous endorsement from the Supreme Court.[43] While it might be an overstatement to claim, as did Taft's major biographer Henry Pringle, that with this opinion, Taft "definitely and specifically revived the Sherman Antitrust Act," it represented a sophisticated reconciliation of existing case law with the ongoing challenges of effective antitrust regulation.[44]

The Addyston Pipe case was decided in 1898 by a three-judge panel that consisted entirely of current or future High Court justices. Supreme Court Justice Harlan presided, joined by judges Taft and Lurton. As president, Taft would later name Lurton to the High Court, the same tribunal to which he himself would be appointed by President Harding in 1921. The United States appealed a dismissal of its claim that an association of pipe manufacturers in violation of the Sherman Antitrust Act had conspired not only to fix prices but also to allocate specific territories in which the various companies could transact business.

Counsel for the association insisted "that the law now recognizes that competition may be so ruinous as to injure the public, and therefore, that contracts made with a view to check such ruinous competition and regulate prices, though in restraint of trade....will be upheld."[45] Speaking for a unanimous panel, Taft denied the contention, noting that "this conclusion is unwarranted by the authorities," from whom he cited in some detail.

Indeed, he wrote, "we can have no doubt that [this] association of defendants, however reasonable the prices they fixed, however great the competition they had to encounter, and however great the necessity for curbing themselves by joint agreement from committing financial suicide by ill-advised competition, was void at common law, because [it was] in restraint of trade, and tending to a monopoly."[46] Following his usual pattern, Taft proceeded to explore the workings of the association, and noted that it did not need to have a "complete monopoly" in order to fall within the Sherman Act's provisions. He cited

[41] Ibid., 513.
[42] Ibid., 521.
[43] 85 F. 271 (1898); 178 U.S. 211 (1899).
[44] Pringle, I, 143.
[45] *United States v. Addyston Pipe and Steel Co.*, 85 F. 271, 283 (1898).
[46] Ibid., 291.

the famous E. C. Knight Case of 1895, in which Chief Justice Fuller had noted that "in order to vitiate a contract or combination, it is not essential that its results should be a complete monopoly. It is sufficient if it really tends to that end, and to so deprive the public of the advantages of free competition."[47] Here, none of the pipe manufacturers who were part of "this pipe-trust combination" were allowed "to send its goods out of the state ... except upon the terms established by the agreement. Can it be doubted that this was a direct restraint upon interstate commerce in those goods?"

Counsel for the association also cited the Knight case, arguing that the agreement that was the basis for the Addyston case was within the parameters of that decision. But Taft would have none of it. He did not need to argue that *Knight* had been wrongly decided. Even if he so felt, and there is no evidence that he did, such a view of a High Court decision from a circuit court of appeals would be unacceptable to contemporary American jurisprudence. Indeed, Taft never even hinted that the Knight case had been subject to criticism. The 1895 holding, he noted, made a crucial distinction between "a restraint upon the business of manufacturing[,] and a restraint upon the trade or commerce between the states in the articles after manufacture." Unlike in *Knight*, manufacturing was not the issue in *Addyston*. Rather, it was "contracts for sale" of articles "to be delivered across state lines, and arrived at after negotiation and preliminary bids – all of which ... do not merely affect interstate commerce, but are interstate commerce."[48]

Here, Taft found himself arguing that the Addyston case better fit within the Sherman Act than had the 1895 holding. In *Knight*, Chief Justice Fuller had held that what the Sherman Act "struck at was combinations, contracts and conspiracies to monopolize trade and commerce among the several states or with foreign nations." In *Addyston*, the agreement was "on its face an extensive scheme to control the whole commerce among 36 states in cast iron pipe, and ... defendants were fully aware of the fact whether they appreciated the application of it to the antitrust law or not."[49] Finally, taking a cue from Chief Justice Marshall, who always insisted that his "landmark" decisions were neither controversial nor innovative, Taft concluded that in *Addyston*, "we do not announce any new doctrine," and if his decision "expands federal jurisdiction ... it is not because such jurisdiction is not within the limits allowed by the constitution of the United States."[50]

The Supreme Court unanimously affirmed Taft's decision, although it emphasized the importance of interference with interstate commerce as an

---

[47] *United States v. E. C. Knight*, 156 U.S. 1 (1895). Three years after this famous decision, drawing a distinction between manufacturing and commerce, and ruling that the Sherman Act applied to the former, but not the latter, conventional legal wisdom held that this distinction had virtually gutted the Sherman Act of any legal significance. As will be seen in *Addyston*, Taft set out to rebut this conclusion.

[48] *Addyston*, 298.

[49] Ibid., 301.

[50] Ibid.

indispensable condition to his holding. Sounding very much like good progressive doctrine, the High Court's opinion proclaimed that "we do not assent to the correctness of the proposition that the constitutional guaranty of liberty to enter into private contracts limits the power of Congress...."[51] The writer was none other than Rufus Peckham, who barely six years later would write the opinion for a badly divided court in *Lochner v. New York*, a decision commonly considered to be one of the landmarks of an excessive judicial concern for liberty of contract.[52] The two opinions in *Addyston* are excellent examples of an intriguing liberal twist in conservative legal doctrine as a whole.

Peckham, for example, could endorse Taft's strictures against an overly aggressive application of private economic greed at the expense of the congressional authority to regulate interstate commerce. But a state regulatory statute that had no apparent connection to interstate commerce represented a very different issue for him, with liberty of contract trumping excessive use of state police power. Hence, in his mind, there probably was no inconsistency between his Addyston decision and his majority opinion in *Lochner* a few years later. Indeed, a lack of concern for property rights was not perceived to be a part of progressive thinking during the era that bears its name. For jurists such as both Taft and Peckham, honesty and efficiency in government, as well as taming "the excesses of capitalism," appeared to be fully compatible with property rights. Moreover, the extent to which progressives desired to undertake "fundamental transformation of the American economic system" remains far from clear.[53]

This conclusion is neither new nor original. More than thirty years ago, the historian John Buenker observed that "the Progressive era was characterized much more by diversity than by unity." Robert Crundon reminds us that "many of the reforms advocated by progressives would be repellent to "contemporary liberal historians." Negative impulses, he notes, such as "imperialism, ... racism, the prohibition and the narrow fundamentalism" could be endorsed by progressives who at the same time might support reforms such as conservation, federal economic regulation, tariff reduction, and the legislative proposals known as the initiative, referendum and recall." Crundon goes so far as to conclude that "to be progressive (in general) was not [necessarily] to be a progressive."[54]

---

[51] *Addyston Pipe and Steel Co. v. United States*, 175 U.S. 211, 228 (1899). As if to make his point even clearer, Justice Peckham added that "it has never been, and in our opinion ought not to be, held that the word [liberty] included the right of an individual to enter into private contracts upon all subjects, no matter what their nature...." Ibid., 229.

[52] 205 U.S. 284 (1905).

[53] William G. Ross, *The Chief Justiceship of Charles Evans Hughes, 1930–1941* (Columbia University: of South Carolina Press, 2007), 4–5.

[54] John D. Buenker, John C. Burnham, and Robert M. Crunden, *Progressivism* (Cambridge, MA: Schenkman Publishing Co., 1977), 108, 112. As will be seen, Crunden's point has special relevance for William Howard Taft, who, as president, supported tariff reduction, conservation, and antitrust regulation, even as he strongly objected to the initiative, referendum,

A final example of Taft's tendency, at least in his first two "careers" on the bench, not to fit neatly into categories such as liberal or conservative is seen in one of his last opinions as a circuit judge. In the 1899 Narramore case, Taft revisited the ongoing issues of contributory negligence and employer obligations.[55] But this case had an interesting twist in that it involved a recently enacted state statute. The law mandated that railroads in Ohio install safety blocks on guard rails and switches. The Narramore case arose when the plaintiff was seriously injured by a railroad car passing over switches on which these safety devices had not been installed. The railroad admitted this fact, but argued that the well-established doctrine of "assumption risk" applied. Because plaintiff knew of the danger from open unprotected switches, and yet continued working, by such action he undertook to assume the risk, thus freeing the railroad from any liability – regardless of the statute.[56]

Speaking for a unanimous court, Taft not only sustained the statute, but also distinguished between assumption of risk and contributory negligence. The claim that Narramore had prior knowledge of the open switches was not relevant. Taft quoted an earlier Ohio decision to the effect that "acquiescence with knowledge is not synonymous with contributory negligence." Moreover, the question of whether or not Narramore used due care should have been submitted to the jury. The clear legislative intent to protect the railroad workers "by positive law" was not to be avoided by invoking the doctrine of assumption of risk. Taft reversed the trial court and ordered a new trial.[57]

As a federal judge, Taft refused to comment publicly on issues of contemporary political concern. The fact that personally he had no interest in politics made this policy all the easier for him to follow. Secure in his career, he still found much on which to react concerning political issues of the day, albeit in private. He noted, for example, the efforts of Mark Hanna – ultimately successful – to orchestrate William McKinley's nomination and election to the presidency in 1896. In 1894, Taft found the Republican congressman to be "a timid statesman," not highly regarded in Washington. Nor did Taft welcome McKinley's nomination. Yet nothing, Taft feared, could prevent it. "He seems to have a great popular ground swell in his favor," and he will win "only to demonstrate his incapacity."[58]

During the summer of 1896, however, Taft's views shifted toward McKinley, especially by comparison with the Democratic nominee, William Jennings

and recall. See also the perceptive comment of John Morton Blum, who concludes that "progressivism, never a neat systematic creed, had almost as many guises as there were different groups … who shared a general purpose, sometimes altruistic, sometimes selfish, to reform American society." John M. Blum, *The Progressive Presidents* (New York: W. W. Norton & Co., 1980), 62.

[55] *Narramore v. Cleveland, C., C. & St. L. Ry. Co.*, 96 F. 298 (1899).

[56] Ibid., 301–303.

[57] Ibid., 304–305. See Pringle 142–143 for some contemporary examples of legal reaction to the Narramore decision.

[58] Pringle, 149–150.

Bryan. According to Taft, the "Democrats are crazy and the crazier they are[,] the surer [of] their defeat."[59] By the fall, he had become a strong supporter of his fellow Ohian, and welcomed his election.

Taft had never abandoned his hope of appointment to the Supreme Court, but he was not too disappointed when late in December 1897, McKinley named Joseph McKenna, in what would be his only appointment to that tribunal. Thus Taft was amazed when in January 1900, he was suddenly summoned to the White House. Taft could not know why the president wished to see him, nor that his tenure as a circuit judge was about to end.

[59] Ibid., 151.

3

Roosevelt and Taft in the Philippines, 1900–1904

TO ACCEPT OR NOT TO ACCEPT?

Taft later recalled his amazement when in January 1900, President McKinley informed him that he wished to appoint the Ohio jurist to the Philippine Commission, a group of civilians charged with establishing and maintaining civil government, even as the American military found itself fighting a native rebellion in the recently acquired island chain.[1] "He might as well have told me that that he wanted me to take a flying machine."[2] Taft had expressed little enthusiasm for the Spanish American War, and vaguely recalled that the United States had paid $20 million to Spain in return for taking control of the Philippines. Affairs there did not interest Taft. Indeed, when McKinley asked him to comment on American policy in the Philippines, he promptly disagreed with McKinley's actions. "I was very much opposed to taking them …," and indeed "deprecated our taking the Philippines because of the assumption of a burden by us contrary to our traditions[,] and at a time when we had quite enough to do at home."[3]

McKinley responded with the observation that he had not wanted them either, "but we have got them[,] and in dealing with them I think I can trust the man who didn't want them better than I can the man who did."[4] He reiterated

---

[1] In fact, Taft would be the head of what was actually a second Philippine Commission. The first group, led by Cornell University President Jacob Schurman, had arrived in Manila in March 1899, shortly after fighting between the Philippine natives and the American occupiers intensified. Schurman's Commission, lacking real authority and hampered by rigid supervision from the military, nevertheless made it clear that the American goal was effective administration, not annexation, with the ultimate prospect of self–government, at least in some form, albeit under American supervision. Pringle, 159.

[2] Pringle, 160.

[3] Ibid. Possibly with prescience, Taft added that "but being there, we must exert ourselves to construct a government which should be adopted to the needs of the people so that they might be developed into a self governing [entity.]"

[4] Ross, 125. Anthony comments on McKinley's initial indecisiveness concerning the Philippines, noting that Mrs. McKinley, with her vigorous support of Methodist missionary work in the

his flattering assessment of Taft's abilities, and added that key members of his administration, including Secretary of War Elihu Root and Secretary of State John Hay, had urged his appointment. Not unreasonably, Taft observed that the president was asking him to give up a life-tenure position in a post that so well-suited him for a very uncertain future. In response, McKinley dangled the prospect of a future Supreme Court appointment before him, and his words concerning Circuit Judge Taft (as reported by Taft to his brothers) are of interest. "If you give up this judicial office at my request[,] you shall not suffer. If I last and the opportunity comes, I shall appoint you.... If I am here, you will be here."[5] Also present at the meeting, Elihu Root took a different tack, and urged Taft to look at the broader picture.

"Now," he said, your country needs you.... You may go on holding the job you have in a humdrum, mediocre way. But here is something that will test you; something in the way of effort and struggle, and the question is, will you take the harder or the easier task?"[6] Typically, Taft hesitated, and turned to his family for advice and support. "The question of course," he wrote to his brothers, "is am I willing and ought I to give up my present position for what is offered *in praesenti* and *in futuro*. The opportunity to do good and help along in a critical state in the country's history is very great ... I confess that I love my present position. Perhaps it is the comfort and dignity and power without worry [that] I like. Ought I to allow this to deter me from accepting an opportunity thrust upon me to accomplish more important and more venturesome tasks with a possible greater reward[?]"[7]

Horace Taft responded positively, writing to Will that "you can do more good in that position in a year than you could on the bench in a dozen...." He added that Will could always get a job in the new prep school that Horace Taft had recently established. "I can give you ... the chair of Christian manhood." But in a more serious vein, he chided his older brother about "the absurdity of being troubled about your future. Even if you were compelled to go back to the Bar and make a little money for a change[,] you would soon have the choice between going on making money and taking a judicial or political office."[8] In the face of consistent encouragement from his brothers as well as Nellie, Taft still hesitated. He sought assurance on one key point in

---

Islands, may have been the ultimate factor in her husband's decision to take responsibility for them. Anthony, 133.

[5] Pringle Papers, Box 28, January 28, 1900. In retrospect, McKinley did not last; he was not "there," and during the remainder of his life – he was assassinated in September, 1901 – had no opportunity to make any more appointments to the High Court other than Joseph McKenna, whom he had nominated in December 1897.

[6] Pringle, 160–161. Perhaps Taft winced at Root's blunt but accurate assessment of his tenure as a circuit court judge.

[7] Pringle Papers, supra. On the bench, Taft had no difficulty in rendering difficult decisions. Outside of that arcane arena, however, his decisiveness sometimes failed him. In this episode, for example, he asked his youngest brother, Horace, to "write fully and frankly."

[8] Pringle Papers, Box 28, January 31, 1900.

a private letter to Root. It warrants some comment, as it is typical of Taft's outlook toward himself.

First, Taft emphasized that "the work to be done is so full of perplexing problems that the responsibility and risk in attempting it will be very great." He then expressed doubt as to his "capacity to meet them[,] but an earnest desire to succeed and hard work may overcome many obstacles." All the more reason, he added, that "if I am to undertake the work ... , I should like to be in a position in which I shall be really responsible for success or failure.... In other words I should like an opportunity commensurate with the responsibility...." The task of the Commission "will be reframing the government and laws, ... retaining what is good and necessary of the old and in deciding how far advanced the people are, to accept the new ... " In short, work for a lawyer. Indirectly, Taft reminded Root again that he would have to resign a life-tenure judicial position, which he loved, for an admittedly risky venture. He asked Root to let him know "whether I am to be, if I accept, the President of the Commission, for it will have a material bearing upon my acceptance."[9] Root responded immediately, with an answer apparently satisfactory to Taft. He accepted the appointment as Commission president, and assumed that the job would last for about one year.[10]

TAFT AND THE ARMY

Taft soon discovered that the Commission had to deal with a problem that was in its way as bothersome as the waves of Filipino rebellion that occurred with some regularity. It was not so much confronting native unrest as coping with the American military presence. Until the country was pacified, the Commission would be unable to carry out its mandate. But who was to determine when this goal had been attained?[11] Taft's effort to resolve this issue was fundamental to the Commission's future. Typically, McKinley left the lines of authority between the military and the civilian Commission unclear. As Taft learned, however, even as he arrived in Manila, the American commander had no doubt as to his powers. That Commander – Arthur MacArthur – also discovered that Taft had a similar perspective on his Commission's authority.

---

[9] Taft to Elihu Root, Root Papers, LOC, February 2, 1900.

[10] In reality, it lasted almost four, brought Taft close to death, and resulted in offers of a High Court appointment from Theodore Roosevelt, which Taft declined, a decision, although surprising given Taft's lifelong ambition to serve on the High Court, is far from inexplicable, as will be seen. The remainder of this chapter explores several aspects of his experiences in the Archipelago that were of major influence in his later career. Of special significance was the relationship between Roosevelt and Taft.

[11] Brian McAllister Linn, *The Philippine War, 1899–1902* (Lawrence: University Press of Kansas, 2000). The best single volume on the history of the American epoch in the Philippines, although marred to some extent by excessive verbiage, is probably Paul Kramer, *The Blood of Government: Race, Empire, the United States, and the Philippines* (New York and Chapel Hill: The University of North Carolina Press, 2006).

Conflict between the two was inevitable, and it started even before Taft disembarked from the boat.[12]

Taft and his fellow commissioners arrived in Manila on June 3, 1900, a typically hot, steamy day. If he had expected General MacArthur, who had been appointed military governor in May, to come on board to pay his respects, he was in for a rude awakening. MacArthur never showed up.[13] Instead, Taft and his commissioners duly appeared at the Ayuntamiento Palace, where they were received, but not welcomed, by the general. His frigidity of manner, Taft later wrote to Nellie, "had made his perspiration stop."[14]

From MacArthur's perspective, Taft and his associates represented little more than an unnecessary nuisance. In his opinion, one shared by most of the military officers around him, the Philippine natives were far from ready for self-government. Indeed, MacArthur regarded them "as opposed to the American Forces[,] and looks at his task as one of conquering eight millions of recalcitrant, treacherous and sullen people."[15] Military rule backed up by the bayonet was more appropriate than any well-intentioned introduction to civil government.[16] On the other hand, Taft brought with him orders from President McKinley, issued through Root, one of which vested his Commission with complete authority over all the financial appropriations MacArthur might require. Moreover, by September 1, 1900, the Commission would assume legislative power and move to establish civilian and provincial governments, even as the military declared each province pacified. Hesitant to act, always skeptical of progress toward pacification, racist in his views of the Philippine people, and worried about congressional reaction to his efforts, MacArthur nevertheless believed himself to be fully capable of governance without civilian interference.[17]

Yet this general – arrogant, opinionated, and narrowly self-educated – met his match in Taft. Indeed, although he did not so state explicitly, the former judge considered the military governor's "lectures tedious, his rhetoric ludicrous, his legal views alarming, and his personality unpleasant."[18] A few

---

[12] It is interesting that MacArthur's difficulty in dealing with civilian authority was apparently inherited by his son, General Douglas MacArthur, whose later involvement with the Philippines, as well as his ultimate removal from military command by President Truman, are beyond the scope of this book.

[13] Pringle, 169.

[14] Ibid., 170.

[15] Taft to Root, Root Papers, LOC, August 18, 1900, 3.

[16] MacArthur frequently argued that it would take at least ten years before all armed insurrection in the Philippines could be suppressed.

[17] Linn, 216. As a survey of the Taft–Root Letters indicates, Taft, rather shrewdly, tried to play the general off against the secretary of war rather than against Taft and his Commission. In such a confrontation, MacArthur could not win, and by the summer of 1901, he conceded as much. In January, Taft had advised Root of "the truth that the military arm is entrenched here[,] and it does not intend to retreat before the advance of the civil government except under distinct orders which it cannot evade." Taft to Root, Root Papers, LOC, January 13, 1901, 2.

[18] Linn, 216.

months after his arrival, Taft wrote to Root, describing his difficulties in dealing with MacArthur. "It is most trying," he noted, "in such a situation as
we have here[,] not to feel that we can consult freely and make suggestions
concerning our common purpose without arousing a[n] ... intense feeling of
fear, lest our suggestions may transgress the fine line between civil and military operation. It is impossible not to do so because we are constantly receiving communications from persons who do not know the distinction[,] but I
have ceased even formally to refer them to the Military Governor for I have
no desire to injure the possibility of good from the suggestion by appearing to
make it myself."[19]

MacArthur insisted that martial law, even if not directly imposed, remained
the standard for military occupation. Taft and his commissioners rejected this
claim out of hand. What MacArthur held, according to Taft, was that "martial law prevail[ing] in a civil government means ... that while the civil officers
... may exercise their appointed functions, such functions may, at any time,
be suspended and are always performed subject to the will of the Military
Commander who is the real ruler of the territory."[20] Moreover, MacArthur
questioned the basic legality of Taft's Commission, regardless of the president's action in creating it.[21]

Taft found the situation both perplexing and frustrating. As he wrote to
Theodore Roosevelt, newly inaugurated as Vice President, "The obstacle presented by the indisposition of the army to give up any power which it has once
enjoyed, and its entire lack of cooperation ... are facts which one should have
counted on, but which I was not sufficiently acquainted with when I came here."[22]
His Commission was in fact serving as "the Legislature of the Military government," an anomaly to be sure, but one that "has worked magnificently." With
military occupation as the only option, rebellion would continue indefinitely.
But with promised opportunities for a real civilian government, motivation for
continued resistance dissipated, even as the Army resisted such changes.[23]

[19] Taft to Root, Root Papers, October 3, 1900. In December, Taft wrote of MacArthur that "it
is exceedingly disagreeable to fuss and fuss with a man who resents your presence and who is
on the keen watch to detect some usurpation of jurisdiction[,] and who is himself suspicious
of any proposition which emanates from you." Ibid., December 27, 1900, 15.
[20] Taft to MacArthur, Pringle Papers, LOC, March 6, 1901.
[21] Taft commented to Root that "it has always been a curious phase of political human nature
to me to observe that men who have not the slightest knowledge of legal principles and do not
claim to have had any legal education feel entirely at home in the construction of the constitution[,] and in using its limitations to support their views and to nullify action, the wisdom
of which they dispute." Taft to Root, March 17, 1901, 7.
[22] Taft to Theodore Roosevelt, Pringle Papers, LOC, May 12, 1901. A few months earlier, doubtless with MacArthur in mind, Roosevelt wrote to Judge William Day, also from Ohio and
destined for appointment to the Supreme Court in place of Taft, after he declined Roosevelt's
offer. The soldier's methods, Roosevelt noted, whether from "the American republic or of a
monarchy ... are necessarily abrupt[,] and he does not seek to give them that appearance of
fairness, which is as important as actual fairness, itself ... " Pringle Papers, December 10,
1900.
[23] Ibid., May 12, 1901.

As for MacArthur's claim that President McKinley had no constitutional power to entrust part of his authority to civilian authority as he did to the Commission, Taft noted in mock amazement that "I have known of the use of the Constitution in arguments for a great many different purposes, but it is the first time I have ever heard of a military commander using it to nullify, or attempt to nullify, the actions of his superior officer in taking away power from him."[24] Earlier, Roosevelt had expressed sympathy and understanding for Taft's problem, while strongly praising his contributions to the Philippines.

"I doubt," wrote the former Rough Rider, "if there is a man alive today who has a higher appreciation of the army than I have; but the older officers of course get ossified, and then they are very difficult to deal with, ... calling for qualities which they have never exercised ... and for a flexibility for which they are not now adapted."[25] What was appropriate in the Philippines was that the "military be an arm, directed by the civil head. In other words, it should be ... the arm, the sword, of the civil government, and that of course means that it should be directed by it."[26]

Taft considered it difficult but not impossible to work with MacArthur, all the more so as the general's tenure as military governor ended in July 1901. Upon his departure, the working relationship between civilian and military improved only slightly because MacArthur's successor, General Adna Chaffee, held similar views. As President of the Commission – Taft's title until he became civil governor in September 1901 – he could point to two disparate elements of his apparently ongoing disagreement with the military. The first involved a rerun of the earlier controversy between MacArthur and Taft over the extent of military jurisdiction in the entire Archipelago, while the second concerned racial views both of the occupiers and the occupied.

Taft's Commission had enacted, among a number of statutes adopted to govern the Philippines, a code of civil procedure, which included a provision for civil courts, complete with authority to issue a writ of habeas corpus.[27] Taft believed that this "right" applied to prisoners held by the military as well as to civilians. In one instance, however, the military command had refused to produce a prisoner in response to an order handed down by the Philippine Supreme Court. Chaffee defended his right to do this in a quasi-legal brief to Taft dated

[24] Ibid. Taft ended his letter by telling "my dear Theodore" that "I look forward with great confidence to your nomination for president....and look forward to voting for you." See what follows for some further comments on the relationship between TR and Taft.

[25] TR to Taft, *Letters of Theodore Roosevelt*, edited by Elting Morison (Cambridge, MA: Harvard University Press, 1951), vol. 3, March 12, 1901, 11. Hereafter cited as Letters, followed by volume and page number.

[26] Ibid., 12. Totally unaware of what the future held, TR told Taft how much "I envy you your work ... though I am enjoying myself ... yet I am not doing any work and do not feel as though I was justifying my existence." Indeed, TR had noted that "I would a great deal rather be your assistant in the Philippines or even Root's assistant in the War Department[,] than be vice-president." Letters, vol. 2, August 6, 1900, 1377. See also TR's letter to Henry Cabot Lodge, ibid., 1136.

[27] By early 1903, the Commission had enacted well over 400 statutes.

October 11, 1901.[28] It reflected, among other things, Chaffee's apparent unfamiliarity with American legal history during and after the Civil War era.

At the outset, Chaffee conceded that most of the main islands had been pacified, but insisted that in actual fact "a state of war exists throughout the entire Archipelago."[29] It followed that "the full power and influence of the Army ... ought not to be lessened by the action of any Civil Court, but permitted to exercise its full function on the theatre of war." Therefore, Taft's Commission had erred in creating civil courts in the Philippines with habeas power. The fault, in other words, was less with the court than with the Commission. Indeed, McKinley "did not intend to delegate to [Taft and his fellow commissioners] authority to pass laws ... that would interfere ... with the exercise of his rightful power as Commander in Chief."[30] Although he did not specifically say so, it seems that Chaffee even doubted whether the President under any circumstances could – let alone would – "cripple his own authority ... necessary for the complete untrammeled and free exercise of his military power...."

Of course, Taft's Commission received its powers from the president, acting as commander in chief. But, insisted Chaffee, "*all* such war powers have not been so delegated."[31] The Commission is "not clothed with plenipotentiary powers" and does not stand "in the place of the Commander in Chief or his Alter Ego." Only civil functions came within the purview of Taft's group, and only those civil functions that had once been exercised by MacArthur and Chaffee had been ceded to Taft.[32] Since MacArthur had previously denied courts the authority claimed in this instance, power to exercise it was beyond the authority of the Commission to grant.

To a great extent, Chaffee's premises were far ahead of his conclusions. He rejected the view of the Court "that because the civil and military authorities here derive their powers from the same source – the war power of the President – therefore they must be co-extensive" as "untenable. First, because the premise is wrong. The Army derives its powers from the Constitution and the laws of Congress." In addition, "only the civil functions ... had

---

[28] Taft and Chaffee felt impelled to report their disagreement to Washington, where Theodore Roosevelt had just become president and was less than enthusiastic about intervening in this controversy. TR responded with separate telegrams – apparently somewhat curt in tone – criticizing the dispute and ordering that the two resolve their differences in the Philippines, presumably without presidential involvement. They did. Pringle, 211–212.

[29] Adna Chaffee to Taft, October 11, 1901, in Root Papers, LOC. Of conditions in the Philippines, Chaffee added "in all parts there may be found sentiments by some of the people ... which are opposed to the governing authority and such sentiments are always found conducive to hostile action. Therefore a state of war exists in a technical sense everywhere in the Islands."

[30] Ibid., 4–5.

[31] Emphasis added.

[32] Ibid., 7. Chaffee noted further that MacArthur had never conceded that civil authorities could call upon the courts for assistance. In fact, "he expressly denied to the civil courts the power to issue writs of habeas corpus to released persons confined under military orders."

been delegated ... , and no military power."[33] The actions of Taft and his Commission were simply *ultra vires*.

Obviously much more at home with legal analysis than General Chaffee was, Taft in his thirteen-page reply easily destroyed Chaffee's arguments. He also provided a cogent explanation of his Commission's purpose in the Islands, one worthy of some discussion. Chaffee's claim that a state of war existed throughout the Philippines received short shrift. With the exception of four or five provinces, it "is certainly not true actually in the rest of the Archipelago."[34] Taft reminded General Chaffee that "the Constitution makes [the President] the Commander in Chief, and within the restrictions of law, the Commanding General is as completely subject to his orders, as is the Commission." Nor could there be any doubt of the president's authority to create courts "in territory conquered or recently in a state of war. "[35] If he did not choose to do this directly, nothing precluded the Chief Executive from delegating such authority to other individuals.

Taft conceded that McKinley had "provided for an anomalous form of military government in these Islands." A peculiar war might need "peculiar remedies." Added the Commission's president, [I believe] that "large parts of the territory would become free from hostilities[,] and that it would greatly aid the army in subduing the remainder, if object lessons in the benefits of American civil government could be offered...." Thus the Commission was empowered to establish governments at the municipal, and provincial levels, followed by some sort of central government "whenever the Commission shall be of opinion that it could be safely transferred from Military to Civil control."[36] Moreover, in his insistence on military independence from the Commission, Chaffee missed the point of McKinley's intentions.

"We have to construe a declaration of principles; a careful working out of concurrent jurisdiction between the civil and the military ... all under the power of the President as Commander in Chief." It would not do to "depend on general questions of military as to whether there is a technical state of actual war here[,] or [on] what the powers of a Commanding General are in the field when he is acting only under general instructions." In fact, McKinley had ordered that "wherever civil governments are constituted under the direction of the Commission," while the military commander controlled the forces, these troops "shall be at all times subject under his orders to the call of the civil authorities for the maintenance of law and order and the enforcement of their authority." Taft could not resist adding that "the *auxiliary function* of the military force in civil governments established by the Commission seems here to be clearly set forth."[37]

[33] Ibid., 7–8.
[34] Taft to Adna Chaffee, October 13, 1901, Root Papers, LOC, 3–4.
[35] Ibid., 5.
[36] Ibid., 7.
[37] Ibid., 8, emphasis added.

The former circuit court jurist further reminded Chaffee that to the greatest extent possible, the Philippine people were to be governed by the fundamental principles of due process, as commonly understood by the American legal order. Taft's Commission was "gradually to establish real civil governments in territory deemed ... fitted for it, and gradually to relegate the Army to the position which it occupies at home in time of peace...."[38] He used the word "real" advisedly. For in "real civil governments, it becomes the power and duty of the Commission to protect the individual from a violation of his civil liberty by furnishing ... the usual means known to Anglo Saxon countries, that of the writ of habeas corpus...." Taft rejected any inclination "to an interference with military affairs," but a civil inquiry into a civil matter did not reach such interference.

Taft's Commission "feels deeply its obligation to the people of the Islands who have joined in bringing about peace, where it exists, to afford them the blessings of civil liberty in as full measure as possible." This includes, "as far as conditions will permit," freedom "from arbitrary arrest by military or other authority." Indeed, "we have promised civil government, and a government in which there is a power which may make arbitrary arrests without being subject to a legal inquiry hardly deserves the name of civil."[39] Further, with only half a dozen out of some eighty-one provinces in partial rebellion, Taft insisted that "peace and good order will be much better maintained by conducting the government on principles of civil government."[40]

But Taft wished to avoid open and sustained conflict with Chaffee, all the more so as President Roosevelt had virtually ordered the two of them to resolve their differences. Taft agreed to amend the code of procedure so as to ban issuance of the writ in those provinces engaged in rebellion, and to provide three exceptions to an order to produce a prisoner held by the military. The commanding general "shall certify that the prisoner is held either (1) as a prisoner of war, (2) as a member of the Army, a civilian employee thereof or a camp follower and subject to its discipline, or (3) as a prisoner committed by a Military Court prior to October, 1902.[41]

Taft explained the great importance of the writ issue in a lengthy follow-up report to Root. The fact is, he wrote, "and the future will demonstrate it, that there in no part of the Archipelago, except in Batangas and Samar, is there the slightest desire on the part of the people for anything but peace. What they dread, however, is military government[,] and that they wish to avoid at all hazards."[42] Here, Taft reiterated a point he had raised with Root earlier. "The

---

[38] Ibid., 9.

[39] Ibid., 10.

[40] Ibid., 11. Taft added, somewhat disingenuously, that issuance of a writ "does not inquire into the merits of a case within the jurisdiction of a military commander and court, but only into the question of jurisdiction....The writ tests the jurisdiction solely and is not a writ of review."

[41] Ibid., 12–13.

[42] Taft to Root, Root Papers, LOC, November 17, 1901, 3.

hunger for civil government cannot be appreciated except by those who live in this community. One gets into a fever of a desire for it."[43] Among the practices of military governance resented by the natives, arbitrary action by a military court was a prime example.

"It is difficult for one who has not lived in the Islands" (Root had not, and Taft had already spent more than a year in residence) "to understand the possibility and frequency in these islands of conspiracies by perjured evidence to convict on unfounded charges." Numerous insurrectos "who have surrendered....[fear] their liability to trial for trumped up charges before military commissions and provost courts." Commonly used by the Spaniards, "such conspiracies, however, are much less easily worked out in a civil tribunal than before a military court."[44]

But Taft's rigorous insistence on proper judicial procedure in civil government, as well as his hostility to military administration, apparently did not extend to equally vigorous condemnation of improper conduct by the occupying American forces. There is no doubt that on a large number of occasions, efforts at "pacification" included incidents such as wholesale destruction of crops and livestock, destruction of private property, and use of torture – such as the infamous "water cure" – against the Philippine rebels.[45] It is also clear that the Philippine rebels employed brutal tactics against the Americans, although the actual extent to which such atrocities occurred on both sides remains debatable. Yet Taft, if not endorsing them, tacitly acquiesced in their occasional application. He wrote to Root, for example, "I fear that the people of Cebu have not had enough of real war yet, and that they must be pretty severely dealt with."[46]

In a similar vein, Taft urged Root to establish Guam as an outpost, to which recalcitrant Filipinos could be exiled. "Transportation to that Island has terrors for the natives that are not exceeded by those of the death penalty." Nothing, he added, could be more effective in the Archipelago after the American presidential election in 1900, "than the conviction of six or seven prominent Filipinos and their deportation to Guam."[47]

---

[43] Ibid., January 9, 1901, 15. See also Taft to Root, August 18, 1900, 11, 12. "It would be difficult, Mr. Secretary, to exaggerate the impatience and the feeling of enmity that exists on the part of the people here who are civilians, whether Americans, English, German, or Filipinos, against military rule. No matter how efficient the government, the abruptness and unconciliatory method of adopting measures, the apparent absence of deliberation and judicial consideration ... have thoroughly tended to bring about this sentiment."

[44] Ibid. Taft was so confident of his position that with some humor, he voiced regret at reaching a compromise with Chafee. "I was pleasantly disappointed," he wrote to Root, "to find that we can probably reach an agreement."

[45] Linn, 220.

[46] Taft to Root, LOC, October 14, 1901, 7. Exactly what Taft meant by this is not clear, but he presumably believed, that at least occasionally, excessive punishments meted out by the military would not be condemned by Taft and his commissioners as inappropriate or excessive.

[47] Ibid, September 21, 1900, 12–13. A few weeks later, Taft urged "again that we be given the opportunity to make Guam a place of confinement for political and other criminals of capital

More will be noted about Taft's attitudes toward the Philippine natives, but in 1901, it was also his own countrymen whom he severely criticized, in particular "the uncontrollable bitterness of Americans here against Filipinos. You know we have the rag tag and bob tail of Americans, who are not only vicious but stupid.... They are constantly stirring up trouble ... they "viciously attack the Commission in every way for appointing Filipinos[,] and sneer at every effort we make."[48] Even more disturbing, however, were visiting congressmen, who used the ongoing controversy over the American presence in the Archipelago for partisan political purposes at home. Among these politicians, Taft singled out a Michigan Republican – Edgar Weeks – for special attention. "It remained for Weeks ... to have an interview in Manila in which he described the Filipinos as nothing but savages, living a savage life and utterly incapable of self-government ... without the slightest knowledge of what independence is." Not only were such comments "altogether extreme and unjust, but even if they had been true, he was a fool to have announced them.... Weeks is an ass, but asses sometimes have a great capacity for mischief."[49]

RACE, RACISM, AND TAFT

Upon his arrival in the Philippines in June 1900, Taft concluded that racism was rampant within the American military authorities. This was not surprising, given the occupying country's own racial prejudices as the new century began. The 60,000 or so volunteers had not left their social values and customs behind on the mainland.[50] Not without reason, Taft was sorry to note, did the feeling exist in large segments of the Philippine people "that should pacification follow and complete control of the Islands be given to the United States, that the Filipinos would be relegated to an inferior class by themselves in a social way."[51] From the outset of his sojourn in the Islands, Taft insisted

importance, because it has the advantage of offering the same terrors as hanging and is by no means so sanguinary." Ibid., October 10, 1900, 2.

[48] Ibid., October 14, 1901, 8.

[49] It might be noted that Taft did not specifically state that Week's comments were untrue. The congressman's diatribe, however, played to the Spanish and Filipino papers opposing Taft's Commission "and intensified the feeling which we have been so anxious to allay." In a similar vein, Taft had written to Root in July, noting the comments of another Republican member of congress, John Hull. During a whirlwind visit to the Philippines, Hull informed Taft that the Commission's work "of organizing the provincial governments has not amounted to anything." Taft marveled, commenting that "the amount that an average Congressman can find out in staying an hour or more at a place concerning conditions that we have been studying for a year passes one's comprehension."" Taft to Root, Root Papers, LOC, October 14, 1901, 8; Ibid., July 4, 1901, 2.

[50] Professor Michael McGerr reminds us that "the early twentieth century became the great age of segregation in the United States, a time of enforced public separations." Michael McGerr, *A Fierce Discontent: The Rise and Fall of the Progressive Movement in America* (New York: Oxford University Press, 2003), 182.

[51] Taft to Root, August 18, 1900, 10.

on a truly integrated political and social framework.[52] In terms of political actions as well as social contacts, the extent to which he and Mrs. Taft pursued this policy was noteworthy.

Whatever his personal views were on the "inferiority" of the Philippine race, widely assumed by the military, Taft as early as June 1900, made it clear that racial discrimination was not acceptable. Thus, while "the ladies of the army ... regard the Filipino ladies and men as 'niggers' and as not fit to be associated with, we propose ... to banish this idea from their mind." The color line, according to his biographer, "was never drawn at the numerous official or unofficial dinners or receptions" required by his office.[53] Nellie Taft recalled that "we insisted on complete racial equality.... We made it a rule from the beginning that neither politics nor race should influence our hospitality in any way."[54] Indeed, as Professor Paul Kramer notes, in the Archipelago "where the racial formation of the war years was characterized by radical exclusion, fiesta politics played an important role in the [Taft Commission's] inclusionary racial formation.... Where U.S. officials danced with the wives of Filipino officials, they constructed a novel symbolic politics of cross-racial empire building that was at odds with wartime politics and, in many ways, at odds with domestic U.S. racial formations."[55]

Regardless of Kramer's apparently positive comments, the significance of Taft's racial "innovation" remains difficult to assess, and this in spite of Theodore Roosevelt's claim in 1902 that Taft "is as free from bigotry as anyone I have ever known."[56] Kramer argues that Taft's actions were in fact based on two negative principles: "calibrated colonialism and an inclusionary racial formation." Both of them were predicated on a gradual and incremental "surrender of power to the Filipinos as the mark of progress." By calibrated colonialism, he means the establishment of "credible, if illusory, markers in time that would signal devolutionary progress...." But calibrated colonialism, he insists, "could succeed only as long as freedom could be both reliably promised and endlessly deferred." It built upon "the endless colonization of the future," contained within "the illusion of impermanence."[57] For Taft, the realities of life in the Archipelago mandated such a policy.

---

[52] A satirical poem circulating in Manila had an American soldier saying:

> I'm only a common soldier-man in the blasted Philippines;
> They say I've got Brown Brothers here, but I dunno what it means.
> I like the word Fraternity, but still I draw the line;
> He may be a brother of William H. Taft, but he ain't no friend of mine.

Quoted in Kramer, 194

[53] Pringle, 174–175.

[54] Anthony, 148.

[55] Kramer, 187. The openness of the Taft receptions "signaled a sharp break with ongoing military encounters as well as with domestic U.S. racial forms." Ibid., 186.

[56] Roosevelt Letters, vol. 3, 308, July 31, 1902.

[57] Kramer, 191. Similarly. Kramer concludes that inclusionary racism "heralded an imperialism of process whose keywords – promise, progress, possibility, capacity, and development – were intended to mask the very empire from which they issued." Ibid., 192.

Taft had been in the Philippines for barely a month when he wrote to Root, describing the Philippine people. The population, he observed, "is made up of a vast mass of ignorant, superstitious people, well intentioned, light hearted, temperate, somewhat cruel ... fond of their families, and deeply wedded to the Catholic Church." Further, "they are generally lacking in moral character; are with some notable exceptions prone to yield to any pecuniary consideration, and are difficult persons out of whom to make an honest government." They are, he concluded, "born politicians; are as ambitious as Satan, and as jealous as possible of each other's preferment."[58]

Taft had previously written Root that "one of the most discouraging things in forming a government in this country is the inherent dishonesty of this race." Years of Spanish rule had taught them "that a legitimate perquisite of officials and of every agent is a 'rake off' on every transaction...." He was not sanguine that filling the key offices – whether municipal, departmental, or central – with Americans would necessarily solve the problem. "The danger is that some of our Americans will succumb to the constant temptation which repeated corrupting offers by the natives and other orientals will present." I must admit, Taft added, "that the dishonesty of this race is only the superlative of the quality of official corruption that prevails in the Orient everywhere."[59]

In August 1900, Taft cited "the indubitable fact ... that the Filipinos are at present so constituted as to be utterly unfit for self government.... They have, if needed to protect themselves, the greatest duplicity...." While they "deal in high sounding phrases concerning liberty and free government[,] they have very little conception of what that means. They cannot resist the temptations to venality, and every office is likely to be used for the personal aggrandizement of the office holder thereof in disregard of public interest."[60] Unfortunately, the judicial system was not immune from these temptations, something of special concern to William Howard Taft.

"The administration of justice through the native judges in Manila," he concluded in January 1901, "stinks to Heaven." Indeed, "the absolute venality of most of the native judges is so well understood that, while our selection of American judges may occasion some wild pyrotechnics of eloquence, everybody will feel that it is absolutely necessary."[61] Taft had already noted the contagion of corruption, particularly in Manila. "Here[.] oriental corruption, through gambling, prostitution and other vices, flourishes in its most luxuriant form, and it is so easy for an American in authority to acquire a great deal of money, with very little possibility of detection, that the real danger in

[58] Taft to Root, July 14, 1900, 2–3.

[59] Taft to Root, July 1, 1900, 4.

[60] Taft to Root, August 18, 1900, 20–21. Taft reiterated these sentiments a few weeks later to Senator John Spooner. "These people are as unfitted for self government as it is possible to imagine. The mass of the people are ignorant and superstitious...." Pringle Papers, September 3, 1900

[61] Taft to Root, 1901, 5–6.

the administration is the inability to secure, not honest Americans, but honest Americans who will not become dishonest under the temptations."[62]

According to Roosevelt's biographer, Edmund Morris, Taft "deeply despised the people he governed."[63] Morris asserts that Taft believed the Filipinos to be "the greatest liars it has ever been my fortune to meet," The great majority were inferior to "the most ignorant negro" and "utterly unfit for self government." Indeed, they would need "the training of fifty or a hundred years before they shall even realize what Anglo-Saxon liberty is."[64] It is one thing to hold opinions such as these cited by Morris. But it is quite another actually to engage in racial discrimination, conduct in which Taft consistently did not indulge while in the Philippines. Whatever he wrote privately, during his tenure on the Archipelago he neither preached nor practiced racism. He lived in a racist era and, like his friend Theodore Roosevelt, was of white, Anglo-Saxon, Protestant descent, and secure in his heritage.

Moreover, in spite of his private comments, Taft wholeheartedly believed in eventual self-rule for the Filipinos. Such was the utimate goal, if not the entire basis, of the American presence in the Islands. When such a step could be taken remained unclear, but Taft never lost sight of it. Whatever negative comments he might make of the Filipino's character, he consistently maintained that "there is in them a capacity for future development, for future preparation for self government."[65] Concurring with Taft, Theodore Roosevelt wrote in 1902 that "I am encouraging in every way the growth of conditions which now make for self government in the Philippines and which, if the Filipino people can take advantage of them, will assuredly put them where some day we shall say that if they desire independence[,] they shall have it. But I cannot be certain as to when that day will be...."[66]

On July 4, 1902, President Roosevelt issued a proclamation to the effect that the Philippine–American war was "officially over." It was the sixth time that American authorities either in Washington or in Manila had demonstrated a "repetitious failure to end the war by fiat." On the other hand, according to *The Washington Post*, "a bad thing cannot be killed too often."[67] Further, by early 1903, the Taft Commission's policy of support for greater

---

[62] Taft to Root, October 21, 1900, 2.

[63] Edmund Morris, *Theodore Rex* (New York: Random House, 2001), 102. Based on an examination of Taft's time in the Archipelago, I have difficulty accepting Morris's *ipse dixit* statement that Taft "despised the people he governed." Besides, even if he did, his conduct reflected a striking lack of discrimination.

[64] Ibid.

[65] Kramer, 199.

[66] Roosevelt Letters, vol. 3, 277 (June 16, 1902)." Writing to a major critic of the American policy in the Philippines, Massachusetts Republican Senator George F. Hoar, Roosevelt emphasized, "Now I do not want to make a promise which may not be kept." In fact, neither Taft nor Roosevelt lived to see independence given to the Archipelago, which did not occur until 1946.

[67] All these quotations are from Kramer, 154–155.

native participation in local government had succeeded, and the military had no choice but to acquiesce in the logic applied by Taft in his earlier dialogue with General Chaffee. When Taft returned to the United States late in 1903, he left behind what Kramer well describes as "an inclusionary racial formation built on interlocking metaphors of family, evolution, and tutelary assimilation."[68]

TR AND TAFT

The relationship between Taft and Theodore Roosevelt was significant, complex, and uneven. It lasted for approximately thirty years, from the time when both had been in Washington – Roosevelt as a member of the Civil Service Commission, Taft as the solicitor general – to 1919, when the former president attended the funeral of the man he had succeeded. Because the ways in which this relationship changed, it seems appropriate to divide examination of it into specific sections, focusing here on Taft and TR prior to 1904. There is no doubt that their early regard for each other was based on a mutuality of viewpoints. TR, for example, applauded Judge Taft's handling of the Pullman strike issues, as well as Cleveland's actions in breaking the strike.[69] Moreover, during Taft's regular visits to Washington while on the circuit court, the stolid jurist became impressed with Roosevelt's seemingly impetuous behavior.

On the other hand, even before leaving for the Philippines, Nellie Taft found herself with a vague but lasting sense of dislike if not distrust for the Roosevelts. Competition is often only in the mind of the beholder, and apparently Nellie Taft – whether it be either for reasons of personal insecurity or of possible political rivalry – was herself unable to react favorably to Roosevelt's charm. As for Edith Roosevelt, "I don't like Mrs. Roosevelt at all. I never did."[70] Taft could not have been unaware of Nellie's sentiments, yet he still tried to aid Roosevelt, especially after McKinley's election in 1896. As did other influential Republicans, Taft pushed for his friend's appointment as assistant secretary of the navy. Although McKinley did in fact select Roosevelt, he commented that "Roosevelt is always in such a state of mind."[71]

Taft observed Roosevelt's vigorous course as war with Spain loomed. He noted the restless assistant secretary's determination to mobilize the American navy, and watched from afar as Roosevelt and his corps of Rough Riders charged up San Juan Hill and down into the governor's mansion in Albany. Having no interest in politics, secure with a lifetime appointment as a federal judge, or so he thought, Taft may have admired Roosevelt for being all

[68] Kramer, 226.
[69] "We have come out of the strike very well; Cleveland did excellent [sic], so did [Attorney General Richard] Olney ... ". Letters, vol. 1, July 22, 1894, 391.
[70] Anthony, 99–100.
[71] Pringle, 153.

that Taft himself was not. He sympathized with the young governor as he confronted the powerful Republican political bosses in Albany. By the summer of 1900, newly ensconced in Manila, Taft may not have been aware that even as he prepared to assume the presidency of the Commission, Roosevelt had coveted such an appointment for himself, rather than the vice presidency, which he considered a dead end.[72] But by August 1900, Roosevelt had been reconciled to apparent political exile. Yet, he wrote Taft, "I had a great deal rather be your assistant in the Philippines or even Root's assistant in the War Department than be vice-president."[73]

There matters stood until September 14, 1901, when McKinley's assassination permanently altered this relationship. Roosevelt had been perfectly sincere when he wrote of Taft that "Taft is about the whitest man I have ever met in politics[,] and I would like to see him President."[74] But now, *Roosevelt* was president, and very early on in his own administration he had already demonstrated that his exercise of power might not be employed in the same manner as that of his predecessor. After barely a month into Roosevelt's administration, Taft reported to his mother that the new president "does not use the same tact in dealing with his subordinates that McKinley did; but I have much confidence in Roosevelt's high conception of civic duty and … of his honesty of purpose and of his courage."[75]

The prospect of a Taft presidency had been raised by others as well as TR, and it amused rather than attracted Taft. "The idea," he wrote to his half-brother Charles, "that a man who had issued injunctions against labor unions almost by the bushel, who has sent at least ten or a dozen violent labor agitators to jail, and who is known as one of the worst judges for the maintenance of government by injunction, could ever become a safe candidate for any party on the presidential ticket, strikes me as intensely ludicrous.… But more than this, the horrors of a modern presidential campaign and the political troubles of the successful candidate for the office … rob [it] of the slightest attraction for me."[76] More will be noted about these views, which Taft apparently never altered, despite his election in 1908. Suffice it here to observe that his campaign and presidency must be considered with these views in mind.

By the fall of 1901, however, Taft had more pressing matters to resolve. He faced very serious health troubles. He had been in the Philippines for almost a year and a half, working with impressive diligence. Never comfortable in hot and humid weather, burdened also with a severe weight problem, Taft became

---

[72] " … [T]he thing I should really like to do would be the first civil Governor General of the Philippines. I believe I could do that job, and it is a job emphatically worth doing.…" Letters, vol. 2, Roosevelt to Henry Cabot Lodge, January 22, 1900, 1136.

[73] Pringle Papers, T to TR, August 6, 1900.

[74] Letters, vol. 2, June 6, 1900, 1325.

[75] Pringle Papers, October 21, 1901. Here, Taft meant the episode – noted earlier – in which Roosevelt ordered General Chafee and Taft to resolve their differences, without his participation.

[76] Ibid., August 27, 1901.

ill with a gastrointestinal infection that required two operations. For a time after the first operation in October, surgeons feared for his life. A second operation took place on Thanksgiving Day, and it became clear that major recovery time was necessary.[77] As Roosevelt and Root were equally concerned, Taft was summoned back to Washington, not only for some rest but also to testify before a congressional committee on the Philippines. After leaving his wife and children in Cincinnati, he arrived in Washington in January 1902, and stayed with the Roots as a temporary guest.

Roosevelt, Root, and Taft engaged in numerous conversations during Taft's two months in Washington. Taft found TR "just the same as he ever was[,] and it is very difficult to realize that he is the President."[78] The subject of appointment to the Supreme Court arose, and Taft reported to Nellie that TR had told him that "he was praying that there would be no vacancy ... until after I had concluded matters in the Philippines." Taft responded that "if he were to offer me a vacancy now, I should decline it."[79] Taft never wavered from this position. However, if TR had been in a position to replace the Chief Justice, events might have turned out differently. But Roosevelt never had that opportunity, and as will be seen, it would fall to Taft to nominate a Chief Justice, the position he himself desired more than any other.

Meanwhile, in March 1902, Taft underwent a third operation, and prepared to return to the Philippines, but with a detour to Italy. His mission was to resolve a complicated dispute with the Roman Catholic Church concerning land in the Philippines, which prior to 1900 had belonged to the Friars.[80] More than seven months after he had left for the United States, on August 22, Taft disembarked at Manila. Bringing word that Congress had both reduced the tariff for Philippine products coming into the United States and enacted a law creating a popular assembly and expanding the civil authority of local governments, Taft emphasized that "I have a deep affection for the Filipino people ... I mean to do everything that in me lies for their benefit[,] and I invoke their sincere and earnest cooperation in the great work of teaching a capable people the art of wise self-government."[81] Regardless of what he had written privately to Root, Taft believed in what he stated to such an extent that he declined at least two opportunities to claim what he desired most, a seat on the United States Supreme Court.

---

[77] Pringle, 214–215.

[78] Ibid., 218.

[79] Ibid., 219. As it happened, Roosevelt was able to fill his first vacancy on the High Court a few months later with the selection of Oliver Wendell Holmes. Both Holmes and his predecessor were from Massachusetts, and there is no evidence that Roosevelt seriously looked outside of that state for his nominee.

[80] This disagreement took years to resolve, but after Taft had returned to Washington as Roosevelt's secretary of war, the United States paid the Church more than $7.5 million for 390,000 acres of farm land. See Pringle, 226–231.

[81] Pringle, 233.

JUSTICE TAFT?

While in Washington, Taft wrote to Nellie that there might be a vacancy on the High Court because Justice Harlan was apparently willing to retire if the president would appoint Harlan's son to a district judgeship. "Personally," Taft noted, "I don't care whether H. retires or not. I would not for a place on that bench give up the work in the Philippines for at least a year and a half longer.... [T]he fact is that it is a bench of old men."[82] Before he left Washington, Taft had discussed anew his current "unavailability" for the Court with Roosevelt.

Taft was therefore shocked to receive a confidential telegram from the president on October 26, 1902, saying that "there will be a vacancy on the Supreme Court to which I earnestly desire to appoint you. It is in my judgment of utmost importance to get our strongest men on the Court at the very earliest opportunity.... You can at this juncture do insofar better service on the Supreme Court than any other man."[83] Roosevelt added that "I feel your duty is on the court unless you have decided not to adopt a judicial career." Here, at last, was an offer of an appointment to Taft that he had sought since his days as a superior court judge in Ohio.

Along with Roosevelt's cable, came a message from Root that his chief's dispatch "causes me grave concern. I am most unwilling to lose you from the Philippines...." But Root was well aware of Taft's medical history there, and it "gives great force to [the] suggestion that you should go on the bench now when you could undoubtedly do great service. That would be better than to take any serious risk of breaking down and having to leave as an invalid...."[84] Taft responded to both messages in twenty-four hours.

To Roosevelt, Taft reiterated his consistent opposition to leaving his post, all the more so as the next two years of Archipelago governance promised to be very challenging. Pestilence, plague, food shortages, lingering native unrest, and religious ferment "all render most unwise the change [of] Governor."[85] Yet he reminded the president that he looked "forward to [a] time when I can accept such an offer[,] but even if it is certain that it can never be repeated[,] I must now decline." Finally, Taft noted that he would not be so firm in tone "if [the] gravity of [the] situation here was not necessarily known to me better than it can be known in Washington." To Root, Taft asserted that "chance has thrown every obstacle in the way of our success[,] but we shall win. I long

---

[82] Pringle Papers, February 6, 1902. Harlan's son was not appointed, His father did not resign, and when he died – still in service – in 1911, his seat was filled by a Taft nominee.

[83] Ibid., October 26, 1902. Roosevelt knew that the legal attack launched at his direction against the latest railroad merger, the Northern Securities case, was headed for the Supreme Court. He may also have been aware of Judge Taft's well-known opinion in the Addyston Pipe Case, a holding that had breathed new life into the Sherman Act. See Chapter 2. Perhaps he envisaged Taft on the bench as a probable judicial ally both in his antitrust campaign and in his efforts to prevent any excesses between capital and labor.

[84] Ibid.

[85] Ibid., October 27, 1902.

for a judicial career but if it must turn on my present decision[,] I am willing to lose it."[86]

Taft's determination to stay on in the Philippines may have been based on more than what he said in his telegrams. In the first place, he had virtually insisted when first offered the appointment in 1900 that it be as president of the Commission. Washington had acquiesced. Now he was the civil governor, and having received consistent and invaluable backing from Root, he may have felt some sense of obligation to the secretary of war. There had also been an implied promise, on Taft's part, to return to Manila. Moreover, his Commission worked well together, and at a sufficient distance from the United States that some real independence of operations was evident. Finally, the timing of Roosevelt's cable bothered Taft, as he indicated in a follow-up letter to Root.

The ongoing dispute concerning the Friars' land in the Philippines had resulted in some harsh criticism of Taft from the American Catholic community. He wondered if the president's sudden move was due to a sense that it might be "embarrassing to him to have me continue at the head of the Government out here....and that my going on the bench might relieve him in this way."[87] The suddenness of Roosevelt's cable, "coming just before the [off year] election" led Taft to conclude "that there might be something in the suspicion. Of course under such circumstances, I would retire, but I could not accept a position on the Supreme Bench. I shouldn't enjoy being kicked upstairs."[88] It seems fair to say that although Taft really desired a High Court appointment more than any other office, he did not deem it valuable enough in 1902 to go against his prior commitments, nor perhaps his ego. Indeed, Taft was so concerned about TR's action that he asked his older brother Henry to meet with TR and Root. A successful corporate attorney, Henry did so, and his candid report to Will offers interesting insights into how they regarded Taft and his future.

The elder Taft reiterated TR's eagerness to have Taft on the High Court "because you will approach all the industrial questions without fear of the ... influence of either the J. P. Morgans or of the labor leaders."[89] Further, the president believed that Taft had successfully met the major challenges facing American governance in the Archipelago. Work remained to be done, but "he does not appreciate that you[r] coming away would create a critical situation." His talk with me," added the elder Taft, "was full of complimentary references to you, and his whole attitude is of that character ... "[90] But if TR

---

[86] Ibid.

[87] Ibid., October 29, 1902.

[88] After hearing about conversations between Taft's older brother, Henry, and Roosevelt, Taft concluded that his concern was groundless. Indeed, Roosevelt was both amused and a bit irritated by Taft's fears. "I have never in my life felt like criticizing anything Will did, but, upon my word, I do feel like criticizing this mental attitude of his!" Roosevelt to Henry Taft, *Letters*, vol. 3, January 19, 1903, 407.

[89] As will be seen in 1910, Taft may well have done just that.

[90] Pringle Papers, January 10, 1903.

was eager and insistent that Taft accept his nomination, neither Root nor his brother endorsed it.

Henry Taft emphasized that "I can't see what difference it would make whether you gave up the work in September … or a year longer." No matter when the departure took place, "you would still find a good many things of importance left to be done.… The break must be made sometime and it would be regarded here that as you had about completed the constructive work, it was not an inopportune time for you to leave the completion of your plans to some one else."[91] Finally, "I really cannot quite reconcile myself with your … choosing a judicial career at your age." On the other hand, "I would not have you embitter your life by seeking to satisfy ambitions in politics[,] and perhaps suffering disappointments … [You] could have a broader influence and leave a deeper impress upon the history of the country if you do not limit the scope of your activities by taking a position on the Bench."[92]

Root was even more emphatic on this point than Henry Taft. "I would advise you not to go on the bench at all.… [I] could not see why you should not be the surest candidate as Roosevelt's successor, at the end of his second term."[93] Henry Taft reminded his brother that "you would prefer being on the Bench to being President." Root's reply was typical. He noted "that the ambition not to be President was one of the easiest things in the world to gratify." While it might be appropriate for William Taft to take the High Court appointment in 1903, and later resign if higher office beckoned, Henry Taft predicted that "if you go on the Supreme Court, it will be with the intention of spending the remaining useful years of your life there, and it seems to me that now is the time for you to choose one career or the other."[94]

The episode with Roosevelt took place in a time of other uncertainties, some of which Taft had cited as justification for his rejecting TR's offer. An additional wrinkle had arisen when Taft received word that Root was anxious to leave the cabinet and resume his much more lucrative private law practice. Taft found the news upsetting. "I need not tell you what a sinking of the heart that announcement has given me, for your presence at the head of affairs in the War Department has been to me always like the shadow of a great rock in a weary land."[95] Root's support had been ongoing, and dependable – with McKinley consistently backing him up as needed. While Taft knew TR quite well, deservedly or not he had gained considerable respect for McKinley since 1900. Now the stability stemming from McKinley and Root seemed to be in flux. "Roosevelt is making a curious president," wrote Taft to Nellie. "His impulsiveness is likely to get him into many troubles which the public will

[91] Ibid.
[92] Ibid.
[93] According to Henry Taft, TR "personally entertained the same view that Mr. Root did, that no man in the country was as likely to succeed him as yourself, although, of course, that was a subject on which predictions were entirely unsafe."
[94] Pringle Papers, January 10, 1903.
[95] Root Papers, LOC, October 4, 1902.

forgive because they think he is honest and desires to do the right thing." Perhaps with TR's autocratic telegram to Taft and Chafee still in mind, Taft added "but the difference between him and McKinley in dispatch of business, in dignity, in judgment, and in tact, only the Cabinet know."[96] But TR was not yet reconciled to losing Taft as his judicial nominee.

To be sure, TR seemingly acquiesced in Taft's decision. "I am quite at a loss whom to appoint to the bench in the place I meant for you. Everything else must give way to putting in the right man; but I can't make up my mind who *is* (sic) the right man."[97] Less than a month later, however, Roosevelt dispatched yet another missive to Taft concerning the High Court appointment. In tone and message, it differed markedly from previous communications – containing an intriguing mixture of firmness, friendship, flattery, and inflexibility, as well as an unmistakable sense of fait accompli. "I am awfully sorry, old man, but ... I find that I shall have to bring you home and put you on the Supreme Court. I am very sorry ... but after all, old fellow, if you will permit me to say so, I am President and see the whole field. The responsibility for any error must ultimately come upon me, and therefore I cannot ... yield to any else's decision if my judgment is against it. After the most careful thought ... I have come irrevocably to the decision that I shall appoint you to the Supreme Court...."[98] Possibly in a manner intended to convey to Taft the futility of protest, Roosevelt added that he had already arranged with Associate Justice Shiras to resign in February 1904, "he consenting to do it on my statement that I intended to appoint you, a statement which I have made to him and the Chief Justice as well as to the others of the Court."[99]

Roosevelt further emphasized that "there is no man whom I could put on the Supreme Court at this time who in any way approaches you, whose appointment would do anything like as much good to the Court...." He would approve Taft's remaining in the Archipelago until August 1904 (shortly, it might be noted, before both the opening of the Supreme Court term and the 1904 election). Finally, he reminded Taft that "as I said, old man, this is one of the cases where the President if he is fit for his position must take the responsibility and put the men on whom he most relies in the particular positions in which he himself thinks they can render the greatest public good. I shall therefore about February first nominate you...."[100]

From Roosevelt's perspective, it can be argued that Taft's appointment made eminently good sense. In the first place, if not yet close friends, the two men had strong respect and regard for each other. Taft was a respected jurist and was "right" on the legitimacy of the Sherman Act. Moreover, TR was concerned about his reelection coming up in 1904. No successor to the

[96] Pringle Papers, February 6, 1902.
[97] Roosevelt to Taft, Letters, vol. 3, October 29, 1902, 372.
[98] Ibid., November 26, 1902, 382.
[99] Ibid., 383.
[100] Ibid.

presidency upon the death of the incumbent had ever won reelection on his own, and there was at least noticeable opposition to Roosevelt, especially in his home state of New York. Roosevelt could only have been aware that some had spoken about rallying around Taft as a viable alternative to the mercurial incumbent. With an opening on the Court, Taft was the right candidate from the right party with the right credentials. Finally, no sitting member of the High Court had ever resigned to accept nomination from a major political party. Roosevelt possibly believed that he could accomplish much by placing Taft on the Court.

In reality, TR had no basis for such concern. Already Taft had written a warm letter to the president, but given the vagaries of trans-Pacific travel, mail delivery was extremely slow, while the cable was not normally used for regular intergovernmental communication. In a letter to "My dear Theodore: (If I may venture once)," Taft sent congratulations "on the personal triumph you won in the settlement of the coal strike[,] and in the great victory of the Republicans in the November elections."[101] He emphasized, correctly, that to gain "a majority of thirty in an off year is unprecedented[,] and shows your hold upon the people. All you have to do, to be elected President ... is to live." As for his own presidential leanings, Taft repeatedly trumpeted his views to his correspondents, and with the same message. "I would not be a candidate or permit my name to be used in any way to prevent [Roosevelt's] nomination. I think his nomination is inevitable and I think it ought to be. If they were to succeed in beating Roosevelt, they would beat the Republican party. More than that[,] I would be the last man that could be helpful to them...."[102] Taft further emphasized that "I am not running for President either in 1904 or 1908."[103] From his perspective in 1903, he meant it.

But Taft did more than urge TR not to nominate him. He enlisted the aid of his fellow commissioners, who wrote to Roosevelt urging that Taft remain in the Philippines. Somehow, word of his pending recall was also leaked to the Manila press, and it "roused the Filipinos to object, and they made such a popular demonstration that the President yielded."[104] Conceding defeat, TR

---

[101] Pringle Papers, December 30, 1902. More than a century after the event, Roosevelt's handling of events to bring about a settlement in the anthracite coal strike of 1902 remains an impressive exercise of presidential influence. Never before had the Chief Executive intervened to use the authority of his office to ensure a settlement rather than merely to break a strike. One of the best analyses of Roosevelt's action is that of John Blum in *The Republican Roosevelt* 2nd ed. (Cambridge, MA: Harvard University Press, 1977). See also Letters, vol. 3, November 6, 1902, 373.

[102] Pringle Papers, April 16, 1903.

[103] Ibid., April 18, 1903. In other words, there was no need at this time for Roosevelt to get Taft out of the way by placing him on the High Court, something Taft did not desire in 1902–1903.

[104] Ibid., January 26, 1903. To Henry Taft, TR wrote that "Will sprung a surprise on me. He must have given the contents of the purport of my letter to a number of the natives, and I received the most fervid telegrams from them as to the effect on the native mind of his withdrawal....I think he has carried his point...." Letters, vol. 3, January 12, 1903, 402.

wrote and cabled Taft that "well, it is all right. In view of the protests from the Philippine People, I do not see how I could take you away.... I most earnestly hope your health will continue good."[105] Taft responded in a tone that bordered on the obsequious. "I beg to express my sincere regret that you should have been embarrassed in finding someone" for the Court appointment, and "I beg to renew my deep gratitude for your kindness and consideration to me."[106]

By the time Roosevelt received this letter, he had already nominated an Ohio Republican – William Day – to the Supreme Court. This action appeared to close the opportunity, precisely as TR had previously warned Taft, for another Ohio appointment, such as himself.[107] Taft applauded TR's choice, writing to a good friend that Day "is not a great lawyer but he is a good lawyer. He is very level-headed, [a] common sense man of courage, loyalty and convictions."[108] He added to TR that Day "is a loyal man, a safe man, and [would] never do anything on the bench to discredit the President responsible for his appointment."[109]

Less than two weeks after Roosevelt assured Taft that "it is all right," he dispatched yet another "personal" letter to him. Again, he asked Taft to return to Washington, but this time to replace Root as secretary of war. Root had served since 1899, and had been the architect of the policies to administer the Philippines. Roosevelt hastened to reassure Taft that as secretary of war, he would still be a key administrator of the Archipelago. Moreover, Root was willing to stay on until early 1904, thus affording Taft ample opportunity to complete a number of projects still pending. TR urged Taft to remember "the aid and comfort you would be to me ... as my counselor and advisor in all the great questions that come up."[110] Similarly, Root urged acceptance, writing that as the secretary of war "you would practically determine the course of our Government towards Philippine affairs."[111]

---

[105] Ibid., January 29, 1903, 413. The episode reflected the marked success that Taft had gained in moving the Philippines toward acceptance of both the American dominance as well as the proffered opportunity to move toward eventual self-government and independence.

[106] Pringle Papers, January 27, 1903.

[107] Actually, in later years, presidents would name multiple justices from the same geographical area with minimal concern and reaction. Thus, President Wilson appointed Brandeis, with another Bostonian, O. W. Holmes, already on the Court, and President Hoover appointed Benjamin Cardozo from New York, with a fellow New Yorker, Harlan Stone, also already on the Court.

[108] Pringle Papers, January 26, 1903.

[109] Ibid, January 27, 1903. Day served on the High Court for almost twenty years, and was still sitting when Taft became Chief Justice in 1921. His most notorious decision may well have been in the case of *Hammer v. Dagenhart*, when for a divided Court, Day declared an act regulating child labor unconstitutional on the grounds that if Congress could enact such a statute, "all freedom of commerce will be at an end ... and thus our system of government be practically destroyed." *Hammer v. Dagenhart*, 247 U.S. 251 (1918), 270–276. I have been unable to locate any reaction by TR to the case.

[110] Letters, vol. 3, February 14, 1903, 425–426.

[111] Root Papers, February 20, 1903.

After a delay of three months, Taft accepted TR's offer in a "My dear Theodore" letter so characteristic of the man that it warrants some discussion. The delay was due to Taft's compulsion to consult with his family before deciding on his own. "I have received ... the opinions of my brothers and Mother ... and they are all strongly in favor of it. I therefore accept your tender[,] and thank you for it."[112] But Taft made it clear that he could not take up his new office until the spring of 1904, pending enactment of a number of statutes necessary for administering the Archipelago. These included a criminal code, an internal revenue act, a general incorporation act, and redistricting for implementing a general assembly. But even as he listed these measures, Taft had to voice his doubts anew. "Now that I have agreed to succeed Mr. Root, I am seized with doubt as to my capacity to take up the enormous problems which he has handled with such signal success. The contrast will prove, I fear, humiliating. However[,] he will have mapped out the policy in most instances, which is much easier to follow than to initiate."[113] Finally, after offering a few observations on politics, Taft added "but I must apologize for running into such a political discussion and taking up your time, with views formed at a great distance and of no significance."[114]

Nellie Taft had strongly supported her husband in his consistent refusals to return to Washington and accept a seat on the High Court, and the question arises as to why she willingly reversed her position. A few points may be noted. Nellie realized that Will, as secretary of war, would be very close to the president and the seat of executive authority. Further, he would be free from all the political constraints that accompanied an appointment to the High Court. Ambitious both for her husband and herself, she saw the presidency in 1908 as a definite possibility for Will.

For his part Roosevelt, by mid-1903, was probably delighted with Taft's response. He would gain an experienced administrator and negotiator, who had performed with marked success in the Philippines. Further, Taft possessed both legal knowledge and training in the law, an area in which TR admittedly was weak. More than that, Taft clearly recognized that he was happy in a position subordinate to the president. In this, the relationship between TR and Taft differed from that between TR and Root. Already a well-respected legal figure, Root stood beyond the president in legal acumen, and both men knew it. He did not need TR; rather it was the other way around. Root did

---

[112] Root Papers, May 9, 1903. Not until consultation had taken place, could or would Taft decide. This compulsion to confer with his family prior to major career moves, a condition that possibly concealed some inner inability to make up his mind, would be of major significance between 1907 and 1912. It also conveyed an external impression of vacillation and self-doubt, even malleability, so different from that exuded by Roosevelt. But by 1903, the lawyerlike function of deliberation, consultation, and thorough consideration before action was too ingrained for Taft to ignore, even had he so desired.

[113] Ibid., 6.

[114] Ibid.

not hesitate to poke fun at the president (or Taft, for that matter), employing humorous sarcasm, something Taft would never do.[115]

For the moment, TR meant what he wrote when he told Taft that "the feeling of admiration and respect for you ... is so great among all those for whose opinion I give a rap, that ... I wanted to put you in what I regarded as an even bigger post, near me." Signing his letter simply as "Faithfully, your friend," TR expressed the hope that "may all that is good ever attend you and yours."[116]

But in 1903, neither Taft nor TR could predict their futures with any certainty. There was no doubt of Taft's total lack of interest in a presidential bid, while TR had confessed that "still less can I tell what the future will bring forth as far as I am personally concerned." As Taft sailed home late in 1903, he had no inkling that in barely eight years, his apparently close friendship with TR would be a thing of the past.

[115] The best-known example of Root's wit as applied to Taft remains his famous telegram in response to Taft's report that as he recovered his health in the Philippines, he had ridden on horse back some twenty miles up a mountain road. Root telegraphed "How is the horse?" Jonathan Lurie, "Chief Justice Taft and Dissents: Down with the Brandeis Briefs," *Journal of Supreme Court History* 32 (2007), 179. As for President Roosevelt, Root commented on one proposal coming from his chief that "it should not suffer from any taint of legality." When TR demanded to know if he had answered certain criticisms of his policies, Root replied "You certainly have, Mr. President. You have shown that you were accused of seduction and you have conclusively proved that you were guilty of rape." Richard W. Leopold, *Elihu Root and the Conservative Tradition.* (Boston: Little, Brown & Co., 1954), 178.

[116] Letters, vol. 3, April 22, 1903, 464–465.

4

The Unwilling Heir, 1904–1908

WILL AS SECRETARY OF WAR

By early February 1904, Taft had returned to Washington and settled in as TR's secretary of war. He understood from conversations with both the president and Elihu Root that he would not have to worry much about administering the war department. Rather he was to function as a troubleshooter for the administration, keep his eyes on the Philippines, and most important, be available to aid TR in his campaign for reelection. Never before had a "succeeding" president (formerly vice president) been reelected on his own to a second full term. Roosevelt knew that history was against him. But he realized that with the death of Ohio Senator Mark Hanna, also in February, there was no Republican politician in a position to mount an effective campaign in opposition to his renomination.

Fresh from almost four years of hands-on administration with varied challenges and minimal interference from Washington, Taft chafed at the emphasis on politics that enveloped TR's conduct of his office in 1904. He wrote to Nellie that his first cabinet meeting "was largely devoted to politics.... It seems to me ... undignified for us to devote so much time to mere political discussion...."[1] On the other hand, he succumbed readily to the famous Roosevelt charm. "He is a very sweet natured man and a very trusting man when he believes in one. I am growing to be very fond of him."[2]

Taft looked at Roosevelt's dogged quest for reelection with a detachment that should be kept in mind when one considers his own course as a candidate for reelection in 1912. "I would not run for president," he announced,

---

[1] Pringle, 258. On April 16, he informed Nellie that the cabinet meeting "was as pleasant and useless as usual." Pringle Papers, April 16, 1904.

[2] Pringle Papers, March 18, 1904. For her part, Nellie Taft never lost her dislike if not distrust of TR, remaining inherently suspicious of his motives. As will be seen, her suspicions became important when Taft had to reach a decision on whether to accept or decline TR's repeated offers of a High Court appointment.

"if you guaranteed the office. It is awful to be made afraid of one's shadow."[3] Try as he might, however, Taft could not escape references to his possible nomination in 1908. After Roosevelt had easily won reelection, Will insisted to an old friend that "I have not the slightest ambition to be president, and believe it utterly impossible.... A national campaign for the presidency is to me a nightmare." What ambition he possessed, he added, "is to go on the Bench."[4]

To yet another correspondent, Taft had earlier offered three reasons "why I decline to be drawn into conjectures" concerning his future candidacy. First was his eight-year record on the federal bench.[5] Second, "I have not the slightest ambition to be in the White House." Third, "by the time that 1908 comes around all thought of selecting me will have disappeared."[6] Yet the issue did not disappear, and as early as April, Taft informed Nellie that "what has surprised me everywhere I have been is the seeming certainty of friends and other people whom I have met that I will be the Republican nominee ... in 1908." Of course, he added, "I cannot regard it as any other than a ridiculous hypothesis...."[7]

Roosevelt's role in these maneuvers even before his own reelection is complex. In August, he informed Taft that he had "told Root that *he* [Root] would in all probability be in the line of succession to the Presidency in 1908.... He said that so far as I was concerned I was out of it[,] because my ambition was to be Chief Justice[,] as he knew."[8] Unless and until this judicial post became vacant, neither Taft nor TR could act. Taft reported to Nellie that one of Chief Justice Fuller's colleagues had told him that "the Chief Justice is getting old and he will have to go soon[,] but I don't think he'll ever resign." Taft's own impression was "that he has no present purpose of retiring at all. The Ch. Justice is as tough as a knot so that if he does not go by resignation, I shall

---

[3] Pringle, 261.

[4] Pringle Papers, November 12, 1904. It should be remembered that Taft had already declined vigorous importuning from TR to accept a seat on the Supreme Court. Had the president been able to offer Taft an appointment as Chief Justice, the appointment/rejection waltz choreographed by Taft and TR might have had a different outcome.

[5] Ibid., February 4, 1904. Where, he added "I dealt out justice to trades-union strikers, and sent them to jail whenever I thought they deserved it. I did more of this probably than any Judge in the United States."

[6] Ibid. But unlike General William T. Sherman of Civil War fame, Taft never issued a direct statement that if nominated he would not run, and if elected he would not serve.

[7] Pringle Papers, April 12, 1904. At some point, the hypothetical scenario, while remaining ridiculous to Taft, became tenable. It would turn into a matter not so much of aspiring to the nomination as acquiescing in its offer and responding to the insistence of his family that he take it.

[8] Ibid., August 3, 1904. TR had written Root, seeking to get him to run for the governorship of New York, which would serve as a springboard to the presidency. Such was the wish, he added "not merely of the New York State Republicans, but practically of all the Republicans of the country in this instance." The letter makes no mention of Taft. It may be that in the spring of 1904, TR had not yet considered Taft as a viable candidate in 1908. Or perhaps he considered Root more desirable. At any rate, Root declined. Letters, vol. 4, 877.

have to whistle for his place."⁹ It remains uncertain as to whether Roosevelt actually made a firm commitment to Taft to appoint him as Chief Justice if the position were open. On more than one occasion, Roosevelt hinted about the possibility to Taft, but he never had the opportunity to do more.

In the meantime, the secretary of war did not forget the Philippines, and when he received word that a military commander sought to build his reputation by a ruthless repression of local disorder, he reacted with firmness, remembering perhaps his earlier difficulties with Generals MacArthur and Chaffee. "What I am determined on, so long as I have any power ... [is] to avoid the bad political effect in the Islands of the use of the Army[,] where it can be avoided." He urged General Corbin to speak with the over-zealous officer "and tell him to possess his soul in patience:

I do not know how long I may remain at the head of the Army, but as long as I do, I shall carry out the policy that I believe to be the best in the Philippine Islands – not the best for making the reputation of brigadier generals ... but the best for the building up of the Civil Government and maintaining its prestige and strength. The prestige of the Army can take care of itself. It will not suffer...."¹⁰

Another issue concerning the Philippines was the ongoing debate as to when it should become independent. Apparently Taft never doubted that at some point, this step would be taken, not as a gift or grant from the United States but as an inherent right possessed by the Philippine people. The timing of such a move remained far from clear in 1904, but it was not, he believed, in the foreseeable future. Thus he opposed all suggestions of immediate independence. As he wrote to Bishop William Lawrence, "When we shall have made a successful government; when we shall have developed and educated the people; when we shall have created an independent public opinion – then the question of what shall be done may well be left to both countries...."¹¹

At the Republican National Convention a few months later, Elihu Root echoed Taft's position. He predicted that the Philippine people "will grow in capacity for self-government, and receiving power as they grow in

---

⁹ Ibid., April 12, 1904. On two occasions as he yearned for the appointment, Taft was stymied (or so he thought) by the consistent refusal of two Chief Justices (Fuller and his replacement Edward White) to resign.

¹⁰ Pringle Papers, September 17, 1904. Taft also insisted on appropriate conduct within the war department, and he included himself. He was quick to reject complimentary railroad passes offered to his family. He wrote to the president of the Pennsylvania Railroad that "I have always found that it greatly aided my peace of mind when sharp issues arise and I am called upon to act in respect to them, to feel that even the slightest appearance of a ground for charging partiality is absent." Ibid., March 24, 1904.

¹¹ Ibid., February 16, 1904. A little more than a year later, Taft was even more emphatic. "The policy of the administration is the indefinite retention of the Philippine Islands for the purpose of developing its prosperity and the self-governing capacity of the Filipino people. The policy rests on the conviction that the people are not now capable of self-government, and will not be for a long period of time; certainly not for a generation, and probably not for a longer time than that:" Ibid., March 16, 1905.

capacity...."[12] So also in his acceptance of the nomination, TR stated of the Philippine people:

"We have already given them a large share in their government, and our purpose is to increase this share as rapidly as they give evidence of increasing fitness for the task.... To withdraw our government from the islands at this time would mean to the average native a loss of his barely won civil freedom. We have established in the islands a government by Americans, assisted by Filipinos. We are steadily striving to transform this into self-government by the Filipinos, assisted by Americans.[13]

During the fall presidential campaign, Taft sometimes found it difficult to reconcile his concerns for the Philippines with the realities of Republican politics. Thus, in several of his speeches, he included statements of support for lower tariffs between the United States and the Islands, especially in rates for tobacco and sugar. He thereby aroused concern from American growers of these commodities, and TR reacted with a suggestion, if not an order, that Taft avoid further comment on a lower tariff. Much to TR's surprise, and possibly to Taft himself, the secretary of war informed his boss "that of course he would not expect me to retract my position, but that if my presence in the Cabinet embarrassed him I would retire at once."[14] The president responded with a letter reflecting both shock and amusement. "Fiddle-dee-dee," he wrote. "I shall never send you another letter of complaint if it produces such awful results. I do not think it worth while again to touch on the tobacco business.... As for your retiring from the Cabinet, upon my word, Will, I think you have nerves, or something!"[15] His short note concluded with instructions that he should "come to breakfast or else to lunch. At any rate, be sure to see me." In a similar vein, shortly before this incident, Roosevelt had not hesitated to give Taft orders concerning his speeches. "Do not in any speech," he instructed Taft, "take any position seeming in the least to be on the defensive. Attack Parker[16] .... show that his proposals are insincere; his statements lacking in candor, and disingenuous."[17]

It seems clear that as his new term commenced, TR appreciated Taft's contributions as a loyal and competent subordinate. In May 1905, shortly before the death of John Hay, McKinley's secretary of state whom TR had retained in office, Roosevelt described Taft to George Otto Trevelyan. "He has no more fear in dealing with the interests of great corporate wealth than he has

---

[12] *Addresses at the 13th Republican National Convention, 1904* (New York: I. H. Blanchard Co., 1904), 63–66.

[13] Ibid., 222–223. "We are," TR insisted, "governing the Philippines in the interests of the Philippine people themselves." Earlier in 1904, TR commented that "we are far more necessary to the Filipinos than the Filipinos are to us." *Letters*, vol. 4, 769. Taft had maintained exactly the same view for the past four years.

[14] Pringle, 261.

[15] *Letters*, vol. 4, 980.

[16] A conservative jurist, Alton Parker was the Democratic presidential nominee in 1904.

[17] *Letters*, vol. 4, 960.

in dealing with the leaders of the most powerful labor unions; and if either go wrong[,] he has not the slightest hesitation in antagonizing them." More than this, "to strength and courage, clear insight, and practical common sense, he adds a very noble and disinterested character."[18]

TR kept his new secretary of war busy. Involved with primary responsibility for the Panama Canal in its early stages of construction; forced to deal with problems in Cuba, where he administered what appeared to be successful American intervention in 1906, resolving tensions between England and Germany; to say nothing of ongoing concern with the Philippines, Taft found himself burdened with challenges. In August 1905, he returned to the Archipelago, this time as TR's representative (Figure 2).

Taft found it necessary to remove, as head of the Commission, his successor, an old acquaintance and former Confederate soldier from Tennessee, Luke Wright. In less than two years, Wright had managed to undo the informal alliance that Taft had cultivated between many natives and the American occupiers. Besides projecting a form of racism that Taft had discouraged and avoided, Wright lacked the patience, forbearance, tact, and understanding "with which Taft had conciliated Filipino elites."[19] Even worse, he had been "unwilling to engage in ... the broader politics of recognition; he and wife openly snubbed Filipino elites socially[,] and refused to acknowledge their demands for political participation."[20] Typically, Taft supported the expansion of the native electorate and the establishment of a Philippine Assembly, even as he urged upon the new legislature a need for cooperation with the Commission (Figure 3). He hinted at what might be forthcoming in the absence of such cooperation. Would the new assembly, he asked, "by neglect, obstruction and absence of useful service, make it necessary to take away its existing powers on the ground that they have been prematurely granted?"[21]

WILL AS PRESIDENTIAL CANDIDATE?

Busy as he invariably was, the issue of the presidency consistently lurked in the background for Taft and also for TR. By December 1905, Taft had moved from active indecision concerning his candidacy to a tentative, passive acceptance. He was not a candidate, he wrote, "in the sense that I expect to do anything, formally or informally, by conference or otherwise, to secure the nomination." But Taft had become infected with the presidential bug. "I presume, however, there are very few men who would refuse to accept the nomination ... and I am not an exception. If it were to come to me with the full understanding ... of the weaknesses that I would have as a candidate, I should not feel that I had any right to decline."[22] Besides, to some extent, at least, he wanted the job!

[18] Ibid., 1175. "He helps me in every way more than I can say...."
[19] Kramer, 291.
[20] Ibid.
[21] Ibid., 305.
[22] Pringle Papers, December 1, 1905.

FIGURE 2. Secretary of War William Howard Taft upon his arrival in Manila, August 5, 1905. Photograph by Harry Fowler Woods. Copyright 2006 by H. F. Woods Camp Trustees. Reproduced by permission.

A few months earlier, in June 1905, Roosevelt compared Root (who had just rejoined the cabinet as secretary of state) to Taft.[23] He wrote to Henry Cabot Lodge that "I am inclined to think that Taft's being from the west,

---

[23] Although Nellie disagreed with his action, rather than expressing any interest in the post for himself, Taft had strongly supported Root's return to the cabinet. Nellie believed that TR should have named Will as Hay's replacement.

FIGURE 3. Secretary of War Taft in the Philippines,1905, shaking hands with a Moro Datu. Photograph by Harry Fowler Woods. Copyright 2006 by H. F. Woods Camp Trustees. Reproduced by permission.

together with his attitude on corporations, would for the moment make him the more available man." Always careful to hedge his comments when discussing his successor, TR added that "of course no one can tell what will be the outcome three years hence."[24] Thus the consistency with which TR lauded Taft's abilities, assistance, and attainments must be matched by the consistency with which he refused to offer a specific endorsement of him. In March 1906, the president had another vacancy to fill on the High Court. Again he turned to Taft, assuming that with administration of the Philippines in hand, Taft's earlier concerns had been satisfied. Again, Taft declined, leaving TR a bit perplexed, even as he seemed to sympathize with Taft's difficulty in having to choose one of two options, either a run for the presidency or a seat for life on the Supreme Court.[25]

He wrote to Will. First, he refused to offer Taft any specific advice on what choice to make. "No other man can take the responsibility of deciding for you what is right and best for you to do." But TR pointed to "the immense importance of the part to be played by the Supreme Court in the next twenty five years," adding that "I do not at all like the social conditions at present." He denounced the "dull, purblind folly of the very rich men; their greed and arrogance, and the way in which they have unduly prospered by the help of the ablest lawyers, and too often through the weakness or shortsightedness of the judges...."[26] And once again, he hedged on whether he would appoint Taft as Chief Justice, assuming he had the opportunity.

Taft's chances might be lessened, "although it probably would not be the case, that I might find some big man like Root or Knox who would consent to take the present vacancy if he knew the Chief Justiceship was open[,] but who would not take it if he knew the appointment was foreclosed; and under such circumstances I would not feel that I had the right to foreclose it."[27] But Roosevelt immediately dismissed his own argument, noting "I do not believe that the big men I have in mind would now go on the bench in any event."[28] Toward the end of his letter to Taft, Roosevelt reiterated that if he could place Taft in the center seat, he "probably would, save in such an event as I speak of above." The letter serves as yet another example of Roosevelt's disinclination simply to endorse Taft as his chosen successor.[29]

---

[24] Letters, vol. 4, 1272.

[25] Actually, with the exception of the claim that his work in the Archipelago was unfinished, all the other arguments as to why Taft should not take a seat on the High Court – which he had considered earlier – were, from his (and his family's) viewpoint, still valid in 1906.

[26] Letters, vol. 5, 183.

[27] Philander Knox, respected and trusted by both Roosevelt and Taft, was TR's first attorney general. He would also serve in Taft's cabinet as secretary of state, but later would clash with his former boss concerning Wilson's League. See Chapter 9.

[28] Letters, vol. 5, 185. If such was the case, one wonders why TR felt it necessary to raise the point at all. Perhaps he was indulging in a sort of cat-and-mouse game.

[29] Ibid., 186–186. In other words, if Taft wanted to sit on the Supreme Court, now was the time. But Taft should understand that if TR could find people of the caliber of Root and Knox

Several possible explanations for this omission can be offered. In the first place, it may well be that with the election not until 1908, TR had not yet made up his mind concerning whom he should support as his replacement. He admired and respected Root, but his secretary of state was well along in years and had an irrevocable link to conservative business elements. Roosevelt respected Charles Evans Hughes, but did not like or trust him. Further, Hughes was emerging as a viable Republican candidate for the governorship of New York. Among Republicans with national reputations, that left only Taft. But TR still hesitated. In July 1905, he wrote of his "anxiety as to who is to take the leadership," and while Root "would carry on the contest very much as Taft and I would ... I do not believe we can persuade people that this would be the case." On the other hand, TR did not want to place Taft on the bench "because just at the moment I am puzzled to see what other leader is developing for the nomination...."[30]

Roosevelt, moreover, appears to have had some doubt concerning the extent to which he should support a candidate. In August, he wrote to William Allen White that "you know how highly I think of Secretary Taft, but I am not going to take a hand in his nomination, for it is none of my business."[31] Finally, it may be that although TR did not articulate such a sentiment, he perceived of Taft only as an outstanding, able, loyal, subordinate. In that capacity, he had excelled, but as a national leader, a maker of policy, and a forger of consensus, one who would inherit Roosevelt's mantle as minister of a "bully pulpit," could Taft survive, let alone excel? Roosevelt may well have had his qualms.[32] Yet, who else if not Taft?

But TR found Taft's lack of enthusiasm – if not interest – bothersome. At a luncheon in October 1905, he had taken Nellie Taft aside and informed her that Will "must be more encouraging."[33] Otherwise he would not receive support that was crucial to his success, and Roosevelt might have to support Hughes. Nellie's report to Taft about this incident prompted Taft to send Roosevelt a letter that cannot have assuaged TR's doubt. Writing while on a campaign swing in the Midwest, and far from being concerned about possible Roosevelt support for Hughes, Taft stated that such action "will awaken no feeling of disappointment on my part."

Roosevelt knew "what my feeling has been in respect to the Presidency." He should also know that "I find on this trip, and find it everywhere, that the strong feeling is not for me but it is for your renomination...." Indeed, " ... the groundswell for your renomination is beginning, not among the politicians,

---

willing to become Chief Justice, he would chose one of them over Taft. Perhaps this position renders TR's oft-repeated encomiums to and about Taft suspect.

[30] Ibid., 329.
[31] Ibid., 354. Of Taft, TR added that he "would be an ideal President."
[32] I see no reason to question Pringle's comment that in spite of all the praise he lavished on Taft, "Roosevelt, in his heart, ever regarded Taft as less capable than himself." Pringle, 275. It may be noted further that TR came to this viewpoint even before Taft was nominated.
[33] Pringle Papers, October 27, 1906.

but among the people...." They, Taft emphasized, "are delighted with your courses. They are anxious to have you given an opportunity to continue for four years longer, and they are not content with any substitute."[34]

In his reply to Taft, TR did not rebut Taft's comments. He simply ignored them. What he had said to Nellie, he noted, was that "you must not be too entirely aloof because if you were it might dishearten your supporters[,] and put us all in such shape that some man like Hughes, or more probably some man from the West, would turn up with so much popular sentiment behind him that there would be no course open but to support him."[35]

In the meantime, as an alternative to his own appointment to the High Court, Taft suggested either William Moody, at that time TR's attorney general, or Horace Lurton, a colleague on the 6th Circuit whom Taft had gotten to know very well. Moody "would be right on all the great questions.... His mind is judicial[,] and his thoughts run clear and with great common sense." But Taft urged Roosevelt to appoint Lurton "in spite of all that can truly be said in favor of Moody." Lurton "is beyond dispute the ablest Circuit Judge on the Bench." A former Confederate soldier and lifelong Democrat, "his appointment will be hailed by the country as the evidence of your non-partisan desire to elevate and strengthen the Supreme Court."[36]

In August 1905, Taft informed Moody that Justice Harlan had given no indication of his readiness to resign, and "I am inclined to think that the old man wants to hang on...."[37] Taft added that "I shall not accept the vacancy made by [Justice] Brown," who had resigned. He remained hopeful, however, that TR "will appoint me to one of the vacancies ... which I feel reasonably certain there will be before the end of his term." He even admitted that no one, "not even my friends, will credit me with any other purpose than to run for the Presidency." But "we have to stand these misconstructions of our actions, and there are worse things than being thought a candidate for that high office."[38]

But Taft remained optimistic that he would not have to face the inevitable consequences of being a candidate. Even as he had written to TR urging that he run again, Will had confided to Nellie that "politics, when I am in it makes

---

34 Ibid., October 31, 1906.

35 Letters, vol. 5, 486–487. " ... [I]f our Kentucky friends felt that you did not really care for the fight, and were not in it, we might find ourselves wholly powerless to support you."

36 Pringle Papers, July 30, 1906. Although he seriously considered Lurton, TR took his time in reaching a decision. In December 1906, he nominated Moody. Unfortunately, his tenure was cut short by illness, and lasted less than three years. In an ironic twist, Lurton would be named to the High Court by Taft in 1909. He would be the oldest appointment thus far in the Court's history.

37 Ibid., August 3, 1906.

38 Ibid. The ease with which Taft added this observation indicates that by August 1906, he was willing to accept the possibility that he might be nominated, even though he did not wish it. As fate mandated, however, Roosevelt would have no more opportunities to make High Court selections after Moody. Taft, on the other hand, would appoint six Supreme Court members, the largest number from any single-term president in U.S. history.

me sick."[39] When he wrote to Root in November, perhaps it was more an expression of his hopes rather than perceptive observations. "My judgment is that the President cannot avoid running again unless he would resist the unanimous call of his party. There is a ground swell in his favor which will be more than his strong will can resist. There is really no second choice where I have been.... So far as you and I are concerned, I think we are well out of it, and whatever may be our ambitions for honorable service, there is a compensation in not having to be exposed to the horrors of a campaign...."[40]

Taft, of course, ignored the fact that at least in public, Roosevelt had never wavered in his determination to fulfill the pledge, uttered shortly after his impressive reelection in 1904, that he would never again accept nomination to national office. He did not believe that TR's statement was irrevocable, all the more so if there were unity among the Republican Party for a third term. From his limited perspective, such was indeed the case. It is significant that in 1906, Taft saw no serious impediment that would prevent TR from running for a third term. What Taft either did not see or else chose to dismiss was the harsh fact that by 1908, major opposition to Roosevelt had coalesced within powerful segments of the Republican Party.[41]

In 1906, Taft also saw himself very much in the Roosevelt mold as a progressive politician. Thus, in March, he accepted "the honor with pleasure" of election as an honorary member of the Roosevelt Republican Club of Cincinnati. Among the "objects" of the organization, which he endorsed, four should be noted:

1. The advocacy of laws providing for the establishment of the merit system in appointment to subordinate offices in the cities, villages, and counties.
2. Advocacy of such changes in the election laws as shall permit a more direct participation by the people in nominations to public elective offices.
3. The separation of municipal affairs from National Party politics.
4. Resistance to and exposure of corruption, and [the] promotion of reform in public affairs.[42]

---

[39] Pringle, 290.

[40] Pringle Papers, November 10, 1906. This letter to Root must be seen in contemporary political context. Taft had the very recent New York gubernatorial race in mind, one in which, with real difficulty, Hughes had managed to defeat William Randolph Hearst. Taft wrongly assumed that Hearst would gain the Democratic nomination in 1908. The prospect that Taft might be competing against "such a dealer in filth as this hideous product of yellow journalism" only strengthened his desire not to involve himself. Let TR handle Hearst! 1906 was not 1908, however, and by the time of the nominating conventions, Hearst had lost too much ground to William Jennings Bryan, anxious to try again after his defeats by McKinley in 1896 and 1900.

[41] It is interesting to note that in 1912, Taft recalled the 1904 pledge with bitterness, whereas in 1906, he had been perfectly willing to dismiss it.

[42] Pringle Papers, March 10, 1906.

Taft did more than write that he was in "thorough sympathy with" these objectives. He added that "eternal vigilance is the price of good government." Politics "ought to be neither distasteful nor degrading, and men who enter [politics] for the purpose of keeping them pure and making them better are engaged in the highest duty."[43]

Perhaps Taft's reluctance to involve himself in "the highest duty" reflected his awareness that he was neither suitable nor suited for national politics. Unwilling to engage himself in a manner similar to TR, he was not strong enough to stand by his repeated statements of a lack of interest in such activities, all the more so as dominant personalities such as Nellie Taft and his brothers – to say nothing of TR – kept pushing him toward a run for the presidency. He wrote to the brewer Adolphus Busch, "You will bear me witness that the situation into which by circumstances I have gradually been brought of being a candidate … was not one which was of my active seeking."[44] By 1907, TR seemed to be moving toward Taft, even if Taft was standing still. Taft's mother reminded her son that "Roosevelt is a good fighter[,] and enjoys it, but the malice of politics would make you miserable. They do not want you as their leader but cannot find anyone more available…."[45] In March 1907, the president instructed cabinet members involved in matters of Ohio patronage "that the judgment of Secretary Taft should be obtained….Mr. Taft is to be consulted as I feel a peculiar regard for his judgment and think it wise to follow it."[46]

MORE HEDGING FROM TR

But in less than a month, TR reverted to his old form. "Of course I do not wish to dictate the nomination. Taft or Root, or any man as good as either, will do for me." He added, "But at present it looks to me as if Taft was the man we ought to unite on. Of course this is private."[47] A month later, TR wrote to his son Kermit of Root and Taft that "they are both really wonderful men. I most earnestly hope and I am inclined to believe that we shall be able to nominate Taft for President. Of course this is to be kept strictly quiet, as I cannot, as President, take any part in getting him the nomination."[48] Finally,

---

[43] Ibid. The progressive tone of these objectives seems obvious today. What role the Club played in Ohio politics for the 1908 election was complex and controversial. It is all the more interesting that in November 1906, Roosevelt wrote to Taft that "the Republican Club has been acting like such a fool in Cincinnati that I wonder if it would be possible for me to disassociate myself from it." Letters, vol. 5, 487, 837.

[44] Pringle Papers, April 26, 1907.

[45] Pringle Papers, January 21, 1907. Although she did not live to see her son nominated, Louise Taft was prescient in her insights.

[46] Letters, vol. 5, March 16, 1907, 625.

[47] Ibid., 651.

[48] Ibid., 655–656. While prolix as Roosevelt was in making such comments, his actual conduct belied them. As will be seen, he worked with great diligence for Taft's nomination.

in July, Roosevelt confronted his ambivalence in a candid letter to William Allen White, and discussed the coming presidential nomination, barely a year away.[49] "I am well aware, "he wrote "that nothing would more certainly ruin Taft's chances than to have it supposed that I was trying to dictate his nomination." On the other hand, like every other voter, he had a right to support his choice and "to try to exercise that choice in favor of the man who will carry out the governmental principles in which I believe with all my heart and soul." Roosevelt insisted that "I am not trying to dictate the choice of anyone, and ... I stand for the kind of man rather than any particular man."[50] Of the available choices, however, "it would seem to me that Taft comes nearer than anyone else to being just the man who ought to be President."

What about Root? "There are some good reasons," TR conceded, "which could be advanced to show that Root would be a better president than Taft, or me, or any one else I know. I could not express too highly my feeling for him." If he was available, one suspects that TR would have preferred Root to any other candidate. "But at present it does not seem to me that there would be much chance of nominating or electing him, and therefore I do not consider him in the running."[51] The same could not be said about Taft. "In point of courage, sagacity, inflexible uprightness and disinterestedness, and wide acquaintance with governmental problems, [Taft] seems to me to stand out above any other man who has yet been named."[52]

TR sent a copy of this letter to Taft, who could now understand the president's lack of enthusiasm for his nomination. One suspects that Will, who had a healthy self-awareness of his own limitations, probably agreed with Roosevelt! By September 1907, TR served out more of the same, telling Taft that "you at the present time seemed more likely than anyone else to be the man upon whom it would be desirable to unite; but of course no one could foretell the events of the next nine months, and ... it was always possible that I should have to alter my judgment...."[53] He wanted Taft to know that "to have it stated that I want you to succeed me both hurts and helps you. It helps you in the West. It hurts you among all the reactionary crowd, both the honest reactionaries and the corrupt financiers and politicians in the East."[54]

---

[49] Although a lifelong Republican, and editor of the Emporia *Gazette* for almost fifty years, like many others, White readily succumbed to the Roosevelt charm, and would later follow him into the Progressive Party.

[50] Ibid., July 30, 1907, 735.

[51] Ibid.

[52] In other words, the best man is not available, so let us take Taft, who just happens to be pretty good. In the meantime, "My chief business is not to nominate the President but to try to do my own work as President for the next eighteen months, and this is a big enough job by itself. I do not want to get into a row with any of the other candidates if I can legitimately keep out of it." Ibid., 736.

[53] Ibid., 780.

[54] Ibid., 781. " ... I am not sorry that the people here in the East – the big financiers and big politicians who are most influential in politics – should get the idea that they may have to take

By September 19, 1907, a subtle change appeared in TR's letters to Taft. Now it became clear that the president would indeed support his secretary of war, and Roosevelt felt tempted "always to write you the gloomy side, because I really believe I am quite as nervous about your campaign as I would be if it were my own." Therefore, "I want you to avoid staying with private individuals in the future. Go to a hotel and give everybody a fair show at you." Although TR continued to admire Taft's courage, "don't talk on delicate subjects where there is a chance of twisting your words, unless it becomes necessary."[55]

Taft's half brother, Charles, had already begun intensive political organization in Ohio on Taft's behalf. But Will emphasized that "I am not getting into a situation where a failure to get the nomination will leave me bitter or indeed disappointed.... If it does not come, the result will be an entirely natural one. The truth is, I think that in your general earnestness and zeal on my behalf, a defeat would be more disappointing to you than to me...."[56]

Roosevelt's consistent refusal to reiterate publicly his disavowal of another nomination troubled many of Taft's supporters. Mabel Boardman, whose family had known the Taft clan for many years, and who would become one of Taft's close confidants during his term, wrote to him that TR "presents a large mystery to the public as to his intentions. For my part, I do not see how he can afford to break his word and run again...."[57] Boardman further noted that the anti-Roosevelt press "have aroused his fighting spirit, but the keeping of a promise is to me a question of honor...." It is a pity, she added, "that with all his good points the President has so bitterly antagonized so many men." Indeed, the negativism toward TR was affecting the presidential campaign as a whole. "Somehow to me the whole contest is distasteful ... dragging down a high office that should be dignified and respected." Reiterating similar comments from Taft's late mother, Boardman warned her friend that even if he gained the office, "it means continual struggle, attack and criticism. If you don't get it[,] I shall be sorry for the country, but glad for your own sake."[58]

Taft was, of course, well aware of the criticisms leveled against the president. He had even received advice that he should distance himself from the incumbent by resigning from the cabinet. Will's response was unequivocal.

If I am to be defeated because I am close to Roosevelt, then I am defeated for [that] reason ... and I ought to be defeated on that account. I very much enjoy being in his

---

you rather than stand me." Such a comment is another example of TR's cat-and-mouse technique as applied to Taft.

[55] Ibid., 796.

[56] Pringle Papers, September 11, 1907. Although there is no reason to question Will's candor, Charles Taft's efforts on behalf of Will continued unabated.

[57] Pringle Papers, November 18, 1907.

[58] Ibid. On December 12, Roosevelt released a statement that his earlier decision "was final and would not be changed." He had been concerned, he wrote to Taft, that "my position was misunderstood, and that it damaged you to have any doubt whether my refusal was really final." Letters, vol. 5, 864.

Cabinet and shall be quite content if the nomination goes elsewhere. He knows and I know, and I don't know who else knows, that if I am President, I will be President myself, and I don't have to convince either himself or myself by leaving the Cabinet.[59]

TR AND WILL CAMPAIGNING

Taft's insistence that he be seen as a key admirer and supporter of TR raises the question of precisely what political/policy positions the president maintained as the 1908 election drew nigh. In January 1908, Roosevelt wrote to his friend the British historian Sir George Trevelyan. During his years as president, "my chief fight has been to prevent the upgrowth in this country of the least attractive and most sordid of all aristocracies ... , a plutocracy, a caste which regards power as expressed only in its basest and most brutal form, that of mere money."[60] One day later, he expanded his views in a lengthy letter to his attorney general, Charles Bonaparte. Two themes may be isolated from TR's extensive comments.

Roosevelt denounced "the representatives of predatory wealth ... accumulated on a giant scale by iniquity, by wrongdoing in many forms, by plain swindling, by oppressing wageworkers, by manipulating securities, by unfair and unwholesome competition, ... in short by conduct abhorrent to every man of ordinarily decent conscience...."[61] Such conduct was offensive not only in itself but also for what it might provoke in American society as a whole. This fear was reflected in TR's second theme, one that he reiterated time and time again during the next decade: "We seek," he emphasized, "to control law-defying wealth, in the first place to prevent its doing evil, and in the next place to avoid the vindictive and dreadful radicalism which, if left uncontrolled, it is certain in the end to arouse."[62] Indeed, "we act in no vindictive spirit, and we are no respecter of persons. If a labor union does what is wrong, we oppose it as fearlessly as we oppose a corporation that does wrong; and we stand with equal stoutness for the rights of the man of wealth and for the rights of the wageworkers; just as much so for one as for the other."[63]

In January 1908, TR delivered his annual message to Congress. In it, among other things, he "attacked Wall Street," and added that domestic prosperity was less important than honesty in both finance and corporate dealing as well as in industry.[64] Rather than being shocked, Taft described TR's proposals as "of a most conservative character." Indeed, no one would be able to

---

[59] Pringle Papers, August 6, 1907. "My strength is largely as his friend, and while I may have some independent strength, it is not nearly so large as that which I get through him."

[60] Letters, vol. 6, January 1, 1908, 882–883.

[61] Ibid., 884.

[62] Ibid., 889.

[63] Ibid., 889–890. See also his comments a few months later to Ray Stannard Baker. "I fight against privilege; I fight for the control of great wealth; I fight against mob rule; I fight for equal opportunities for all." Ibid., June 3, 1908, 1049.

[64] Pringle, 344.

find anything in the message as "to shake in the slightest the guaranties of life, liberty and property secured by the Constitution."[65] Similarly, when the Republican Convention later convened in Chicago, Taft had prepared a plank for the platform critical of judges who abused their injunctive powers in labor disputes. Well known himself as a judge who had not hesitated to enjoin labor leaders from secondary boycotts and to send a number of such individuals to prison, nevertheless Taft by 1908 found himself opposing those judges who had "by hasty and ill considered issue of injunctions, without notice or hearing, incurred the just criticism of laboring men engaged in a lawful strike."[66]

But the conservative wing of his party would have none of their nominee's objections to "this reckless use of ex parte injunctions." Both TR and Taft had to accept a watered-down plank, which in the end said nothing about such abuse from the courts. American Federation of Labor president Samuel Gompers was accurate when he noted that organized labor had been "thrown down, repudiated and relegated to the discard [sic] by the Republican Party."[67] It might be observed that TR had agreed to the dilution of Taft's original plank, and urged its acceptance upon Taft.

To a certain extent, but not – one thinks – as much as Taft imagined, he found himself in agreement with TR. Concerning rights of labor, perhaps a different issue in his mind than for rights of labor unions, Taft stated on numerous occasions that "I believe there ought to be no favored class in litigation at all, that a man who has property and a man who has labor to sell shall stand on equality in court, and that every man shall be entitled to be protected by all the writs and remedies that the law affords, by an impartial judiciary."[68]

Similarly, in a letter to a supporter written on August 15, 1908, Taft insisted that his purpose as president would be "to protect those who comply with the law in the rights secured to them by the Constitution and statutes of the country; and I believe myself able to assure ... others that neither special interests nor particular clamor will prevent my treating squarely the people, the shippers, the carriers, the wage-earners and the capitalists."[69] Taft then added a sentence that, as will be seen, he would reiterate with minor variation many times during the next four years. It reveals that even before his election, Taft did not perceive of his term as a carbon copy of TR's. If either did, and apparently TR was more persuaded on this point than Taft, it was an early contribution to the eventual disintegration of their friendship. With Roosevelt's term

---

[65] Ibid.
[66] Ibid., 350.
[67] Letters, vol. 6, June 15, 1908, 1077.
[68] Ross, 200. On the other hand, TR worried about how organized labor in general perceived Taft. Concerning a forthcoming paper on his labor positions, Roosevelt urged Taft to consult some of the Western radicals about it. "I do not think that La Follette would give you anything worth having, but it is possible that [Iowa Governor Albert] Cummins might." Letters, vol. 6, September 1, 1908, 1203–1204.
[69] Pringle Papers, August 15, 1908.

ending, Taft believed that now is the time "for the constructive work needed to secure the enforcement of the law, the protection of those who keep within it, and the punishment of those who violate it; and more than all, a sufficiently clear guide for those who would keep within the law as to the limits of their action."[70]

Roosevelt denied that he was trying to dictate Taft's nomination. Yet, as he wrote to his son Kermit, "I believe ... that Taft, far more than any other public man of prominence, represents the principles for which I stand; ... and I would hold myself false to my duty if I sat supine and let the men who have taken such joy in my refusal to run again select some candidate whose success would mean the undoing of what I have sought to achieve."[71] But while he ultimately supported Taft, TR never described him in the terms he employed a few weeks later to portray his relationship with Henry Cabot Lodge. The senator from Massachusetts "was my closest friend, personally, politically, and in every other way, and occupied toward me a relation that no other man has ever occupied or ever will occupy"[72] (Figure 4).

Nevertheless, TR rejoiced in Taft's nomination on the first ballot at the Republican Convention. To be sure, it followed an uproarious demonstration at the mention of Roosevelt's name by Henry Cabot Lodge, one that lasted for some forty-nine minutes – almost twice as long as a similar outburst for Taft when his name was later placed in nomination.[73] The nomination now an accomplished fact, TR boasted to Trevelyan that "I had thrown myself heart and soul into the business of nominating Taft[,] ... that he stood for exactly the same principles and policies that I did.... He and I view public questions exactly alike. In fact, I think it has been very rare that two public men have ever been so much as one in all the essentials of their beliefs and practices."[74]

But the president saw possible difficulties ahead for his candidate. He observed to his son-in-law, Nicholas Longworth, that "I am not very much

---

[70] Ibid. TR had emphasized using the law to protect working Americans from the abuses of capital, while Taft emphasized protecting the rights of all, within the law.

[71] Ibid., 916. For an example of TR's actions in support of Taft's nomination, see his letter to Augustus Gardner, ibid, February 10, 1908, 936–937. As for the only other feasible Republican possibility with any sort of national reputation, New York Governor Charles Evans Hughes was "a fairly good man, (but not a big man) and an inordinately conceited one." Indeed, TR likened Hughes to a "psalm singing son of a bitch." Edmund Morris, "Theodore Roosevelt, President," 32 *American Heritage*," 1981, 6. Another presidential hopeful, Senator Robert La Follette, was "an entirely worthless Senator." Letters, vol. 6, May 30, 1908, 1044.

[72] Ibid., February 10, 1908, 935.

[73] Whether these ovations were spontaneous or contrived remains unclear. Taft's manager assured his candidate that TR's sustained cheers "meant nothing." Pringle, 352. Of the ovation for her husband, Nellie Taft emphasized that "I ... want it to last more than forty-nine minutes. I want to get even for the scare that Roosevelt cheer ... gave me yesterday." Ross, 197.

[74] Letters, vol. 6, June 19, 1908, 1085. Barely two years later, TR would back away from this position. Further, while too much should not be made of the discrepancy between TR's popularity and that of his successor, as manifest during the convention, from that time on until 1912, Taft remained very much aware of it.

HARPER'S WEEKLY

A JOURNAL OF CIVILIZATION

VOL. LII.   New York, October 10, 1908   No. 2703

Copyright, 1908, by Harper & Brothers. All rights reserved

T. R. "Our Candidate is the Strongest Man I Know"

HE NEEDS TO BE

FIGURE 4. Cartoon from *Harper's Weekly*, October 10, 1908. The cartoonist's negative attitude toward TR might be noted. Taft is portrayed as a solid, strong individual, able to put up with a restive, if not bothersome, campaign nuisance, who won't leave the nominee alone. Reproduced by permission of HarpWeek, LLC.

pleased with the way Taft's campaign is being handled ... I do wish that Taft would put more energy and fight into the matter ... "[75] On the same day, he sent a "personal" letter to Taft. "I do think," he wrote, "that there is urgent need that you should dominate more than you have yet done the National Committee; that it should be much more active than it has yet been ... , and above all, you should take the most aggressive kind of attitude towards Bryan, hitting him hard."[76]

Taft was probably not surprised to receive such a letter from Roosevelt, all the more so as he had read others like it. His answer to one of them well indicates how much he differed from TR in his approach to politics. In August 1908, he had replied to one correspondent "that you think I am not sufficiently aggressive in my speeches ... but I cannot be more aggressive than my nature makes me. That is the advantage and disadvantage of having been on the Bench. I can't call names and I can't use adjectives when I don't think the case calls for them, so you will have to get along with that kind of candidate." None knew better than Taft "the strength that the President has by reason of those qualities which are the antithesis of the judicial, but so it is with me, and if the people don't like that kind of man then they have got to take another."[77]

Never an enthusiastic campaigner, Taft during the fall of 1908, received letter after letter from TR. The president constantly reminded him how he had run his campaign in 1904, forgetting perhaps that Taft had played a very important role in it. As noted earlier, Roosevelt on the one hand would urge Taft to be more forceful and aggressive, while on the other, he thought "it essential that your personality should be put with all possible force into the campaign."[78] When Taft so desired, however, he acted regardless of Roosevelt. Thus he insisted that one donor who had offered a campaign contribution of $50,000 reduce it to $10,000 because "the size of the subscription will be misunderstood and the inferences drawn from it will not be just or kind either to you or to me." Roosevelt's reaction was that "really, I think you are

---

[75] Ibid., September 21, 1908, 1244. A week earlier, TR had intimated to Taft that his energy employed playing golf might be put to better use during his campaign. "I don't suppose you will have the chance to play until after election, and whether you have the chance or not, I hope you won't." Ibid., September 14, 1908, 1234. Taft continued to play golf during the campaign, regardless of TR's wishes.

[76] Ibid., September 21, 1908, 1247. One day later, he emphasized to Lyman Abbott, "Oh Lord, I do get angry now and then over the campaign....but certainly I would like to put more snap into the business." Ibid., 1248–1249. "If a man wishes to win," he added, "it is absolutely necessary that he shall knock out his opponent when he has the latter groggy." In reality, what TR desired, of course, was that Taft be a 1908 version of the president.

[77] Pringle Papers, August 11, 1908. One month later, TR put it more forcefully. "Let them realize the truth, which is that for all your gentleness and kindliness and generous good nature, there never existed a man who was a better fighter when the need arose. The trouble is that you would always rather fight for a principle or for a friend than for yourself. Now hit at them...." Letters, vol. 6, 1908, 1231.

[78] Ibid., 1195, August 24, 1908.

oversensitive."[79] Ultimately, the Taft campaign raised a little over $1.5 million, compared with more than than $2 million for TR in 1904.

VICTORY

Not an inspiring speaker, Taft traveled across the country for some forty days, always with a worried President cajoling, critiquing, and commenting in the background as the campaign came to an end. Indeed, Pringle does not exaggerate when he states that "Taft was relatively forgotten in the campaign."[80] Essentially Taft ran on TR's record although, as noted earlier, he called for completing and perfecting "the machinery" that would protect legitimate business even as it "restrained and punished" the lawbreaker. *The Wall Street Journal* further distinguished between TR and Taft when it observed that Taft was "neither a reactionary nor a revolutionist, neither a Bourbon nor a Jacobin."[81] Not a colorful or eloquent speaker as was his opponent, Democrat William Jennings Bryan, who was seeking the presidency for a third time, Taft capitalized on Bryan's ill-considered proposal to nationalize the railroads. Moreover, against a three-time candidate, Republicans knew what to expect from Bryan (Figure 5).

The fall election resulted in Taft's clear victory, with more than a million vote majority over Bryan. If TR was delighted that his candidate did so well in the electoral vote (321–162), perhaps he should have been troubled by the fact that Taft's popular lead over Bryan was less than half of TR's rout of Parker four years before, even though Taft received more Republican votes than had TR. Also, Taft lost several states that TR had carried in 1904. Yet, in November 1908, TR gave no indication that anything might be amiss concerning an election four years off. Repeatedly, he reaffirmed to many a correspondent that "Taft will carry on the work … His policies, principles, purposes and ideals are the same as mine….I have the profound satisfaction of knowing that he will do all in his power to further every one of the great causes for which I have fought[,] and that he will persevere in every one of the great governmental policies in which I most firmly believe."[82]

But TR's rhetoric concerning the identical symmetry of Taft's views with his own was not as accurate as he hoped and predicted. A far more effective politician than Taft, Roosevelt nevertheless by the last year of his term, faced major internal dissent within his own party. It involved the party stand on the tariff and the emergence of Midwest reform elements, specifically targeting the entrenched House Speaker, Joseph Cannon. As president, Roosevelt spoke to power. Recognizing Cannon's strengths, and capitalizing on his weaknesses, TR had achieved successes in railroad regulation and public health

---

[79] Pringle, 360.
[80] Ibid., 366.
[81] Ibid., 366.
[82] Letters, vol. 6, November 6, 1908, 1328.

SOMEWHAT OBSCURED, BUT STILL VISIBLE

FIGURE 5. Cartoon from *Harper's Weekly*, October 24, 1908. As the 1908 presidential campaign wound down, it appeared to some, including the cartoonist, that Taft as a candidate–along with his solid and calm personality–was being obscured, but not quite concealed, by TR's loud rhetoric on his behalf. Reproduced by permission of HarpWeek, LLC.

reform, but at the cost of tariff reform, which he employed as a bargaining chip, and interparty opposition to Cannon, which he quietly encouraged even as he declined to endorse it himself.

Taft made no secret of his distaste for the Speaker's tactics, including his crude cynicism concerning both the common good and possible tariff reform. Shortly after his election, Taft indicated that Cannon ought to be forced out. TR had already been urged by a number of House insurgents to "start a backfire against that miserable antediluvian nuisance."[83] But both Roosevelt and Root wondered who might take Cannon's place if he were driven from office. If the vast majority of Republican congressmen wanted Cannon, he observed to Taft, "I do not believe it would be well to have him in the position of the sullen and hostile floor leader bound to bring your administration to grief, even though you were able to put someone else in as Speaker."

At first, Taft seemed firm in his opposition to Cannon, even as Root warned the president-elect that "it would be very unfortunate to have the idea get out that you wanted to beat Cannon and are not able to do it. "[84] Writing to Root about the 1908 Republican commitment to tariff reduction, Taft emphasized that "I am willing to have it understood that my attitude is one of hostility to Cannon and the whole crowd unless they are coming in to do the square thing."[85] Yet the Cannon "problem," as well as the issue of genuine commitment to tariff reduction, were linked together. Late in November 1908, Taft noted to one correspondent that "I am confronted in the beginning of my administration with what seems to be something of a party crisis. I do not wish to do anything rash, but neither do I wish to omit any legitimate effort as the head of the party to prevent a fatal reactionary mistake."[86] But in the last few months of Roosevelt's term, Taft may well have feared being out in front on the tariff issue, but without a following behind him. Acting on TR's advice, he reached in December what he thought was an understanding with Cannon. In return for not interfering with House reorganization, Cannon and his supporters would not block efforts to deal with the tariff, or so he thought.[87]

Promptly accused of selling out to Cannon, Taft replied that the election of the Speaker rested with the House, not the president. He added that "I might go in and make a fight to affect the organization of the House ... "[88] But such a step might be an unfortunate precedent, especially if it resulted in defeat, "which would only make the situation worse," and if it resulted in victory "it would leave a recalcitrant and ugly minority quite capable of defeating any legislation which I desired, and producing a lack of cooperation that would

---

[83] Ibid., November 10, 1908, 1340–1341.
[84] Pringle, 405.
[85] Pringle Papers, November 25, 1908.
[86] Ibid., November 23, 1908.
[87] According to Taft, Cannon observed that "he was entirely in sympathy with my efforts to carry out the pledges of the Chicago platform, and that he would assist me as loyally as possible." To Taft's discomfort, Cannon's later actions belied his words. Pringle, 406.
[88] Pringle Papers, December 6, 1908.

result in no progress whatever."[89] Later to be faulted by his critics for surrendering to Cannon, Taft could have replied with complete justification that TR had urged him not to confront the House Speaker.

In spite of the fact that Roosevelt repeatedly emphasized the similarity of perspective between himself and Taft, one suspects that by such constant repetition of the point, he sought more to convince himself of what he knew was not really the case. But the two men possessed contrasting personalities. The dynamic, active, impetuous, spontaneous, and impulsive president – although he was politically sophisticated – differed from the ponderous, judicious, lawyerlike, phlegmatic if not lethargic secretary of war, even though there was never any question of Taft's utter loyalty to his boss. Taft's reaction to TR's final annual message to Congress and his comments on courts and judges well demonstrates the point.

Mention has already been made of Taft's oft-cited devotion to courts and judges. The president-elect was not sympathetic to Roosevelt's comments on the role of the judiciary in twentieth-century America. "I have gone over the President's message," he wrote, "and could wish that he had said nothing on the subject." On the other hand, along with Moody and Root, he had critiqued it, and "I believe that a good many objectionable things have been stricken out of it...." Taft told the President "I would rather he did not say anything on the subject," but this was not to be. "I knew that his mind was made up[,] that this was the last message he would write and that he must give consideration to the subject which has occupied him heretofore."[90]

Judges should realize, according to TR, that "every time they interpret contract, property, vested rights, [and] due process of law ... they necessarily enact into law parts of a system of social philosophy; and as such interpretation is fundamental, they give direction to all lawmaking."[91] The judge "who owes his election to pandering to demagogic sentiments or class hatreds and prejudices, and the judge who owes either his selection or his appointment to the money or the favor of a great corporation, are alike unworthy to sit on the bench, are alike traitors to the people; and no profundity of legal learning, or correctness of abstract conviction ... , can serve as an offset to such shortcomings."[92]

Responding to William Allen White's compliments concerning his message, TR emphasized that there are many judges "who are entirely unfit to occupy the positions they do, [Supreme Court Justice David] Brewer being a striking example of this kind." One suspects that Roosevelt never showed this letter to Taft. But TR added an intriguing final sentence in his letter to White. "Meanwhile I do wish that you would write in the most emphatic manner to Taft. It could only do good."[93]

[89] Ibid.
[90] Ibid., November 21, 1908.
[91] Letters, vol. 6, November 30, 1908, 1392. Taft saw such results from an independent judiciary as absolutely essential to constitutional government.
[92] Ibid.
[93] Ibid., 1393.

As TR prepared to surrender his office, Taft prepared to build his new administration, and if the outgoing president overemphasized his pleasure in the transition, he also spoke in different tones to those closest to him. A few days before he left office, TR had written to Taft about his forthcoming inaugural address. "I did not wish unreservedly to praise it until I had carefully gone thru it. Now I have gone thru it carefully and I have no suggestion to make."[94] With one day remaining in his term, TR saluted Gifford Pinchot, his comrade-in-arms concerning conservation. "As long as I live," TR wrote, "I shall feel for you a mixture of respect and admiration and of affectionate regard. I am a better man for having known you ... and I cannot think of a man in the country whose loss would be a more real misfortune to the Nation than yours would be."[95] One looks in vain to Roosevelt for a similar sentiment concerning Will Taft. In less than one year, and already well along the route to an irrevocable rupture with the former president, Taft would dismiss Pinchot from office.

[94] Ibid., February 26, 1909, 1538. Indeed, "It is simply fine in every way. I cannot imagine a better inaugural." As will be seen, after its delivery, TR added yet another positive comment about his address to Taft. See the following.

[95] Ibid., March 2, 1909, 1541.

PART TWO

THE PRESIDENCY

5

President Taft

Tensions and Travail, 1909–1910

TENSIONS SO SOON

The first indication that all was not well between TR and his successor came even before Taft's inauguration. Perhaps unconsciously, Roosevelt at first may have assumed that nothing was different between him and Taft. But in fact, as Roosevelt ultimately recognized, their relationship had indeed irrevocably changed. The loyal and responsive subordinate was now the president-elect, while TR – buffeted by an increasingly fractious legislature – faced the inevitable waning of his power as March 4 1909, drew nigh. Initially, Taft had indicated that he intended to adopt Roosevelt's cabinet as his own. "I did not see," he stated to his aide Archie Butt, "how I could do anything else but retain all the old members of the Cabinet who had been associated with me."[1] How much influence Helen Taft exercised over her husband's cabinet choices remains a matter of conjecture. However, she is on record as having stated in one instance, "I could not believe you to be serious when you mentioned that man's name. He is perfectly awful and his family are even worse. I won't even talk about it.[2]"

Fleeing to Hot Springs, Virginia for some rest after his election, Taft apparently reconsidered. By late December, he had selected former Attorney General (and future Pennsylvania Senator) Philander Knox as Secretary of State. As to other positions, he observed to Knox that "I am trying ... to act as judicially as possible, and to free myself from considerations of friendly association as far as I can and remain a decent man with red blood in me."[3] The net result of these efforts was a cabinet with only two holdovers from Roosevelt's administration. Yet Taft hesitated to inform those who would not be retained. Early in January, TR bluntly suggested that "now I think it would be well for you

---

[1] Pringle, 384.

[2] Manners, 70. The identity of this subject of Nellie's wrath remains unclear.

[3] Pringle Papers, December 23, 1908. Taft had invited Elihu Root to reclaim his old cabinet post as secretary of state, but Root declined, pleading ill health. Henry Cabot Lodge also declined the appointment. Knox was Taft's third choice as secretary of state.

to write them all at once that you do not intend to reappoint them....I do not think they ought to be left in doubt"[4] (Figure 6).

TR added that "of course I am perfectly willing to tell them if you will write to me to do so, but I do not think I ought to tell them unless I have some direct communication from you."[5] Taft responded promptly with a note almost curt in tone in which he stated to the president that "I think I ought to do it myself." After further discussion with Knox, "I shall do something definite in the way of action towards those who are now in office."[6] Taft signed the letter "sincerely yours" in spite of the fact that in his previous correspondence with TR, he had habitually used much more cordial language.[7] Roosevelt commented to James Garfield, his secretary of the interior and probably his closest friend in his cabinet, that "something has come over Will, he is changed, he is not the same man."[8]

Indeed, Garfield observed in his diary on January 4 that "Sen[ator] Lodge has been with Taft and brings back word that he has completely changed his mind about the making of his cabinet[,] and now thinks he ought to keep no one. In fact Lodge thought he even resented the intimation that the President's policies and friends were helpful to him. It is evident that hostile influences are at work with Taft and are estranging him from the President."[9] More than a week later, Garfield reported that there was "still no news from Taft who seems now to [want] no conference nor even association with the President and his friends – an astounding condition of affairs and wholly without reasonable explanation."[10]

Shortly thereafter, Garfield referred to legislative opposition to TR. "The congressional fight against the President more bitter[, and] anything he particularly wants they will refuse if they dare." Taft's silence on this issue troubled Garfield. "If only Taft would speak out and let them know such an assault on Roosevelt will not make the assailants friends of Taft, the fight would end and things be done."[11] Finally, on January 25, Garfield mentioned a letter from Taft informing him that he would not remain in the cabinet. "Taft's letter

[4] Letters, vol. 6, January 4, 1909, 1458.

[5] Ibid.

[6] Mabel Boardman Papers, April 15, 1912, enclosure dated January 8, 1909. In the spring of 1912, with Roosevelt now a declared presidential candidate, the issue of Taft's alleged promise to retain Roosevelt's cabinet in 1909 received public attention. Taft sent Boardman copies of his earlier correspondence with Roosevelt, which clearly revealed an absence of any such commitment, at least in writing.

[7] On January 2, for example, Taft had signed a letter to TR: "Believe me, my dear Theodore, Affectionately yours...." Pringle Papers, January 2, 1909.

[8] William Manners, *TR and Will: A Friendship that Split the Republican Party* (New York: Harcourt, Brace and World, 1969), 73. Son of the late president assassinated in 1881, Garfield had become a devoted friend and partisan of TR's. Together with Gifford Pinchot, TR and Garfield had orchestrated the Roosevelt policy of national conservation.

[9] Garfield Diaries, LOC, January 4, 1909.

[10] Ibid., January 12, 1909.

[11] Ibid., January 18, 1909.

FIGURE 6. President-elect Taft and his daughter Helen, ca. 1908. This portrait was apparently one of the most popular images taken of Taft prior to his becoming president. Courtesy of Library of Congress Prints and Photographs Collection.

curiously weak and not sincere. Evidently difficult for him to write because was not willing to tell his real reasons for deserting the first plan to keep most of the present cabinet."[12]

In accordance with his letter to Roosevelt, Taft notified those in the previous administration who were not to be retained. His letter to Garfield, replete with vapid generalizations and unconvincing explanations, may be considered typical. Taft stated that "the duties of a new administration are quite different from those of a retiring administration" and "require that the complexion of the new cabinet should be somewhat different from the old because of a difference of function that the new administration is to perform in carrying out the policies of the old." In selecting the cabinet, Taft added, "I have tried to act as judicially as possible[,] and to free myself altogether from the personal aspect, which has embarrassed me...." He concluded by informing Garfield "that you are young enough to make it better for you not to continue in the cabinet at this time ... And perhaps in doing what seems ungracious ... I am doing the best for you."[13]

In his letter to Garfield, Taft reiterated what he had written five months before in his formal acceptance message to the Republican Convention, actually delivered after it had concluded. It warrants a brief examination because the statement reveals that Taft was indeed prepared to move in a different direction from Roosevelt, even though he fully accepted the "party's declaration ... that it intends to continue his policies. "[14] Indeed, he lauded the sincerity of TR's "efforts to command respect for the law, to secure equality of all before the law, and to save the country from dangers of a plutocratic government, towards which we were fast tending." But "we should be blind," Taft added, "if we did not recognize that the moral standards set by President Roosevelt will not continue to be observed by those whom cupidity ... may tempt, unless the requisite machinery is introduced into the law[,] which shall in its practical operation maintain these standards and secure the country against a departure from them."[15]

The purpose of Taft's administration "is distinct from, and a progressive development" of that already undertaken by Roosevelt. "The chief function of the next Administration is to complete and perfect the machinery by which these standards may be maintained, by which the lawbreakers may be promptly restrained and punished, but which shall operate with sufficient accuracy and

[12] Ibid., January 25, 1909.

[13] Pringle Papers, January 22, 1909. In March 1910, Taft indicated what may have been the real reason for not retaining Garfield. "Pinchot dominated Garfield. It was one reason why I did not retain [him] in the cabinet. I did not want Pinchot to run the Interior Department and the Agricultural Department as well." Taft to Karger, March 12, 1910, Folder 4, Taft–Karger Correspondence, Cincinnati Museum, Center. See also Lewis Gould, *The William Howard Taft Presidency* (Lawrence: University Press of Kansas, 2009), 27.

[14] http://www.presidency.uscb.edu. See "Taft, Address Accepting the Republican Presidential Nomination, July 28, 1908," 2.

[15] Ibid.

dispatch to interfere with legitimate business as little as possible."[16] Taft did not minimize the challenge he faced. This "practical[,] constructive and difficult work of those who follow Mr. Roosevelt is to devise the ways and means by which the high level of business integrity and obedience to law which he has established may be maintained[,] and departures from it restrained without undue interference with legitimate business."[17]

Taft's points demonstrate the very different approaches to government held by the new and the former Chief Executives. They also well reflect Taft's emphasis on a legalistic approach to executive leadership. If Roosevelt had been result-oriented, Taft primarily focused on proper methodology, although both men may have sought the same goals. For Taft, implementing some of Roosevelt's policies would require legislative mandates, not executive directives. The necessary new laws required careful drafting.

Who would be better equipped to draft such remedial statutes than successful corporate lawyers? Taft nominated six of them to his cabinet, and observed that they all took substantial pay cuts to serve in his administration.[18] Moreover, they had in the past represented and understood corporate wealth, "the present combination, its evils, and the method by which they can be properly restrained." Leaders of Congress, especially Speaker Joe Cannon and Senator Nelson Aldrich, might well be receptive to proposals from such individuals. But they "would certainly oppose recommendations made by a Cabinet consisting of the more radical element of the party," as typified by James Garfield.[19] Taft's inability to be candid with TR's outgoing secretary of the interior necessitated the vapid platitudes noted earlier in his letter to Garfield.

"I am going to be criticized," correctly stated the incoming president, "for putting corporation lawyers into my Cabinet." Yet they were "as good lawyers as there are in the country. And being first-class lawyers, they have a good deal of corporate employment."[20] As noted, they moved in the same circles as Cannon and Aldrich, not Garfield – a point not lost on Henry Adams, who asked, "If the new President is bent on making a clean sweep of Roosevelt's men, why did we elect him expressly to carry out the Roosevelt regime?"[21]

---

[16] Ibid., 2–3. Roosevelt had emphasized punishing the corporate wrongdoer. Taft, on the other hand, emphasized the immediate need to enable "those anxious to obey the Federal statutes to know just what are the bounds of their lawful action." TR was interested in prompt punishment, while Will Taft was interested (always) in proper procedure.

[17] Ibid.

[18] For example, George Wickersham, Taft's nominee for attorney general, saw his salary reduced from $100,000 a year to the cabinet stipend of $12,000. Besides Wickersham, Knox (State), Jacob Dickinson (War), Charles Hitchcock (Postmaster General), Charles Nagel (Commerce and Labor), Richard Ballinger (Interior), were all lawyers.

[19] Pringle Papers, February 23, 1909.

[20] Ibid.

[21] Manners, 74.

As he prepared to assume the presidency, Taft experienced real doubts as to his success in that office. To Roosevelt he confided that "I look forward to the future with much hesitation and doubt as to what is to happen."[22] In retrospect, he realized how different his administrative responsibilities had been in the Philippines from what he now confronted, "and I don't know that I shall rise to the occasion or not."[23] He could say in all honesty that he had neither sought nor welcomed the presidency. Now that it was his, he faced the future with ambivalence and gloomy resignation, rather than real enthusiasm, noting that the interval between his election and inauguration might "be a period of stagnation [in] Washington."[24]

During this hiatus, Taft indicated his fear of "undue interference" with legitimate corporate enterprise, even as he voiced what appeared to be a surprisingly militant stand on the tariff. Actually there was nothing inconsistent in his concern for big business and his apparent insistence that the tariff be lowered. "I foresee," he wrote on January 5, 1909, "that I am going to have a fight right through my administration on the subject, but I am ready for it. I believe the people are with me, and before I get through I think I will have downed Cannon and Aldrich too, if Aldrich [is] in the way, or else will have broken up the party...."[25] As will be seen, Taft backed away from major confrontation with the Republican leadership on the tariff. His initial vigorous rhetoric was only that. The result was a divided party, and by consistently siding with Aldrich and Cannon, Taft made a major contribution to the division.

In a similar vein, and at the same time, Taft voiced early frustration at the tendency of federal judges and justices to remain in office longer than they should. "I am afraid that we can't enact anything that will drive the old codgers off the bench; I wish we could."[26] But again, the incoming president later repudiated his own words. During his single term, in which he selected more High Court justices than any other president since Washington, Taft appointed the oldest member of the Supreme Court thus far in its history. Further, in 1921, he would openly and successfully lobby for his own appointment as Chief Justice, even though he was almost sixty-five years old at the time.

Yet all this lay ahead of the incoming president. For now, perhaps either because of and/or in spite of signs of friction between TR and Taft, or possibly as a token of friendship, Roosevelt invited Taft and Nellie to spend the night of March 3 at the White House. Privately, TR had already noted to a confidant

---

[22] Pringle Papers, January 5, 1909.

[23] Pringle, 381.

[24] Letters, vol. 6, January 10, 1909, 1473. On hearing this, TR commented to his son Kermit that "I have felt like wiring [Taft] that the period of stagnation continues to rage with uninterrupted violence." Ibid.

[25] Pringle Papers, January 5, 1909.

[26] Ibid., January 7, 1909.

that although Taft would try hard, " … he is weak … "[27] Taft responded that "people have attempted to represent that you and I were in some way at odds during the last three months, where as you and I know that there has not been the slightest difference between us, and I welcome the opportunity to stay the last night of your administration under the White House roof to make as emphatic as possible the refutation of any such suggestion."[28]

March 4, 1909, brought one of the worst winter storms to buffet Washington. "I knew," remarked TR, "there would be a blizzard when I went out." For his part, Taft observed that "even the elements do protest."[29] Nevertheless, he turned to his inaugural address, a solid and thoughtful if uninspiring analysis, which warrants some attention, as it focused on what Taft saw as the goals for his administration now beginning.

Again Taft praised his predecessor, as he pledged to continue what TR had started. "I should be untrue to myself, to my promises, and to the declarations of the party platform on which I was elected … , if I did not make the maintenance and enforcement of those reforms a most important feature of my administration."[30] Again he reiterated the dual emphasis he had noted in his speech of acceptance about six months earlier. First, that Roosevelt's reforms must be "lasting," and second, to secure "freedom from alarm on the part of those pursuing proper and progressive business methods, further legislation and executive action are needed." Big business needs to understand "those things that may be done[,] and those that are prohibited.… Such a plan must include the right of the people to avail themselves of those methods of combining capital deemed necessary to reach the highest degrees of economic efficiency, at the same time differentiating between combinations based upon legitimate economic reasons," and those formed for monopolistic greed."[31]

If Roosevelt had shown no inclination to move on the tariff, Taft, at least in this earliest phase of his presidency, demonstrated determination. He described it as "a matter of most pressing importance," and stated that "I shall call Congress into extra session," in order to consider its revision. Aware that Congress could easily take up other items during the special session, he added that "it would seem wise to attempt no other legislation at the extra session. I venture this as a suggestion only, for the course to be taken by Congress, upon

[27] Pringle, 392.

[28] Ibid. In spite of Taft's sentiments, which TR acknowledged in kind, actually both men could only have realized that already there had been disagreements between them, although more in terms of personnel rather than on policy. The fact that Taft replied to TR's invitation as he did indicates a desire to deny what both sensed to be the truth. Tension was also noticeable during the final dinner party, although it was a very small group. Ibid., 393. March 3, 1909, was apparently the last night Roosevelt ever spent at the White House.

[29] Ibid., 394. "I always said it would be a cold day when I got to be President of the United States." Ross, 208.

[30] http://www.presidency.ucsb.edu. William Howard Taft, Inaugural Address, March 4, 1909, 1.

[31] Ibid.

the call of the Executive, is wholly within its discretion."[32] The new president reminded Congress that "the scope of a modern government in what it can and ought to accomplish for its people has been widened far beyond the principles laid down by the old 'laissez faire' school of political writers, and this widening has met popular approval."[33] He also stated that "the putting into force of laws which shall secure the conservation of our resources ... including the most important work of saving and restoring our forests ... are all proper government functions...."[34]

Taft devoted almost half a dozen paragraphs to the South, focusing in particular on racial relations there. His comments well illustrated his flirtation with progressive views, which often concealed a racist and conservative bias. Fully aware that the Democratic "solid South" was now a reality, Taft hoped to increase "the already good feeling between the South and other sections of the country." He looked forward as well to "an increase in the tolerance of political views of all kinds[,] and their advocacy throughout the South."[35] He conceded that although in the South the Fifteenth Amendment "has not been generally observed in the past, it ought to be observed." But he immediately added, "It is clear to all that the domination of an ignorant, irresponsible element can be prevented by constitutional laws which shall exclude from voting both negroes and whites not having education or other qualifications thought to be necessary for a proper electorate."[36]

Again Taft extolled the Fifteenth Amendment. "It is a great protection to the negro. It never will be repealed, and it never ought to be repealed." Yet "it is not the disposition or within the province of the Federal Government to interfere with the regulation by Southern States of their own domestic affairs." Taft looked for a greater improvement of the negro "as a productive member of society, on the farm, and in the shop, and in other occupations [which] may come."[37] As for appointment of blacks to federal office, the new president carefully hedged his support. When applied to "their distinguished men," such patronage "is properly taken as an encouragement and an appreciation of their progress," to be "pursued when suitable occasion offers." But President Taft tacked on a caveat in a typically lengthy and turgid sentence:

But it may well admit of doubt whether ... an appointment of one of their number to a local office in a community in which the race feeling is so widespread and acute as

---

[32] Ibid. As will be seen, on a philosophical level, Taft's conception of the authority inherent in the presidential office contrasted dramatically with that of Roosevelt. Roosevelt's personality made it easy for him to exercise and indeed expand presidential power. Either through disinclination or inability, Taft, with a few rare exceptions, could not imitate his predecessor.

[33] Here Taft demonstrated at least some minimal sympathy with the progressives in his own party, but later events indicated that it did not consistently extend to active support.

[34] Taft Inaugural Address, 2.

[35] Ibid., 4.

[36] Ibid. In other words, the South was free to exclude an "ignorant" black electorate from voting, assuming that the same action would be taken against "ignorant" whites.

[37] Ibid., 5. Clearly Taft had embraced Booker T. Washington's 1905 controversial "cast down your bucket" conception of blacks' progress in white society.

to interfere with the ease and facility with which the local government business can be done by the appointee is of sufficient benefit by way of encouragement to the race to outweigh the recurrence and increase of race feeling which such an appointment is likely to engender.[38]

Claiming that "personally, I have not the slightest race prejudice or feeling," Taft predicted voting "by those of this race who are intelligent and well to do will be acquiesced in, and the right to vote will be withheld only from the ignorant and irresponsible of both races."[39] Thus Taft indicated that Southern steps toward barring impoverished and uneducated blacks from the franchise, already well in hand, were acceptable – assuming that ignorant and poor whites were also to be disenfranchised – although he offered no evidence that he was prepared to ascertain whether or not this was true.[40]

Well before his inaugural, Taft had already informed Booker T. Washington that he had "quite definite ideas" concerning the Southern race question, "but I am not sure how they conform to what you may deem an appropriate expression of them."[41] On February 23, 1909, he wrote a correspondent in Missouri that "I am going to take a decided step in respect to Southern negro appointments. I am not going to put in places of such prominence in the South where the race feeling is strong, Negroes whose appointment will only tend to increase that race feeling; but I shall look about and make appointments in the North and recognize the negro as often as I can."[42]

In a telling comment, Taft added that "I have to meet Booker T. Washington ... and ... presume that he will object to my stand in this regard, but I am convinced that it is in the interest of the negro as it is in the interest of the public at large, and that it will allay race feeling in the interest of the struggle of the negro for industrial position in the North." Two points should be noted here. First, Taft stated that he *had* to meet with Washington, not that he *wished* to do so. Second, and he would reiterate this position in his inaugural address, Taft consistently linked progress for the blacks with their place in the industrial order. As was observed in Chapter 3, Taft had demonstrated a considerably stronger commitment to racial progress from 1900 to 1903 while in the Philippines. But much had changed by 1909, and concerned now for keeping on good terms with a Southern constituency, Taft backtracked from TR's racial practices, which, while they might have been called progressive in 1905, in no way resemble modern meanings of the term.

[38] Ibid. Taft was indeed a child of his time, and the first decade of the twentieth century remains both the dawn of the progressive period and at the same time an era of heightened racist intensity. He cannot be removed from it.

[39] Ibid. He had said the same thing during an interview with a group of colored citizens in Chicago on April 4, 1908. " ... with respect to the ignorance of the white man as compared with the ignorance of the colored man ... they both have to be excluded on the same ground...." Pringle Papers, April 4, 1908.

[40] I have been unable to find any examples of where Taft either was aware of or acquiesced in the disenfranchisement of any white male voters.

[41] Pringle Papers, November 23, 1908.

[42] Ibid., February 23, 1909.

During the course of his inaugural address, in addition to calling for a reduction of the tariff, Taft also paid tribute to TR's efforts on behalf of labor, especially railway workers. He noted that Congress had made interstate carriers liable to their employees "for injuries sustained in the course of employment...."[43] Further, it had cast aside the outmoded practices of the fellow-servant rule and contributory negligence. The legislature had also passed "a model child labor law for the District of Columbia." He added that "I hope to promote the enactment of further legislation of this character."

Finally, as if to demonstrate that he was by no means committed to all progressive measures, Taft reaffirmed his unshakeable conviction that courts must retain their authority to issue injunctions in industrial disputes.[44] "As to that, my convictions are fixed." He had no doubt that to hold business not to be "a property or pecuniary right ... is utterly without foundation on precedent or reason." Employing a secondary boycott in strikes "is an instrument of tyranny, and ought not to be made legitimate."[45] Behind these claims had been an interesting controversy between Taft and the platform committee of his own party.

Although Taft candidly conceded that as a judge he had not hesitated to enjoin the secondary boycott when he felt it appropriate to so rule, both he and Roosevelt had publicly criticized what Taft called "this reckless use of ex parte injunctions," especially in strikes.[46] He proposed that in their platform for the 1908 campaign, the Republicans oppose such a practice, and defended his proposal from criticism by concerned party regulars. To one such individual he wrote that "I am bound to say that there has been abuse in this matter." With unintended understatement, Taft added that "I yield to no man in my respect for the courts ... but I am most anxious that in order to secure their continued position of independence and power, we shall remove the slightest reason for criticism against them."[47]

He was even more emphatic to his campaign manager. "I yield to no one in my respect to the courts and would rather cut my hand off than to take power away from them [that is] needed to protect rights of property...." But "the courts have by hasty and ill considered issue of injunctions, without notice or hearing, incurred the just criticism of laboring men engaged in [a] [l]awful strike." A statute that would require hearing and consideration prior to issuing injunctions, while not restricting essential judicial authority in any way, "is right and ought to be adopted."[48] Taft "deemed it of

---

[43] Taft, Inaugural Address, 5.
[44] Ibid. See Chapter 2.
[45] Inaugural Address, 6.
[46] Ibid. Pringle, 350.
[47] Pringle Papers, June 15, 1908.
[48] Ibid. To another correspondent, Taft urged that the platform contain a suggestion for a "change in the procedure in the United States Courts which will prevent this reckless issue of exparte injunction." Ibid., June 14, 1908.

the utmost importance to adopt the plank," all the more so as Roosevelt strongly supported it.[49]

Although the Republican conservatives and business interests opposed both Taft and Roosevelt on the injunction issue, TR had urged the Convention to endorse what he considered not "an anti-injunction plank at all, but a singularly moderate and reasonable provision which in its essence merely asks that judges shall think before they act, but which does not in any way hamper their action when once they have thought."[50] The "old guard" remained unyielding, however, and ultimately both TR and Taft had to accept a watered-down substitute. It pledged the Republicans to "uphold at all times the authority and integrity of the courts," and made vague reference to a need to define "more accurately" the rules of procedure dealing with writs of injunction. For opposing reasons, both the Association of Manufacturers and Samuel Gompers denounced the final version. Gompers was both accurate and candid when he stated that organized labor "had been thrown down, repudiated and relegated to the discard [sic] by the Republican party."[51] In his inaugural address, Taft made no mention of the in-fighting over the tariff plank, but he stated that the party platform called for "the formulation in a statute of the conditions under which a temporary injunction ought to issue." Such a statute, he added, "can and ought to be framed to embody the best modern practice...."[52]

So Taft's inaugural address passed into history. In a number of instances, it reflected progressive views. Taft had called for tariff reduction, had endorsed continued federal efforts at conservation, and had supported more regulation concerning safety for railroad workers. Even his comments on racial relations and voting restrictions were in line with typical progressive sentiment of the period, even though they seem very unprogressive to us today.[53] Applause broke out in the crowded Senate chamber as Taft ended his address, and TR shook hands with his successor, calling the speech "a great state document."[54] The two men were not to meet again until June 30, 1910. Roosevelt traveled first to Africa to hunt wild game, and then to Europe. "I trust," supposedly observed J. P. Morgan, that "the first lion he meets will do his duty."[55] In the meantime, Taft was on his own.

[49] See Ross, *A Muted Fury*, 73–74.

[50] Roosevelt, *Letters*, Vol. 6, June 16, 1908, 1078. In a telegram to Henry Cabot Lodge, Roosevelt noted that "It is just as weak and unwise to yield to the demands of the Manufacturers' Association when they are wrong[,] as to yield to the demands of [Samuel] Gompers [president of the American Federation of Labor] when he is wrong." Ibid.

[51] Ibid., 1077.

[52] Taft, Inaugural Address, 6.

[53] See Michael McGerr, *A Fierce Discontent: The Rise and Fall of the Progressive Movement in America* (New York: Oxford University Press, 2005), 182–218.

[54] Pringle, 396

[55] http:www.pithypedia.com. "J. P. Morgan on Teddy Roosevelt's safari." For a slight variation in the quotation, see also Matthew Josephson, *The Robber Barons: The Great American Capitalists 1861–1901* (New York: Harcourt, Brace & World, Inc, 1962), 451.

PRESIDENTIAL METHODOLOGY

The new president could not allow TR to sail without sending him a fare-well letter, replete with expressions of foreboding. "I have no doubt," he wrote, "that when you return you will find me very much under suspicion by our friends in the West." Here, Taft was referring to the restless progressive Republicans, who although nominally in the GOP, were increasingly at bitter loggerheads with the Eastern conservative wing of the party. But Taft reit-erated prior advice from Root and Roosevelt himself when he added that he would be making a "capital error" if he alienated "the good will of those with-out whom I can do nothing" in terms of promised legislation."[56] He referred specifically to Cannon in the House and Aldrich in the Senate.[57]

Taft went on to compare himself unfavorably with TR with, as it later turned out, real prescience. "Of course I have not the prestige which you had or the popular support in any such measure as you had...." Moreover, "I have not the facility for educating the public as you had through talks with corre-spondents, and I fear a large part of the public will feel as if I had fallen away from your ideals...."[58] Acknowledging the accuracy of Taft's self-perceptions, one might ask why – if he was so well aware of them – did he make no effort to gain some rapport with the press? As will be seen, he demonstrated a con-sistent lack of interest in building such links, which could have been of great value. Meanwhile, "I can never forget that the power that I now exercise was a voluntary transfer from you to me, and that I am under obligation to you...."[59]

But Taft appears to have had some difficulty understanding what this obli-gation implied. Less then four months into his presidency, he removed Henry White as ambassador to France. It mattered not that TR had repeatedly told Taft of his admiration for White's skill as a diplomat. Nor did it matter that Taft had apparently assured Roosevelt that he would retain White, without question. He never explained the reasons for his action. Yet this incident, early in Taft's term, riled TR, and the way he responded to it in a letter to White can be considered prophetic. It is true that Taft had not "promised" to

---

[56] Pringle, 400–401.

[57] A member of the House for almost thirty years, Cannon was a capable, cynical, and calculat-ing congressional veteran. By 1909, as Speaker, he appeared to rule the lower chamber almost as a fiefdom. In fact, however, Cannon's days of absolute power were numbered. Barely a year after Taft's inauguration, a coalition of congressional malcontents led by George Norris brought "Cannonism" to an end, not, however, before the wily Speaker taught Taft a lesson in legislative legerdemain as the tariff controversy unfolded. See the following.

[58] Pringle, 400–401.

[59] Ibid. Not surprisingly, Roosevelt felt it necessary to reply that "everything will turn out all right, old man." But in less than a year, Taft had slipped in his estimation. Of Root, TR wrote to Andrew Carnegie, "You know how I trust him; he was *the* man of my cabinet, the man on whom I most relied, ... as great a cabinet officer as we have ever had...." Letters, vol. 7, February 18, 1910, 48 (emphasis in original). It is interesting that TR makes no mention of President Taft.

retain White. Indeed, his pledge to Roosevelt "was, of course, not a promise[,] anymore than my statement that I would not run again for President was a promise."[60]

Perhaps it is unfair to conclude, as did Stanford historian Thomas Bailey, that "an aura of fumble, bumble, and stumble" characterized Taft's presidency.[61] Examination of his proposals and actions evinces an initial firmness, albeit one that was frequently transformed and hampered by malleability. During his first year in office, it appeared that Taft had to ask not so much what *would* TR do under similar circumstances, as what *will* TR do when he returns home in some fifteen months. His presence, either looming or actual, seemed to hang over Taft's tenure.

THE TARIFF

Today, as Lewis Gould well notes, the tariff battle of 1909 "seems an arcane dispute over an outmoded public policy."[62] But at that time, the philosophy of protectionism represented the gospel of the Republican Party. According to its supporters, it had produced industrial power, economic wealth, "social cohesion, and an alluring vision of a bright economic future."[63] In reality, however, the tariff no longer held the same appeal for Western Republicans as it did for the Eastern establishment. It had become a divisive issue within the party, and those who wanted unity within the GOP hesitated to take it up.

Thus, for several possible reasons, including political expediency, Roosevelt had consistently avoided the perennial controversy of the tariff. Taft, to the contrary, had pledged a special session of Congress to deal specifically with it. For him, the party platform came close to a form of a quasi-contract between it and the electorate, and in his view, the Republicans had called for lower rates. Despite other Republican statements to the contrary, the new president emphasized his obligation to the fulfillment of the platform's pledges, resulting in heavy cost to his popularity, as will be seen. The way in which he handled the tariff, a perennial divisive issue, typifies the difference between Roosevelt and Taft in working with the legislature. Taft had limited practical experience in this area, unlike TR, who had been a member of the New York Assembly, as well as governor of New York. Moreover, TR had a very different concept of executive leadership.

TR's ability to deal with the legislature is well known. He would bombard the lawmakers with messages, communicate with them personally, and hector them to accept his wishes, relishing the give-and-take of political discourse,

---

[60] *Letters*, vol. 7, July 21, 1909, 21. So early in Taft's tenure did TR articulate the claim that his notorious act of renunciation was in fact not that fixed.

[61] Thomas A. Bailey, *Presidential Greatness* (New York: Appleton-Century-Crofts, 1966), 309.

[62] Lewis L. Gould, *Four Hats in the Ring: The 1912 Election and the Birth of Modern American Politics* (Lawrence: University Press of Kansas, 2008), 8.

[63] Ibid., 9.

always reserving the right to go public, to utilize his "bully pulpit" as the penultimate means of legislative persuasion. Such techniques were apparently foreign to Taft, and if summoning Congress for a special session dealing with tariff reform provided a suitable opportunity to demonstrate leadership early in his term, the result was unfortunate. Donald Anderson has well described Taft's failure to effectively press for a lower tariff. According to Anderson, Taft made no effort to dramatize his views, no sense of urgency resonated within his short and "innocuous message," issued no "ringing declaration of principle," no "cry for redemption of campaign promises to keep faith" with the voters.[64] Indeed, the tariff episode represents an excellent example of Taft's ideas concerning limited executive leadership, demonstrated during the first six months of his term.

On the other hand, it will not do to claim that Taft was ignorant when it came to dealing with Congress. As Roosevelt's secretary of war, as well as through his earlier work in the Philippines, he possessed firsthand familiarity with TR's successes and failures on Capitol Hill. The brevity of his message and his "hands off" approach to Congress as it took up tariff reduction reflected rather a particular philosophy of executive governance that characterized much of his administration. Looking back on his difficulties during his first year in office, Taft claimed in 1915 that "our President has no initiative in respect to legislation given him by law except that of mere recommendation, and no method of entering into the argument and discussion of the proposed legislation while pending in Congress, except that of a formal message or address."[65] The former president noted further that when a new president is elected, the result is usually a Congress with a majority of his own party.

What Taft called "the natural party cohesion and loyalty," together with "a certain power and prestige which the President has when he enters office," usually enable the new Chief Executive to exercise "much influence in the framing and passage of legislation to fulfill party promises," especially during his first congressional session.[66] Taft may have assumed that such cohesion and loyalty made any direct dealing with Congress unnecessary. He also had been assured by Cannon and Aldrich, or so he thought, that the leadership was committed to substantial tariff reduction.[67] Further, both men had strongly urged Taft to keep his distance from the House as it took up the tariff measure. Later, when the bill was before Conference committee, there would be ample opportunity for direct presidential involvement.[68]

While committed to tariff reduction, the new president lacked fundamental knowledge of the complexities involved in such legislation. Compared with

---

[64] D. Anderson, 104.
[65] *Collected Works of William Howard Taft*, edited by David Burton, vol. VI (Athens: Ohio University Press, 2003), 18.
[66] Ibid.
[67] It appears that either Taft had overestimated assurances of cooperation from Cannon and Aldrich, or that he was intentionally misled by the much more experienced politicians.
[68] Anderson, 100–101.

Cannon and Aldrich, he was ill-equipped to deal with such complexities. Lodge wrote to Roosevelt that Taft "knows little of the questions and the arguments and the conditions which beset the various industries."[69] With minimal involvement from the White House, less than a month after the special session had convened, the House on April 9, 1909, sent its version of the tariff revision to the Senate. That it contained some reductions cannot be doubted, and on the whole, Taft found it acceptable. Although it did not reduce rates to the extent he desired, the bill "contains much of what I approve."[70] But if the House proposed, the Senate disposed, and Taft watched in growing dismay as Aldrich's committee orchestrated an emasculation of the House bill.[71]

There was another reason why Taft had made minimal effort to shape the House tariff bill. Even as the Congressmen considered the measure, they were involved in the latest version of the effort to reduce Speaker Cannon's control over the legislative process. Before he became president, Taft had been both candid and critical in his assessment of Cannon's "reign." It was one thing to vent in private correspondence with Root and Roosevelt, both of whom had advised caution in dealing with Cannon. But it was quite another to support the insurgents as they sought to revise the House rules while the tariff bill was pending.[72] Taft not only reduced his rhetoric; he also backed away from the insurgents who urged him to support their cause. "I do not think it a good time to meddle," he wrote. "I may have to use the very machinery they are denouncing to pass a tariff bill. And a tariff bill must be passed."[73] The House insurgents would increase in number, and their harsh criticism of Taft kept pace. When they finally succeeded in 1910 in reforming the rules, thus muzzling Cannon, it would be accomplished while Taft was away from Washington – and without his support, as will be seen.

If Taft was willing to leave much of the tariff legislation to the House, the same cannot be said for those provisions relating to the Philippines. Here he exercised effective leadership, resulting in legislation that placed almost all Philippine imports on the free list. Donald Anderson suggests three reasons as to why Taft was so successful, and they indicate that when Taft really cared about a matter, he could be quite effective; even as he intentionally intruded in the deliberations of Congress.

In the first place, based on prior experiences, Taft was more familiar with conditions in the Philippines than were most members of Congress. Further, he was no stranger to tariff controversy concerning the Islands, and had urged tariff reforms there for almost ten years. Finally, he was willing to fight in Congress for what he sought, and the Philippine tariff measure, as he put it,

[69] Pringle, 427.

[70] Ibid., 428.

[71] It took the form of more than 800 amendments.

[72] Cannon had made it clear to Taft that if he were defeated, the president's legislative program would be in jeopardy. Anderson, 102.

[73] Ibid.

remained "pretty dear to my heart."[74] Taft persisted in his efforts, and in this instance he made effective use of the "politics" so familiar to his predecessor. On the other hand, Taft's success with the Philippine tariff provisions made it all the more unlikely that he would veto the tariff measure as a whole.[75] Thus the availability of a threatened veto as a weapon to force congressional acceptance of lower tariff rates in general was dissipated.[76] Yet Taft's failure to provide as decisive leadership here, as had been the case in the Philippine provisions, did not mean that he had surrendered to protectionists in his party – or so he thought.

The House tariff measure had been mildly reductionist, while the Senate version raised the rates on about 600 items.[77] Nevertheless, it appeared certain that additional revenue would have to be raised, and on April 1, 1909, Senator Joseph Bailey proposed an addition to the tariff legislation in the form of an income tax – 3 percent on incomes above $5,000. Although Taft, in company with most progressives, supported an income tax, he had difficulty with Bailey's amendment. Strange as it may sound, the proposal offended his sense of legal propriety. Well aware of the 1895 Supreme Court decision calling an income tax unconstitutional, Taft saw congressional moves toward reenacting such a bill as a tactic "which exposes the court to very severe criticism whatever it does." Far better to accept the holding "and submit to the people the question of a constitutional amendment."[78] Indeed, Taft urged Congress both to enact a corporate income tax and endorse an amendment providing for a personal income tax. Congress acquiesced in both measures.

Taft thus persuaded Congress not only to impose a new mode of "national supervision over corporations," but to frame a constitutional amendment that is correctly described as one of the three progressive constitutional amendments – the other two involving direct election of senators and the franchise for women. The income tax amendment moved quickly through the requisite number of states, and before Taft left the presidency, was declared ratified by his Secretary of State, Philander Knox. It might be noted that the progressives in Congress did not propose the income tax amendment. It came from Taft, and reflected his respect for proper legal procedure. But the credit

---

[74] Ibid, 108.

[75] Writing to Nellie, the president emphasized the "possibility of great improvement" in the pending tariff measure as "one of the reasons why I should be very reluctant to veto the bill." Ibid., 107.

[76] Taft wrote to his brother, "Of course, I could make a lot of cheap popularity for the time being by vetoing the bill, but it would leave us in a mess out of which I do not see how we could get, and the only person who would gain popularity would be your humble servant, and that at the expense of the party and the men who have thus far stood with me loyally." Ibid., 112.

[77] Pringle 432.

[78] Ibid, 433. Passage of a personal income-tax statute without an amendment would "be a great public injury, thus to involve the Supreme Court and injure its prestige, whatever its decision." Anderson, 109.

Taft deserved for proposing and endorsing this amendment was lost in the mounting public controversy over the tariff.

The Senate's "revision" of the House version differed so much from the original bill that it required a conference committee of both houses to produce a final measure. Cannon and Aldrich took care to pack the committee with confirmed protectionists. Privately, but not publicly, Taft objected. "I don't think," he wrote to his brother, "that Cannon played square,"[79] All during the hot and humid summer of 1909, the committee wrangled. Taft continued to emphasize in public that his party was committed to tariff reduction. In June, he stated that "if the Republican Party does not live up to what the people expect of it, it will be relegated to 'His Majesty's opposition.'"[80]

Although Taft took an uncompromising stand on only a few of the hundreds of provisions in the schedule, and although the conferees acceded only to a few of his preferences, the tariff bill that emerged from the conference committee was essentially the Senate version.[81] Nevertheless, Taft endorsed the Payne–Aldrich tariff. Though neither "a perfect bill" nor "a complete compliance with promises made," still it was "a sincere effort on the part of the Republican Party to make a downward revision."[82] Taft might well have reflected on what these words implied, but all during the summer he had been deprived of his most influential consultant, confidant, and erstwhile critic, his wife. In May, Nellie Taft had suffered some form of cerebral hemorrhage, which left her able to comprehend, but temporarily restricted in speech.[83] She began a long, slow period of convalescence, and her husband – weary of involved and complicated tariff negotiations – spent many hours at her side, patiently working with Nellie to help her regain her speech. By the early summer, Nellie relocated to Beverly, Massachusetts, where she slowly but steadily convalesced, while her sweating husband remained in the sweltering capital.

Meanwhile, it quickly became clear that the Payne–Aldrich tariff of 1909 satisfied very few interests, and split an already fractured GOP. Doctrinaire protectionists felt it had reduced some rates to an unacceptable level, while Western Republicans argued that Taft, by his consistent support for Cannon and Aldrich, had sold them out. But believing that as long as the ilk of Cannon and Aldrich controlled Congress, the beleaguered Chief Executive insisted that although a reduced tariff schedules was preferable, there were a number of other legislative items that needed congressional action, and he knew this would be impossible if he did not cooperate with the established leadership.[84]

---

[79] Pringle, 436

[80] Ibid., 438–439.

[81] Manners wrote that in dealing with Taft, "Aldrich was always ready to make a small concession for a large advantage." Manners, 99.

[82] Pringle, 445

[83] The incident is sympathetically described in Pringle, 442–444.

[84] During 1909, in spite of earlier hints of support, Taft kept his distance from the insurgents. Much less successful than TR in keeping the Republicans reasonably unified, the president privately voiced his resentment of insurgents such as Senator Albert Beveridge. The Indiana

He was persuaded that a presidential cross-country trip was now appropriate. During this journey, and with increasing enthusiasm, Taft explained and defended the controversial new tariff law, forgetting how measured his comments had been as he signed the bill.

The 13,000 mile tour, the first of a number that characterized Taft's presidency, lasted almost two months, from September to November 10, 1909, during which time the president delivered more than 250 speeches. These he dictated, often during train travel between stations. Never fond of speech writing, Taft avoided preparing his presentations for as long as he could, sometimes with very unfortunate results. In Minnesota, for example, without considering the political implications of his words, he stated that "I am bound to say that the Payne bill is the best bill the Republican party has ever passed."[85] To the Midwest Republican insurgents, such a comment seemed not only stupid, but also offensive, as was Taft's consistent endorsement along his route of "Old Guard" Republicans, matched only by his studied refusal to support any insurgents.

Even as Taft undertook this tour, the second major controversy of his still new administration was taking shape. Although the results of his efforts on tariff reduction were mixed at best, and did the chief executive little good politically, at least he had tried, unlike TR, who had left the tariff issue alone, except to employ it as bargaining chip with congressional leaders over issues of greater concern to him. Indeed, from his hunting camp in Kenya, Roosevelt endorsed the end result, writing to Lodge that "you have come as well as we could hope on the tariff question."[86] TR's views on the tariff, whatever they were, had not been a factor in the resulting legislation. The next difficulty for Taft, however, directly concerned the former president, and would play a major role in the ultimate rupture of their once relatively close relationship. It involved TR's intimate friend, Gifford Pinchot, nominally the Chief Forester in the Forest Service.

BALLINGER AND PINCHOT

Although not close, Taft and Pinchot were acquainted with each other. While Taft sympathized with TR's enthusiasm for conservation, he worried about what he considered the legality of the way his boss occasionally had attained his conservation goals, ignoring both the law and later the clear instructions of Congress, when, for example, toward the end of TR's tenure, Congress specifically banned further blocking of public lands from private development

erstwhile Republican was "a selfish pig," one who "tires me awfully," and is "so self-centered and so self absorbed." Pringle, 430–431.

[85] Ibid., 454 Perhaps, Taft recalled late in 1911, "the comparative would have been a better description than the superlative." Ibid., 456. But in 1909, the president considered this speech as "the best thing I have done." Ibid.

[86] Letters, vol. 7, September 10, 1909, 28.

in a number of Western states. TR, enthusiastically abetted by his Interior Secretary James Garfield, and Pinchot had taken a series of executive actions during the interval before the law went in to effect. They ensured that some 16 million acres, "enough acreage to create twenty one new national forests," was withdrawn from development, in defiance of congressional action.[87]

Further, Taft had observed the close camaraderie between TR, Garfield, and Pinchot. In particular, he noted the way Pinchot would go over the head of his superior, directly to TR. Such informality offended Taft's commitment to what might be called the process of order.[88] Nevertheless, he seems to have harbored no deep-seated animosity toward Pinchot as he began his presidency, and had the chief forester gone about his normal business, following appropriate channels of communication, the story might have had a different outcome. Indeed, even before Taft's inaugural, Pinchot had strongly endorsed the new president-elect. "[T]he election of Mr. Taft was the best thing that could have happened to the Forest Service, and the work of Conservation. Mr. Taft committed himself thoroughly to the Conservation policy ... and we all look forward to great progress in the next four years."[89]

The later Ballinger–Pinchot imbroglio had its origins not so much in Pinchot's conduct as in that of a minor official in the General Land Office named Louis Glavis, one who wholeheartedly shared Pinchot's enthusiastic commitment to conservation. Glavis had been investigating attempts by the Guggenheim interests to obtain certain mining rights in the Alaskan interior. Federal officials also found evidence of a scheme to sell these lands to a Morgan–Guggenheim syndicate. Shortly before he became Taft's secretary of the interior, Richard Ballinger had represented the syndicate before the same Land Office in which he had been a commissioner in 1907 and 1908. Glavis continued his painstaking investigation, even as Ballinger joined Taft's cabinet in 1909. Apparently impatient to see both the investigation ended and his former clients cleared, Secretary Ballinger "removed Glavis from the investigation."[90] At this point, Glavis turned in August to Pinchot, who, on paper at least, as the chief forester in the Department of Agriculture supposedly had nothing to do with the entire episode.

But in fact, anything involving open land and a clash between conservation and the potential for industrial development did indeed concern Pinchot, who, as has been noted, was no respecter of procedure. He had become so accustomed to direct presidential access and to bypassing his nominal superior, the secretary of agriculture, to say nothing of Ballinger, that he sent Glavis

---

[87] Manners, 107.

[88] Taft noted to Nellie that "the heads of the Departments are the persons through whom I must act, and unless the bureau chiefs are responsible to the heads[,] it makes government of an efficient character impossible." Anderson, 74. In other words, Pinchot would have to work with the secretary of the interior, something he ultimately refused to do.

[89] Gifford Pinchot Papers, LOC, Box 126, January 9, 1909.

[90] Melvin Urofsky, *Louis D. Brandeis: A Life* (New York: Pantheon Books, 2009), 254; Gould, 68–69.

directly to Taft, thereby again breaking the chain of command. He even wrote two letters of introduction for Glavis to present to Taft. On vacation in Beverly, Massachusetts, worried about the health of Nellie, and busily preparing for a cross-country tour on which he had to deliver numerous speeches defending the recently enacted Payne–Aldrich tariff, Taft had little interest in what appeared to be a feud between Ballinger and Glavis, In reality, it represented the culmination of long-simmering antagonism between Pinchot and Ballinger, now a member of Taft's cabinet.[91] As requested, on August 18, 1909, Taft met with Glavis, listened to his arguments, and invited the subjects of his complaint – especially Ballinger – to respond.

By mid-August, with the controversy apparently not yet between Pinchot and Ballinger, but rather between Ballinger and the young subordinate who had objected to Ballinger's actions, Pinchot began to consider the secretary's decisions as not only contrary to the goals of conservation, but also as destructive of TR's conservation policies. Yet Pinchot could still note that "I could not attack President Taft's policies because I know him to be in sympathy with the Roosevelt policies for which I stand."[92] So too, by August, Taft realized that in fact the conflict was between his secretary of the interior and one of TR's closest associates.

Ballinger traveled to Beverly in September, and spent two days in consultation with Taft. Also in attendance was Oscar Lawler, an assistant attorney general connected to Ballinger's department. Taft took several days to consider the extensive number of documents he had received from both Glavis and Ballinger. With his cross-country trip about to begin, Taft asked Lawler to prepare a memorandum on the matter "as if he were President."[93] Finally, Taft's atttorney general appeared, and with Taft, prepared both the response to Glavis and a lengthy report about the claims and counterclaims. Even as he left on his trip, Taft dispatched letters to both Ballinger and Pinchot, hoping – in vain – that they would put an end to the controversy.

The president vindicated Ballinger's actions and dismissed the charges leveled against him by Glavis as "only shreds of suspicions without any substantial evidence to sustain" them.[94] He sent a very different note to Pinchot. In a "My dear Gifford" letter, Taft observed that "you do not give to Mr. Ballinger the confidence and trust which I do." Moreover, "I think you have allowed your enthusiastic interest in the cause of conservation, and your impatience at legal obstacles and difficulties, to mislead you...." But Taft reassured his chief forester "that I am thoroughly in sympathy with all of these policies and propose to do everything that I can to maintain them, insisting only that the action for which I become responsible ... shall be within the law."[95]

[91] Ibid., 69–70.
[92] Pinchot Papers, August 12, 1909.
[93] Gould, 70. He also ordered Glavis dismissed from government service.
[94] Ibid., 71.
[95] Pinchot Papers, September 13, 1909.

Pinchot, however, had little respect and less liking for Taft's replacement of Garfield as his secretary of the interior, even though Ballinger had earned a fine reputation as a reform mayor of Seattle. As Taft tried to resolve the tariff imbroglio, acrimony between Pinchot and his superior became public. Now Taft wrote again, this time to "My dear Mr. Pinchot." I am bound to say, noted the president, "that you have not by anything you have suggested ... shaken in the slightest my confidence in Secretary Ballinger's good faith...." Further, "I do not ask any further correspondence on this subject, unless you insist on it." Finally, Taft urged Pinchot to use "your influence to prevent further conflict between the Departments by published criticisms in the newspapers."[96]

To his credit, Pinchot promptly advised his district administrator that "it is just now peculiarly necessary to guard with the utmost care against any yielding to requests for information which might be construed as furnishing material for an attack on any public officer."[97] Taft replied that he was "very glad to note what you are doing in this regard. I feel sure that with some self-restraint we can come out all right in this business...."[98] Thus Taft, who had sustained his secretary of the interior and ordered the dismissal of Glavis, still sought to retain Pinchot in his administration. But he sensed that keeping Ballinger and Pinchot under one roof seemed impossible, and if the chief forester "is looking for martyrdom ... it may be necessary to give it to him...."[99]

Apparently such is what Pinchot sought. He encouraged Glavis to go public with a lengthy account of his dispute with Ballinger, one that appeared in a muckraking journal, *Collier's*; authorized members of his department to leak anti-Ballinger material to the press; and finally, he deliberately defied a direct order from Taft that no one in his administration was to comment publicly on the matter. Pinchot wrote a letter to a Republican senator in which he supported Glavis and indicted Ballinger "as a foe of conservation."[100] He implied that the Roosevelt accomplishments in this field were being undone.[101] The letter was read on January 6, 1910, on the Senate floor – as Pinchot no doubt intended – and his dismissal promptly followed. By no means, however, did it end the controversy, which warrants further analysis.

Pinchot responded to his dismissal with a letter to Taft, which, perhaps after some reflection, he did not send. He refused to concede that the respect due the presidential office "is incompatible [with] the right to an honest opinion ... especially when I believe that the reason you were mistaken is because you did not have all the facts. If such an examination of the actions and motives of any public servant is wrong, then our system of Government is condemned

---

[96] Ibid., November 24, 1909.

[97] Ibid., November 26, 1909.

[98] Ibid., November 27, 1909.

[99] Gould, 71.

[100] Urofsky, 257.

[101] Much has been written about the Ballinger–Pinchot controversy, which has been thoroughly analyzed by James L. Pennick Jr., in *Progressive Politics and Conservation: The Ballinger–Pinchot Affair* (Chicago: University of Chicago Press, 1968).

in advance."[102] Some observers were quick to see the shadow of Roosevelt looming over the episode. One writer noted that "this upheaval means one of two things. Either the insurgents will gain control of the republican party and nominate a man of the Roosevelt stamp[,] or a new party will be formed. Taft is a 'dead one.' He's nailed himself into his own coffin."[103] The "bulk of the people," observed another correspondent, "believe that the President has been steadily getting into it, one foot after another, until he has made a mess of the whole business, and undoubtedly the chances of the Democrats have brightened day by day."[104]

An editorial, unsigned and undated, concluded that Taft "has been made to believe Pinchot has the backing of a pro-Roosevelt, anti-Taft element that must be crushed in its incipiency if the big President is to feel at all secure in his seat in the saddle. Unquestionably such reports have influenced Mr. Taft and have warped his judgment. Besides inciting him to desperate measures for the rebuke of Pinchot[,] they have excited him into taking most partisan action in defense of Ballinger."[105] The writer was prescient to an impressive extent, and seen in this light, the episode becomes even more significant.

In the first place, Pinchot who had retained his office when Taft began his term, remained an outspoken admirer of Taft's predecessor. Thus he saw any criticism from Taft as an attack on the former president. On the other hand, the new incumbent had made it clear that while he accepted the goal of conservation as laudable, it had to be attained through lawful process, specifically authorized by Congress.[106] If that process required undoing some of the actions taken by TR and Pinchot, so be it. Pinchot conceded candidly that results interested him much more than procedure. "Legal technicalities seldom help people," emphasized this non-lawyer. "Law is not absolute," in that "it needs to be construed," and "strict construction necessarily favors the great interests as against the people...."[107]

In the second place, Taft could only have been well aware how closely Roosevelt had identified himself with Pinchot, and such awareness made him determined to avoid if at all possible antagonizing his temperamental chief forester. On September 24, 1909, for example, Taft and Pinchot visited together. Taft emphasized that "he must have unity of action in his administration," to which Pinchot responded that "I fully understood that[,] and yet it might be necessary to fight." According to Pinchot's recollections, admittedly many years later, he added that "I would not make trouble if I could avoid it, but

---

[102] Pinchot Papers, January 9, 1910. Two days earlier, Taft had ordered Pinchot's dismissal as chief forester.

[103] Ibid., January 11, 1910.

[104] Ibid., January 8, 1910.

[105] Ibid., Box 435.

[106] Perhaps with Pinchot in mind, as this dispute simmered. In June, Taft wrote to California Congressman William Kent that "it is a very dangerous method of upholding reform to violate the law in so doing, even on the ground of high moral principle." Anderson, 73.

[107] Bromley, 195.

might be forced to, and he might be forced to fire me."[108] Yet Pinchot went out of his way to irritate the president. He talked to whomever would listen about conservation and the progressive policies of TR. William Manners observed that for Pinchot, dismissal "seemed a provocative prospect." Maybe, wrote Pinchot, "my head is coming off, but if it does I shall try to be like a gentleman in the Arabian Nights whose most important remarks were made after decapitation."[109] For his part, Taft was well aware that dismissing Pinchot would inevitably result in "an open rupture between Roosevelt and myself," something he sought to avoid. But if it occurred, Taft wanted to ensure that it would not happen "through any action of mine." As to the dissident chief forester, "I am going to give Pinchot as much rope as he wants, and I think you will find that he will hang himself."[110]

But Pinchot and Garfield wrote to TR that "not until now have we felt like interfering with your hunting of African beasts by telling you anything about the beasts in this country who have been coming again into the open since you left."[111] The letter discussed Taft's tariff travails and his difficulties with the insurgents. "We understand that Taft is now keenly anxious for a second term, wishing to be elected on his own record rather than upon yours, and that he views your return with great apprehension. "But Taft ought to realize that "the only way he can make a record" for his reelection "is to carry out in spirit the promises which made his election possible. If he does not do that he may well fear your return."[112]

Meanwhile, Ballinger had requested and been promised a congressional investigation into the accusations leveled against him, and pending its outcome, Taft ordered all executive departments to say nothing about the case.[113] As we noted, Pinchot's blatant defiance of this order took the form of a long, open letter to Iowa Senator Jonathan Dolliver, emphasizing the proper motives that had guided the federal employees who had brought their accusations against Ballinger, and implying that Taft had been misinformed about the true facts of the case. Elihu Root, senator from New York, advised Taft that "there is only one thing for you to do now, and that you must do at once."[114] He did, and on January 7, 1910, Taft notified Pinchot that "by your own conduct you have destroyed your usefulness as a helpful subordinate of the government," and

---

[108] Pinchot Papers, Box 438; from a transcription of notes, supposedly taken on September 24, 1909, and typed on September 18, 1935.

[109] Manners, 119.

[110] Ibid., 118. Writing to Charles Taft, Will implied here that Pinchot would have to go too far before he would dismiss him.

[111] Pinchot Papers, Box 437. There is no date on the carbon, but a handwritten note states "Fall 1909."

[112] Ibid.

[113] For a perceptive account of the case, see Melvin Urofsky, *Louis D. Brandeis: A Life* (New York: Pantheon Books), 254–276.

[114] Pringle, 508.

ordered him removed from office.[115] Garfield's reaction was predictable. "It is astonishing that we ever should have been so mistaken in Taft."[116]

Conducted in a highly partisan atmosphere, the congressional inquiry lasted until mid-May 1910. It furnished few additional insights into the mélange of claims and counterclaims that characterized the entire controversy. But it involved Louis Brandeis, the nationally known attorney from Boston who in 1916 would be appointed to the Supreme Court by Woodrow Wilson. Brandeis served as counsel to *Collier's*, which had published the Glavis article on Ballinger. Brandeis discovered that Taft had misdated his findings on the Glavis–Pinchot dispute, and while very careful to impute no improper motive to the president, Brandeis believed on a personal level that Taft had demeaned the nature of his office. More a result of ineptitude rather than intrigue, revelation of the misdating highly embarrassed Taft, who never forgot Brandeis and his role in the episode.[117] By a strict party line vote, the congressional inquiry found that although Ballinger had demonstrated no improper conduct, the same could not be said about Glavis and Pinchot.

Echoes of the Ballinger–Pinchot imbroglio reverberated for the remainder of Taft's tenure in the White House. While Ballinger continued in the cabinet for the remainder of 1910, ultimately Taft accepted his resignation, as will be seen. Further, when Taft's term drew to a close, it would become clear that he had proven to be a greater friend to conservation in his four years as president than had TR in his almost eight years.[118] In so doing, however, he followed the lead of Congress rather than imposing his executive authority.

Meanwhile, far from chastened, Pinchot seems to have welcomed his removal. He continued speaking out on conservation, and invoking the name and works of Theodore Roosevelt. In February, 1910, he and Garfield also wrote the former president another long letter that denounced Taft for surrounding himself "with Reactionaries," maintaining a "vicious political atmosphere," and demonstrating "a most surprising weakness and indecision."[119] Reading much like an indictment, this letter deserves some attention, as it reveals how Taft by 1910 had alienated rather than placated the progressive wing of his own party.

According to Pinchot and Garfield, and speaking of TR, Taft "changed his attitude markedly toward yourself [TR] and your friends immediately after his election," and "he replaced your cabinet by one composed principally of corporation lawyers out of sympathy with the Roosevelt policies." It is true, Taft "has repeatedly reaffirmed his intention to carry out these policies, but

[115] Ibid, 509.

[116] Garfield Diaries, January 16, 1910.

[117] Urofsky, 267–274. The incident did not, however, prevent either Brandeis or Taft from working well together as colleagues on the High Court when Taft arrived there in 1921. See the following.

[118] Ibid., 271. Taft withdrew more public lands, but with much less notoriety, than did TR.

[119] Letters., vol. 7, note 1, p. 50. Another TR correspondent was more articulate concerning Taft, who, according to Lucius Swift, was "a damn, pig-headed blunderer." Ibid.

we cannot accept the word in place of and in face of the deed." Thus there were two key aspects to the Pinchot–Garfield missive: the first specified the various mistakes and missteps committed by Taft, while the second emphasized his betrayal of what TR stood for. Taft "has created an attitude with reference to yourself and the policies for which you stand such that his partisans and defenders find their commonest ground for defence [sic] and attack in setting the two Administrations over [and] against each other...." Finally, Taft "has lost the confidence of the great mass of the people ... by aligning himself with the special interests which have always opposed you," and "if our fears should turn out to be justified, your disappointment we realize will be even keener than ours."[120]

Not content merely to write, Pinchot sailed for Europe, and visited with TR in Italy. Both Henry Cabot Lodge and Elihu Root advised TR not to see Pinchot, but to no avail. Yet Roosevelt wrote of Pinchot's missive to Dolliver that "of course in any event he ought not to have sent it."[121] Moreover, while Roosevelt in his written reply to Pinchot refused to fault Taft, he stated that "it is a very ungracious thing for an ex-President to criticize his successor."[122] Of course, what transpired in the conversations between Root, Pinchot, and TR cannot be known. But there is no doubt that less than one year into Taft's term, TR had commented to a number of his correspondents about the prospects of his return to the White House – and this even before he had returned to the United States.[123]

Indeed, Roosevelt may well have received an unbalanced account of affairs in Washington if only because letters from Garfield and Pinchot, not to mention Henry Cabot Lodge, more than filled the vacuum caused by the almost total lack of communication between Taft and TR. One May 26, 1910, after more than a year of silence, Taft finally wrote a poignant letter to TR, stating that in the year and three months since he had taken office, "I have had a hard time. I do not know that I have had harder luck than other Presidents, but I do know that thus far I have succeeded far less than have others." Instead of explaining his actions and rebutting his critics as the Ballinger–Pinchot dispute played out, Will acknowledged only that this incident "has given me a great deal of personal pain and suffering." But he refused to go further, to explain let alone justify his actions. "I am not going to say a word to you on

---

[120] Garfield Papers, LOC, February, 1910 [specific date not clear]. In his diary for January 7, 1910, Garfied had observed that Taft "goes deeper into trouble each week ... , yielding to those who are clearly opposed to the great policies upon and for which Taft was elected."

[121] Letters, March 4, 1910, 52. Here, TR echoed Lodge, who had commented that Pinchot "was all wrong" in writing to Dolliver.

[122] Letters, March 1, 910, 51.

[123] Pinchot described his visit to TR in glowing terms, but less then two weeks after his visit, while still in Europe, he wrote to TR that "it seemed to me much wiser not to meet you again on this side. One meeting commits you to nothing; two might be taken to mean more things about your attitude than ought to come out just yet." Pinchot Papers, Box 121, April 23, 1910.

that subject. You will have to look into that wholly by yourself without influence by the parties[,] if you would find the truth...."[124]

There are a number of possible explanations for Taft's otherwise inexplicable silence. Perhaps he felt uncomfortable confessing to the man who orchestrated his nomination what appeared to many observers to be an abject failure of presidential leadership. Perhaps he believed that the correctness of his action was self-evident, thus needing no justification. Perhaps he still sensed Roosevelt's lingering presidential persona, even though TR had been out of office for some fifteen months. Taft closed by inviting TR to spend a few days at the White House – an offer that TR first deferred, and then rejected.

Even before he received Taft's letter, however, Roosevelt had written an amazing mea culpa concerning his successor to Lodge.[125] He observed that leaders such as Taft, Aldrich, and Cannon who, it will be recalled, TR had strongly advised Taft to work with rather than antagonize, "have totally misestimated the character of the movement which we now have to face in American life." For "a year after Taft took office, for a year and a quarter after he had been elected, I would not let myself think ill of anything he did. I finally had to admit that he had gone wrong on certain points; and I then also had to admit to myself that deep down underneath I had all along known he was wrong, on points as to which I had tried to deceive myself, by loudly proclaiming to myself that he was right."[126]

A number of comments should be made here concerning this letter. As we saw in Chapter 5, Taft became president largely if not solely because of TR. Roosevelt had selected him, coached him, spoken for him, repeatedly endorsed him, emphasizing how much Taft would and did follow the Roosevelt precepts. If TR is to be believed in this 1910 missive, much of his past conduct represented hypocritical duplicity on his part. TR confessed to Lodge how stupid he had been, and how from the beginning he had known in his heart that Taft would not work out well. Maybe so.

If such was the case, one might inquire why TR had foisted Taft upon the country. More to the point, this letter demonstrates that in an age without the benefit of antibiotics, Roosevelt could find no way to bring down his own lingering presidential fervor, talk around it though he did. In fact, Roosevelt had loved his presidency, and did not willingly relinquish it – although thrilled with victory in 1904, he had stated that he would not serve another term. Already by 1910, however, he was denying that this firm promise was any such

---

[124] Pringle Papers, May 26, 1910.

[125] Somehow, Lodge, arrogant and distant in manner, would retain his lasting friendship with TR until Roosevelt's death in January 1919, no mean feat considering what the future held for both men, and something impossible for both Taft and Root. Thomas Reed, Republican from Maine, and a former Speaker of the House, aptly described Lodge as "thin soil highly cultivated." Robert L. Beisner, *Twelve against Empire: The Anti-Imperialists, 1898–1900* (New York: McGraw-Hill Book Co., 1968), 205.

[126] Letters, vol. 7, 89, May 5, 1910.

thing. In truth, his discontent with Taft had started well before Will had taken the oath of office. Unfortunately, worse was in store for the incumbent, when TR made a triumphant return to America in mid-June 1910. Within a year, Roosevelt's sentiments would become public knowledge, leaving Taft worried and fearful for the future.

6

Jockeying on the Court, 1910–1911

Even as the Ballinger–Pinchot controversy received nationwide attention, Taft encountered – if not created – further problems early in 1910 that only exacerbated the subtle but real tension between him and TR, even though the latter was not scheduled to return to the United States until June. It will be recalled that prior to his inauguration, Taft had been extremely critical of Joseph Cannon. But he also had refused to support the House insurgents as they sought to end Cannon's domination. All this had changed when Taft tried to get a reduced tariff through Congress. Now he backed away from earlier presidential aspirations to bring about Cannon's ouster as House Speaker. He maintained that supporting Cannon would be a small price to pay for the Speaker's supposedly promised endorsement of Taft's legislative program. Taft's original position of disinterest concerning the insurgents became a matter of basic hostility. Indeed, by January 1910, it became clear that he would offer neither encouragement nor aid to the House insurgents in any way, even going so far as to deny them access to traditional patronage sources. A spokesman for the insurgents, Republican congressman – George Norris soon to become Senator from Nebraska – confronted Taft on this issue.

He reminded Taft that in reality, the insurgents were not in opposed to Taft's legislative agenda. Far from it. Rather, we "stand for but one proposition – a change in the rules of the House that will take away from the Speaker some of his power which we believe to be unreasonable, detrimental to good government, and at times tyrannical." Taft might try to withhold patronage from the insurgents, but it would do little good. "We have gone into this movement on principle because we believe it is right, and will not be enticed away from it by the promise of political patronage or be driven therefrom [sic] by the threat of its withdrawal."[1] Thus Norris tried to persuade Taft to separate opposition to Cannon from the support for Taft's basic policies, but

[1] Pringle Papers, January 6, 1910.

with no success.[2] Missing Norris's point, Taft denied that he was withholding patronage from the insurgents.[3]

By March 1910, Norris had constructed a coalition of insurgent Republicans and sympathetic Democrats. With Taft away from Washington, and unable to interfere, Norris suddenly proposed a resolution calling for an elected Rules Committee, rather than one appointed by the Speaker. A lengthy debate ensued, one that Taft observed from a distance, and that ended in a victory for the insurgents.[4] In spite of Norris's letters, Taft failed to understand the significance of Cannon's defeat, worrying only about its implication for his legislative goals. "If this fight in the House," he wrote to Nellie, "results in the humiliation of Cannon and his removal from the Rules Committee, I don't know what may happen in respect to the organization of the House, and whether we can keep a Republican majority sufficiently loyal and disciplined to pass the legislation which we promised." On the other hand, he added that "it would please me very much if they could effect a compromise by which the old man [the contemporary title frequently applied to Cannon] would not be eliminated from the Rules Committee even though they enlarge [it]...."[5]

In several instances, Taft's response was typical of the man. In the first place, it reflected his desire not to antagonize anyone if at all possible, especially those in power. Further, it revealed his lawyerlike belief that the Republican platform represented a virtual contract that the Party was bound to fulfill. He did not support Norris's efforts, but he did not openly oppose the results they brought – an end to Cannon's autocracy, the introduction of election to standing committees rather than appointment by the Speaker, and an enlarged Rules Committee. Yet he remained hostile to the insurgents, and may well have had them in mind when shortly after the Cannon defeat, he wrote that "this reckless, violent, unmeasured abuse, without knowing on what ground, without definition or limit ought not to be encouraged and certainly will get no help from me."[6]

Thus, in barely one year as president, Taft had managed to split his party over the tariff, thereby antagonizing Midwestern republicans, offended others – including the conservation lobby – with his handling of the Ballinger–Pinchot controversy, and stand on the sidelines as disgruntled members of his own party effectively curtailed the Speaker's authority. Surely he meant well, but his actions – as well as his inaction – revealed a strange lack of insight into

---

[2] Ibid, January 10, 1910.

[3] Pringle, 612–613.

[4] Advising Taft to stay away, Attorney General Wickersham acknowledged receipt of word from the president about the Cannon showdown that he "never contemplated coming back" to deal with it. Nor did he, and the insurgents did not forget that they owed Taft nothing concerning their victory. Pringle Papers, March 19, 1901. George Wickersham had been a former law partner of Taft's brother, Henry Taft.

[5] Pringle Papers, March 17, 1910.

[6] Pringle, 558. Taft blamed the insurgents in general and Pinchot in particular for the troubles surrounding Richard Ballinger, whom he stubbornly defended long after the controversy had subsided.

the political aspects of the presidency. Indeed, Taft seems to have had virtually no interest in the political consequences of his own actions. From early on in his administration to its close, he displayed a sense of fatalism about them all the more intriguing because he was fully aware of the negative impact. Yet he would refuse to act in any way that might alleviate them.

There was one area, however, in which Taft felt much more secure. He might have lacked understanding concerning the intricacies of the tariff; he might have failed to explore the more subtle complexities of the Ballinger–Pinchot imbroglio; and he may well have demonstrated callous indifference to the significant issues lurking behind the insurgents' battle against Cannon, but in matters of the judiciary, he was truly at home. No president has ever been elected with as much judicial experience as that possessed by Taft. Further, it will be recalled that he and TR had exchanged candid opinions concerning the Court and its need for rejuvenation, even as Taft consistently declined TR's offers of appointment to it. During his first year alone, Taft appointed two new justices of the High Court, and before the end of his term he had selected a total of six Supreme Court jurists, more than any other single–term president in American history.[7] With one exception, he did not spend a lot of time on his selections. But, as will be discussed later, the exception turned out to be very significant for the president, although the ultimate results did not occur until a little more than eight years after Taft left the presidency. Although he did not know it, two of his choices would still be on the Court in 1921 when Taft became Chief Justice.

JUDGING JUSTICES

A lifelong Republican, Taft described himself in 1916 as a believer in "progressive conservatism." While this description may be less than accurate when applied to his later years as Chief Justice, it has some validity for his six selections to the High Court, as well as for his presidency as a whole. Party labels were not important to him, as seen in the fact that half of his choices were Democrats. Two came from the circuit courts of appeal. One was already on the High Court, and Taft was the first president to elevate a sitting justice to the center seat as Chief Justice.[8] One came from the highest judicial post in New Jersey. One was a distinguished scholar in the legal history of Georgia, and one was selected while serving a second term as a reform-minded governor

---

[7] Such are the vicissitudes of history. In four years, Jimmy Carter was not able to appoint a single justice to the High Court, whereas in eight years, Bill Clinton named two. FDR completed his first term without a single appointment to the Supreme Court, yet by mid-1943, on the eve of his nomination for a fourth term, he had remade the Court with his selection of nine justices.

[8] This has happened only three times in our Supreme Court history. Following Taft, President Roosevelt elevated Justice Harlan Stone in 1941 and President Reagan elevated Justice William Rehnquist in 1986.

of New York. All were able lawyers, well-established in their field, and at least two – Hughes and Pitney – can be placed within the progressive purview.

While sitting on the Court of Appeals for the 6th Circuit, Taft was associated with Horace Lurton, who joined that court in 1893. The two became close friends, and served together until Taft resigned in 1900 to take on the administration of the Philippines. Lurton took over as presiding judge, and was still there when Taft became president. Two months into his term, Will wrote to his old friend that "the condition of the Supreme Court is pitiable, and yet those old fools hold on with a tenacity that is most discouraging." The Chief Justice "is almost senile," Justice Harlan "does no work," Justice Brewer "is so deaf that he cannot hear and has got beyond the point of the commonest accuracy in writing his opinions." Indeed, "Brewer and Harlan sleep almost through all the arguments."[9] A few months later, Taft vented to Henry Cabot Lodge of "the outrage that the four men on the bench who are over seventy should continue there...."[10]

The first vacancy for Taft occurred when Rufus Peckham, author of the controversial bakers' hours case, *Lochner v. New York* (1905), passed away in October 1909.[11] Taft turned immediately to Lurton as a replacement, in spite of what Taft had written him about age. Now this issue became a personal one for the president, as his intended nominee was sixty-five years old. Taft's attorney general, George Wickersham, objected. He reminded the president that his support among lawyers was based on the assumption that he "would be conscientious in the selection of judges" to build up the High Court "to the place that it formerly occupied," and that by appointing Lurton, "so soon to be seventy ...," Taft would "sacrifice the needs of the country and the needs of the Court to a personal feeling."[12]

Honest to a fault, Taft realized that Wickersham was right, but he also knew that thus far in his young administration, very little had gone well. The tariff battle had been difficult, Nellie was recovering from a stroke, the Pinchot–Ballinger matter was at hand, promising no positive benefit to Taft however it was resolved. For the president, Lurton's nomination represented an opportunity to do something that brought him real pleasure, an act that took account

[9] Pringle, 529–530.

[10] Ibid. What goes around comes around, and ultimately Taft himself remained on the High Court past the age of seventy-two, until early 1930, and served with a number of colleagues who were well over seventy. These included, among others, Oliver Wendell Holmes, Louis Brandeis, and Willis Van Devanter.

[11] It might be noted that both Taft and Elihu Root believed that *Lochner* had been wrongly decided. See Root to Taft, October 14, 1910, and Taft to Root, October 15, 1910, Root Papers, LOC.

[12] Pringle 531. Previously, Taft had tried to persuade TR to appoint Lurton to the Court as a replacement for Henry Billings Brown, who resigned in 1906. Taft appears almost to have succeeded, until Henry Cabot Lodge pointed out to Roosevelt that Lurton had found against the government in virtually every case his Court heard concerning federal power under the Commerce clause. I have been unable to locate any reaction from TR concerning Lurton's appointment four years later.

of both professional expertise (Taft was well acquainted with Lurton's judicial abilities) and personal friendship. He heard but rejected Wickersham's views, and made the appointment on December 13, 1909. Apparently untroubled by considerations of age, the Senate confirmed him by voice vote one week later. Lurton was a former Confederate soldier, a Southern Democrat, and the oldest jurist ever appointed to the Supreme Court – and all this from a Republican president.

Lurton wrote a letter to Taft acknowledging his deep gratification that Taft had not "passed me over in favor of a younger man," even though he had been urged to do so. "This consideration," he added, "shall ever be present with me, and I shall endeavor ... to so discharge my duty on the Bench and to that Court by retiring before my activities become impaired."[13] Taft promptly replied to his former colleague that "it is just the simple truth to tell you that the chief pleasure of my administration, as I have contemplated it in the past, has been to commission you as a Justice of the Supreme Court...." While he cited Wickersham's concerns, Taft had become convinced "that I had the right to gratify my personal predilection by doing what I have done...."[14]

Not surprisingly, the shadow of TR hovered over most of Taft's appointments to the High Court. His second opportunity came with the death of Justice Brewer, who passed away on March 28, 1910. Less than one month later, Taft turned to Charles Evans Hughes, a moderate with some characteristics as a progressive. Currently serving his second term as governor of New York, Hughes was struggling with a recalcitrant legislature. Both Taft and TR were familiar with Hughes, who had flirted with a run for the presidential nomination later won by Taft. Roosevelt appears to have had a negative impression of Hughes, in spite of his public endorsement and praise for the governor. Early in 1908, he commented that many Republicans opposed to him had gravitated toward Hughes, who was "a fairly good man (but not a big man) and an inordinately conceited one" and "not knee-high to Taft in any way."[15] Taft and Roosevelt were well aware also of Hughes's incredible legal intellect, and perhaps there was a bit of jealousy in TR's assessment of his fellow New Yorker – mentioned in Chapter 4 – as "a psalm singing son of a bitch."[16]

On April 22, 1910, Taft wrote to Hughes that his appointment "will strengthen the bench as a lawyer and a jurist with a great power of application,"

[13] Horace Lurton Papers, LOC, December 22, 1909.
[14] Ibid., December 26, 1909. Lurton served only four and a half years on the High Court, until July 1914. While his brief tenure reflected the conservative consensus widely shared by both Southern Democrats and Eastern Republicans, Lurton found himself joining Justice O. W. Holmes in dissent in a number of cases. There seems to have been a streak of progressivism in Lurton's jurisprudence.
[15] Letters, vol. 7, January 27, 1908, 916.
[16] Edmund Morris, "Theodore Roosevelt, President," in 32 *American Heritage* (1981), 6. Hughes may have worn his rectitude more openly than many others. Morris adds that "but then Charles Evans Hughes tended to invite such descriptions."

and also that "you will strengthen the bench in the confidence of the people."[17] "I believe as strongly as possible," Taft added, "that you are likely to be nominated and elected President sometime in the future unless you go upon the bench." With impressive prescience, Taft added that "the chief justiceship is soon likely to be vacant[,] and I should never regard the practice of never promoting associate justices as one to be followed. Though, of course, this suggestion is only that by accepting the present position you do not bar yourself from the other, should it fall vacant in my term." Was this sentence an intimation that Hughes would have a lock on the selection, should the vacancy occur? Perhaps Taft may have so considered it, because he added an intriguing afterthought before he sent the letter to Hughes.

The governor should not misconstrue what Taft was saying. "I mean that if the office were now open, I should offer it to you[,] and it is probable that if it were to become vacant during my term, I should promote you to it." Sounding much like TR in discussing the same possibility with Taft several years before, the president added a caveat. "Of course, conditions change so that it would not be right for me to ... promise what I would do in the future. Nor, on the other hand, would I have you think that your declination now would prevent my offering you the higher post, should conditions remain as they are."[18]

Hughes did not deliberate for very long, and only two days later, accepted Taft's offer of appointment. He also noted that "your expressions regarding the Chief-Justiceship are understood and most warmly appreciated. You properly reserve entire freedom with respect to it, and I accept the offer you now make without wishing you to feel committed in the slightest degree. Should the vacancy occur during your term, I, in common with all our citizens, would desire you to act freely and without embarrassment in accordance with your best judgment at that time."[19] From Europe, Roosevelt endorsed Taft's choice. "Hughes' nomination is excellent, and I think he will make a fine judge."[20] Although promptly confirmed by the Senate, Hughes remained in Albany and did not take the oath of office until October 10, 1910. So matters stood until Chief Justice Fuller died, appropriately enough, on July 4, 1910.

Within three days, Taft received a letter from the editor in chief of *The Outlook*, Lyman Abbott. Theodore Roosevelt had already become a

---

[17] Pringle, 532.

[18] Ibid. Taft also made it clear that if he accepted, Hughes would not have to resign as governor of New York until the fall. Thus Hughes could complete most of his term, and remain in New York until the second week of October. Taft's equivocation is similar to that of TR's earlier writing on whether or not he would support Taft as his successor.

[19] Pringle Papers, April 24, 1910. Taft had to have been aware that in appointing Hughes to the High Court, he apparently removed a potential rival for his 1912 renomination.

[20] Letters, vol. 7, May 5, 1910, 80. "I only hope," added TR, "that he has awakened to the fact that ... there must be a very radical change in the attitude of our judges to public questions. I verily believe that the conduct of the bench, in failing to move with the times ... rather than turning to broad principles of justice and equity, is one of the chief elements in producing the present popular discontent. I do hope Hughes will realize this."

contributing editor to the magazine, but Abbott made it clear that he was "writing it on my own motion without the suggestion of any one else."[21] He urged the appointment of Hughes as Chief Justice "since it is impossible for you to appoint yourself to that office." While "there may be some Judge who would be better able than he to bring the new Bench – for it will be practically new when you are through with your appointments – into a cooperative mood, ... but certainly ... he would be admirably fitted to do that greatly needed work ...." Abbott expressed his hope that he was not "over-stepping the limits of friendship in saying this to you personally instead of saying it in the columns of *The Outlook*, which, it does not seem to me, is the proper place for saying it, if it is to be said at all."[22]

Abbott's letter probably echoed Taft's own perceptions of Hughes. Moreover, Taft was quite prepared to appoint a new Chief Justice from among the sitting members of the Court, a step that no previous President had ever taken.[23] Nevertheless, he pondered and procrastinated. Indeed, more than five months passed before the president finally made his choice, and it was not Charles Evans Hughes. Considering that Taft had made his first two selections rather promptly, why did he take so long?

There are several explanations for this lengthy delay. In the first place, while the Chief Justice might be *primus inter pares*, in a different sense the position was not an ordinary High Court appointment. Taft had a feel for the administrative responsibilities that in his judgment were part and parcel of the Chief Justiceship. The office required, as he put it, "constant attention to the business of the court and to the reform of its methods.[24] His undoubted legal brilliance to one side, did Hughes possess such skills?[25] As had also been the case with TR, Taft was eager to place Elihu Root on the High Court. He had genuine affection for the man, and total respect for his legal skills. But Taft well recalled that Root had firmly discouraged any offers of judicial appointments from TR, and he saw no prospect of any change of mind. More important than all these considerations was the fact that Root had turned sixty-five. Having surmounted the age barrier with Lurton – and against the advice of his own attorney general – Taft had no desire to revisit this controversy again.

---

[21] Pringle Papers, July 7, 1910. Abbott apparently did not use the official *Outlook* letterhead, and there is no mention of TR.

[22] Ibid.

[23] Later, Taft noted that "there has been a tradition that no Associate Justice ... should ever be promoted to the Chief Justiceship. This was on the ground that an Associate Justice should divest himself of all ambition when he takes his seat on the bench, in order that he may not be diverted by it from the devotion to his duties. I am not in sympathy with that tradition. I believe that the stimulus in question should remain, leaving every Associate Justice the hope that some day he may preside over the court." Taft to Karger, December 12, 1910, Taft–Karger Correspondence, Box 1, Folder 8, Cincinnati Museum Center.

[24] Pringle, 534

[25] Although Taft did not live to see it, the answer to this question was a resounding yes. Hughes succeeded Taft as Chief Justice in 1930.

Another factor that Taft considered was the preference of Theodore Roosevelt. The two met face to face on only two occasions during the summer and fall of 1910, and it appears that the subject of the vacancy on the High Court was not discussed. Others, besides Lyman Abbott, were more forthcoming. The publisher S. S. McClure, for example, suggested that "Root be made a member of the cabinet, Mr. Knox resigning, and that Mr. Roosevelt be appointed or elected senator in Mr. Knox's place. Then, ... with Root in the cabinet and Roosevelt in the Senate, Hughes on the Supreme bench, all working together, the administration would be greatly strengthened."[26]

Taft's knowledge of TR's preference concerning the Chief Justiceship may have come from three letters, all written by New York Republican Amasa Thornton. On November 25, 1910, he reported TR's comment that "the promotion of Mr. Justice [Edward D.] White would be the best possible thing." I know, Thorton added, "how it would help you and in that way our party ... I appeal to you to help strengthen our line ... Please for all our sakes promote Justice White."[27] Four days later. Thornton sent another letter reminding Taft that "I am sure I know how [Roosevelt] feels. An appointment that would please him I think is more desirable than one that he might consider as an affront...."[28] Three days later came yet a third letter. Roosevelt "is very much opposed to the promotion of Justice Hughes to the Chief Justiceship[,] and I believe if you do that it will add perplexity to a situation...."[29] Before writing to Taft, Thorton had addressed a separate note to Charles Norton. He told Taft's secretary, "I am sure Mr. Roosevelt would be greatly dissatisfied with the promotion of Mr. Hughes ... You seem to have political sense and I think you can see what an advantage it will be to everyone to have Mr. Roosevelt heartily back of the President."[30]

By the fall of 1910, Taft had determined to appoint the new Chief Justice from within the Court. Two other justices were interested besides Hughes. Justice Harlan sought the position as a sort of tribute to his length of service, now thirty-three years. But Taft brusquely rejected the idea out of hand. If Root would not be selected, primarily because of age, surely appointment of a justice already older than Root was not appropriate. Justice Edward White,

---

[26] Pringle Papers, October 11, 1910. McClure addressed these proposals to Taft's secretary, Charles Norton. There is apparently no evidence that the president ever saw McClure's fanciful missive.

[27] Ibid., November 25, 1910. As will be seen, Taft by this date, had reconciled himself to the severance of friendly relations with Roosevelt.

[28] Ibid., November 29, 1910.

[29] Ibid., December 2, 1910. Here, Thornton may have been referring to the widespread losses suffered by the Republicans in the recent election. For the first time since the Cleveland era, the Republicans had lost control of the House of Representatives, something Taft had glumly predicted.

[30] Ibid., December 1, 1910. Norton was actually less than effective as Taft's secretary, and ultimately gave way to Charles Hilles, who served Taft for the remainder of his term. Hilles also coordinated Taft's "Southern strategy," which aimed at ensuring that a majority of Southern Republican delegates would support his renomination, as indeed they did.

a former Democratic Senator from Louisiana, also desired the center seat. Adding to his doubts concerning Hughes, Taft received a delegation of Senators from the Judiciary Committee. They reminded the president that Hughes had never appeared before the Supreme Court and had held his seat for barely two months.[31] Earlier, the president asked his attorney general to take an informal and confidential poll of the Court. The result was a clear preference for White.[32] Still Taft hesitated, even as statements of Roosevelt's preference for White reached him. On Sunday, December 11, 1910, the White House called Hughes and asked that he visit with the president. But less than half an hour later, the appointment was cancelled, and the next morning Hughes – along with numerous newspaper readers – learned that Justice White's name would be submitted to the Senate.[33]

These events and considerations help to explain Taft's ultimate choice. But an additional factor may have been even more significant. As a young lawyer, he had made no secret of his devotion to courts and judging, and had rhapsodized, "I love judges, and I love courts. They are my ideas that typify on earth what we shall meet hereafter in heaven under a just God."[34] Even more attractive to him was the position of Chief Justice, and there is little doubt that had the opportunity presented itself, TR would have named Taft to the center seat. It may well be that as Taft pondered whom to appoint as Chief Justice Fuller's replacement, unspoken actuarial considerations constituted the deciding factor against Hughes.

Taft was mindful that he was fifty-three years old, Hughes a mere forty-eight, and White sixty-five. If appointed, Hughes might well outlive Taft (as indeed he did.) White, on the other hand, was seventeen years older than Hughes, and could reasonably be expected to last another ten or fifteen years. The conclusion was self-evident. Taft would have no chance of succeeding Hughes – all things being equal. But with White as Chief Justice, he might yet have an opportunity to take his place, given the vicissitudes of time. One suspects that when all the other considerations were added to this one, White became the logical choice, and Taft made it. Again, he was honest in his comment as he signed White's commission of office. "There is nothing I would have loved more than being Chief Justice of the United States. I cannot help seeing the irony in the fact that I who desired that office so much, should now be signing the commission of another man."[35]

In fact, on December 12, 1910, Taft sent three nominations to the High Court. While Taft considered the conundrum of the Chief Justiceship, another court vacancy occurred when Justice William Moody was forced to retire

[31] Merlo J. Pusey, *Charles Evans Hughes*, vol. 1 (New York: Macmillan Co., 1951), 278–281.
[32] Pringle, 534–535.
[33] Pusy, ibid.
[34] J. Anderson, *Taft*, 259.
[35] Pringle, 535. The fact that TR favored the selection might have been seen by Taft as an additional reason for selecting White.

because of a crippling illness. One of the youngest members of the Court, he had been TR's attorney general. Moody had filled the seat that Taft had earlier sought for his friend Horace Lurton. Taft's choice was Willis Van Devanter, a member of the 8th Circuit Court of Appeals, to which he had been appointed by Roosevelt in 1903. A conservative jurist, his strength was less in the drafting of written opinions than the intellectual process by which the legal issues were resolved by his brethren. Van Devanter remained on the Court for twenty-seven years, including Taft's entire tenure as Chief Justice.

With White nominated for the center seat, Taft had yet another appointment, his fifth, to the Court. To fill the seat vacated by White, Taft named another Southern Democrat, Joseph Rucker Lamar, a childhood friend, it might be noted, of Woodrow Wilson's. One would like to think that Taft was acquainted with Lamar's reputation as a truly distinguished legal figure, but the truth may be more prosaic. Taft first met Lamar on the golf links in Augusta, Georgia, where he vacationed in 1909 after his election but before his inauguration. In 1910, Taft recalled his visit with Lamar, and after receiving enthusiastic comments about his outstanding reputation as lawyer and legal scholar, appointed Lamar to the High Court.[36] In less than one year, Taft had selected four new members of the Court, plus White, who had moved to the Chief Justiceship.

Although Justice Harlan died in October 1911, Taft did not make what turned out to be his final appointment until 1912. By then, the split with Roosevelt had become a reality, and Taft knew that TR would seek the presidential nomination at the forthcoming Republican Convention. Further, TR now espoused what he called the "new nationalism," about which more will be said later.

Having appointed three justices from the South, Taft looked northward, and after Secretary of State Philander Knox declined an appointment, he apparently sought to undercut TR's obvious tilt toward the insurgents by selecting a candidate who as a committed Republican still reflected some key progressive values. Thus he might appeal to similarly minded Republican voters. He found such a man in Mahlon Pitney, and as had also been the case with Lamar, Taft first met his future choice on the golf course.

A New Jersey native, Pitney had graduated from Princeton in 1879 along with Woodrow Wilson. Alone among Taft's appointments, Pitney never attended law school, but read law under his father's tutelage. Admitted to the bar, he is unique among modern members of the High Court in that he never

---

[36] As he had hinted in his inaugural address, Taft was eager to gain Southern support for his Republican administration. He may well have thought that appointing two Southern jurists to the High Court would help. It didn't, and Taft conceded in the end, that while he was well regarded in the South, apparently his Southern friends "would do anything for him but vote Republican." Lewis Gould, *The William Howard Taft Presidency* (Lawrence: University Press of Kansas, 2009), 131. For further comment concerning Gould's important study, see the Bibliographical Note at the end of the present volume.

earned a law degree, although he later did receive an honorary degree. A two-term member of Congress, he had returned to New Jersey in 1898 and built both a very successful law practice and a favorable political record, hoping to become governor. Indeed, he was elected president of the New Jersey Senate, and appeared to be on track for the Republican gubernatorial nomination in 1901. Instead, he was appointed to the New Jersey Supreme Court, "bringing an end to his career in elective politics."[37]

Simple politics seems to have played a greater role in Pitney's appointment than in any of Taft's other choices. Essentially a conservative, Pitney still reflected some key progressive values. One was the role of the courts and judges. William G. Ross has well observed that "reverence for the law and acceptance of judicial review was particularly engrained in the progressive movement because so many progressives were lawyers."[38] It was one thing to criticize abuses of judicial review, but it was quite another to call for an end to the practice. And rare was the progressive who did so.[39]

Further, like the president, Pitney was strongly opposed to the secondary boycott. Moreover, he distinguished between organized labor and unorganized laborers, often finding against the former but in favor of the latter. As had been true of Taft as a judge, so Pitney feared both the widely perceived monopolistic tendencies of national unions, and the abuses perpetrated by insufficiently regulated business enterprise such as the railroads – a frequent target of Pitney's judicial disapproval. If there was ambivalence in this position, it was widely shared. In company with many progressives, he probably objected to what Jane Addams labeled "negative action" on the part of organized labor.[40] Hostile to organized labor, but sympathetic to non-union laborers, Pitney understood that while some reformers such as TR minimized class differences, labor organizers "wanted to draw the working class together and set it apart from other classes."[41] In short, Pitney's unfavorable attitude toward organized labor was fully compatible with mainstream progressive views. [42]

Taft remained proud of his six appointments. There seems no reason to doubt Henry Pringle's conclusion that Taft "did not allow the stain of political expediency to discolor any [high court] appointments that he made." On the other hand, his choices resulted from a variety of motives. But Taft was mistaken in his assumption that his judicial majority would contribute to

---

[37] Michal R. Belknap, "Mr. Justice Pitney and Progressivism," 16 *Seton Hall Law Review* 381–423, 389 (1986).

[38] William G. Ross, *A Muted Fury: Populists, Progressives, and Labor Unions Confront the Courts* (Princeton: Princeton University Press, 1994), 90–91. If judicial review were restricted, what could takes its place but expanded legislative authority, and progressives feared legislatures dominated by immigrant interests.

[39] Ibid.

[40] McGerr, *A Fierce Discontent*, 134. Addams believed that strikes, such as a national railroad strike, for example, inconvenienced the public. "A [labor] movement cannot be carried on by negating other acts; it must have a positive force." Ibid.

[41] Ibid., 135.

[42] Belknap, 381–384.

doctrinal longevity, no matter who might succeed him. Lurton and Lamar died during Woodrow Wilson's administration, and Justice Charles Evans Hughes resigned from the Court in 1916 to run against the incumbent president. By 1916, then, half of Taft's choices were no longer on the bench. Wilson would name only three justices to the Supreme Court, and one of them – James McReynolds – turned out to be even more conservative than Taft had envisioned. Wilson's other two selections, Louis Brandeis and John Hessin Clarke, were much more liberal.

It is thus a real stretch to claim that Taft's High Court appointments "benefited conservatism in the 1920's and 1930."[43] If the Supreme Court was conservative during this period, it was due to justices selected by presidents other than Taft. President Wilson – through his choice of McReynolds, and Harding through his appointments including Taft as Chief Justice – made the Court what it became to a much greater extent than Taft's original choices.[44]

DRIFTING APART

The period between June 1910, when Roosevelt made a triumphant return to the United States, and September 1911, at which time it was clear that he would surely accept and indeed even seek the 1912 Republican presidential nomination, marked a pivotal period in Taft's term. As I noted in the Preface, never before or since had an incumbent – who had not willingly sought election in the first place – confronted the presence of his predecessor, increasingly eager to reclaim his position. American political history could offer Taft little guidance, and virtually no historical comparisons into relationships such as the one between Taft and the man who had orchestrated his election in the first place. Until TR tried to regain the White House, no former American president had ever made such a determined effort to keep his chosen successor from reelection.[45]

Both men were ambivalent concerning their future political plans. They said the right things to each other during the two occasions on which they met in 1910, but the tension between them was obvious and palpable, and conversation between them appears to have shied away from matters of substance. Both had caused the tension – their complete lack of communication from March 1909 through May 1910 was a mutual action. As Lewis Gould well notes, there is only one reason why Taft could not have kept TR in his confidence, just as there is only one reason why TR did not communicate with

---

[43] Gould. 214

[44] On the other hand, it is clear that as Chief Justice, Taft may have influenced some of the selections made to the High Court by Presidents Harding and Coolidge.

[45] Thus far in our history, only two former presidents have returned to Washington to serve in elected office – John Quincy Adams later distinguished himself as a member of Congress, and Andrew Johnson, surviving his impeachment by the narrowest of margins, came back to Washington as a senator from Tennessee in 1875, although he died barely four months into his term.

Taft from the wilds of Africa.[46] Indeed, TR maintained an extensive correspondence while he was abroad. The reason is simply that neither man wished to write to the other.

Each expected the other to make the first move toward reestablishment of their prior relationship. But neither took that vital step, and in the resulting vacuum, tensions, latent hostility, and bitterness (often in the guise of self-interest) festered. While TR in private made no secret of his dissatisfaction with Taft's performance, still he informed Henry Cabot Lodge that "I very earnestly hope that Taft will retrieve himself yet...." But if that proved impossible, "I most emphatically desire that I shall not be put in the position of having to run for the Presidency.... Therefore my present feeling is that Taft should be the next nominee...." As he had so often written concerning Taft in the past, however, TR immediately qualified what he had just stated. "Of course things may entirely change, and my attitude change with them."[47]

Rebuffed in his repeated invitations to TR to revisit the White House, Taft maintained a civil tone in his correspondence with Roosevelt during the second half of 1910. Perhaps in some way he sensed what lay ahead for both men, although if he was prescient, it was for the wrong reasons! Late in November, he informed TR of the impressive progress that had been made on the Panama Canal, a project on which Taft had labored in close association with his president. Now the canal was reaching completion, and in all probability a ship would be able to navigate through the passage by "July 1, 1913 – a date [on] which both you and I will be private citizens[,] and we can then visit the Canal together and see the completion of that which you initiated and carried on to a full prospect of success, and in which, under you, I have taken an interested part."[48]

Others worried about TR and Will. Mabel Boardman, both a close friend of the Taft family's, and a devoted confidant of the president, wrote to the editors of *The Outlook*. She raised some questions concerning the even-handedness with which the periodical treated Taft. She received a lengthy reply from EFB on behalf of the editors. He reminded Boardman that *The Outlook* had not hesitated to criticize TR "as vigorously as we have criticized Mr. Taft whenever we have disagreed [with] him." Further, EFB predicted that Boardman would find Roosevelt "as independent in criticism as ever, but also as loyal, whenever he can be, to Mr. Taft, personally and politically." Finally, he stated to Ms. Boardman that "the Taft administration has not

---

[46] Gould, 103.

[47] Letters, vol. 7, April 11, 1910, 73.

[48] Pringle Papers, November 30, 1910. This was not the first time, nor probably the last time, that Taft had expressed a longing for what once had been. In June, after a luncheon with TR, Taft had remarked to him that the visit "has taken me back to some of those dear old afternoons when I was Will and you were Mr. President." Pringle, 555. During the visit, Taft inadvertently put his finger on an underlying cause of what lay ahead. He told TR that "I can never think of you save as Mr. President." Ibid, 554. One suspects that, increasingly, as Taft's term ran its course, TR saw no reason to discourage Will from such thinking.

been without its failings," and pointed to the president's "repeated absences from Washington...."[49]

Like many others, Taft awaited some word as to what position TR would take concerning his administration. The silence grew deafening, but TR said nothing in public about the Taft presidency. Taft's brother observed that "the issuance of sibylline leaves from Oyster Bay" were far from clear, "but I still have confidence ... that neither inclination nor interest will lead the sage of Sagamore Hill to widen the breach caused in large part by his wild-eyed friends...."[50]

In August, 1910, Mabel Boardman asked of a Republican congressman from Kansas, "Is it not strange that since [Roosevelt's] return[,] so far not one single word of commendation of President Taft has he uttered in public." Did TR "desire to see in his successor a man who was merely a puppet of his own ... ?" Boardman was willing to give Roosevelt the benefit of the doubt, "but I do believe that his love of power, his triumphant procession through Europe, his popularity at home have made it difficult to for him to brook [sic] any rival near the throne."[51]

After the Republican loss of the House, Boardman received a lengthy hand-written reply from Victor Murdock, who although a Republican in name was among the Kansas politicians who were gravitating toward Roosevelt.[52] His letter is of special interest because Murdock was well aware of Boardman's friendship with Taft. Indeed, Murdock wrote that "for a long time I have had the impression that you, pre-eminently among those notable in Washington, have had more than ordinary voice and direction in some of the larger affairs of the nation...." He was eager to tell Ms. Boardman "the other side." In describing how he perceived the state of national politics in 1910, he may well have assumed that Boardman would make his views known to Taft.

Murdock assured Boardman that "there is no attack from property in the design of anyone.... There is no assault upon the purity of constitutional forms of government anywhere." But, he added, "everywhere there is a restive impeachment of maldistribution of awards, and of distortion of constitutional forms.... Every executive act which invades legislative function is being duly noted; every perversion of legislative function through the brutalities of excessive personal power, as exhibited by Cannon ... or otherwise; every inadequacy for justice exhibited by the higher courts, serene under the callous [sic]

---

[49] Mabel Boardman Papers, LOC, July 1, 1910. Thus far, I have been unable to identify EFB.

[50] Ibid., Henry Taft to Boardman, July 10, 1910. Even the president worried about what TR was planning. "The sage at Oyster Bay is keeping the people in doubt as to just what he proposes to do." Pringle, 552.

[51] Boardman Papers, August 24, 1910. If, she added, TR really believed in the "square deal," "he can show to President Taft the same fine loyalty that Mr. Taft has shown towards him." Taft, "with all his friendship for Col. Roosevelt is not and never will be any man's tool."

[52] Murdock sat in Congress from 1903 to 1915, failed to gain a nomination as a candidate for the U.S. Senate, and served as chairman of the National Committee of the Progressive Party in 1915–1916.

of word and evading technicality, each is being set down in the indictment
the public is drawing slowly through the years. And the politicians generally
do not seem to know it ... the country itself is still in a measure unaware of
how widespread the impulse is."[53] Murdock further informed Boardman that
the existing interests, "political or otherwise, which believe that these public
aspirations can be cajoled, diverted or worn out by inducing the electorate
to indulge in a mechanical see-saw from one political party to the other, are
fatally misreading the signs of the time. The change in the people is not secondary, it is primary. It is not transitory, it is epochal." Finally, Murdock cau-
tioned Boardman that the "public men or the party which reads it differently,
does not read it right. And public men and parties will thrive only in the measure in which they vitalize the national impulse by giving it expression." He
concluded by referring again to Boardman's friendship with Taft, and hoped
that "given a fine sense of his great mentality, and the splendid integrity which
ennobles it, perhaps events from this time forward [would] work for him...."
The correspondence between Boardman and Murdock should be understood
in the light of Roosevelt's actions after his return from Europe in June, 1910.

It soon became very clear that while TR declined to visit Taft in the White
House, during the summer and early fall of 1910 he welcomed a steady stream
of insurgents, and former officials in his administration, notably Pinchot and
James Garfield, to Oyster Bay. In July, TR sent a letter to Garfield that indicates that he still remained ambivalent about Taft. "I do hope," he wrote,
"that you will make every effort to get Regulars and Insurgents together on
a platform which shall not denounce the [Taft] administration, and which
yet shall be progressive." Pinchot ought to reconcile himself to the "probability that two years hence he will find himself, however reluctantly, obliged to
support Taft's renomination." With intriguing prescience, TR insisted that
"I most earnestly wish to avoid a split ... , and that to assume too extreme a
position, which will turn the Insurgents into merely an extreme minor faction,
would be of great damage not only to them, but to the Republican Party, without compensating benefits."[54]

But TR did more than this. During the campaign for the 1910 congressional elections, he actively supported and spoke for a number of Republican
candidates, especially in the Midwest, who were opposed to Taft, a point not
lost on Elihu Root. He wrote to Roosevelt that "you are speaking in a lot of
states where your speeches help the men who have attacked Taft." Such hostile critics as "Beveridge in Indiana, Cummins in Iowa, Bristow in Kansas,
Lafollette in Wisconsin, and Clapp in Minnesota are all drawing strength
from you." Yet Ohio remained "the most important state where you can help
Taft's friends, and....a speech by you in Cleveland ... would be a service
to the Republican party as a whole." Your "help in Ohio," added Root in a

---

[53] Ibid., December 2, 1910.
[54] Garfield Papers, July 16, 1910. This, of course, is exactly what happened, due less to Garfield
than to TR himself.

tone that few others used in correspondence with TR, "would be generally regarded as a fair and manly thing. I think it would be a good thing for you and ... for the party."[55]

Roosevelt replied a few days later, and emphasized to Root that he had been speaking for both those "who have supported Taft" as well as those who "on some point left him – just as I think I would have done in their places." But "I am bitterly disappointed with Taft, and consider much of his course absolutely inexplicable...."[56] More than that, he added, "I have never had a more unpleasant summer. The sordid baseness of most of the so-called Regulars, who now regard themselves as especially the Taft men, and the wild irresponsible folly of the ultra-Insurgents, make a situation which is very unpleasant.... [T]he men who are both sane and progressive, the men who make up the strength of the party, have been left so at sea during these months in which Taft has put himself ... in the hands of Aldrich, Cannon, Ballinger and Wickersham, that they have themselves tended to become either sordid on the one hand, or wild on the other."[57] But TR insisted that he saw no alternative to his current course, which was "striving to re-unite the party and to help the Republicans retain control of Congress ... while at the same time endeavoring to see that this control ... was in the hands of sensible and honorable men who were progressives[,] and were not of a bourbon reactionary type."[58] He might support Taft in 1912, "and if I do support him it will be under no illusion...."

During his cross-country tour, TR avoided attacking Taft, but he criticized national conditions in 1910. He did not mince words concerning the courts, the federal institution dearest to the president. In employing the phrase "the new nationalism," a sort of political platform aimed at Republicans in the fall of 1910 and beyond, TR stated that "it demands of the judiciary that it shall be interested primarily in human welfare rather than in property.... I believe in shaping the ends of government to protect property as well as human welfare. Normally ... the ends are the same, but whenever the alternative must be faced I am for men and not for property...."[59]

Roosevelt singled out the Lochner case (1905) for particular criticism. He described the case as typical of the judicial "type of mind (it may be perfectly honest, but is absolutely fossilized) which declines to allow us to work for the betterment of conditions among the wage earners on the ground that we must not interfere with the liberty of a girl to work under conditions which jeopardize life and limb, or the liberty of a man to work under conditions which ruin

[55] Root Papers, LOC, October 19, 1910.
[56] Ibid., October 21, 1910.
[57] Ibid.
[58] Ibid.
[59] "The true friend of property, the true conservative, is he who insists that property shall be the servant and not the master of the commonwealth." Robert S. La Forte, "Theodore Roosevelt's Osawatomie Speech," 32 *Kansas Historical Quarterly*, 187–200 (1966). In fact, most of the speech was drafted for Roosevelt by Gifford Pinchot.

his health after a limited number of years.... Such decisions, arbitrarily and irresponsibly limiting the power of the people, are of course fundamentally hostile to every species of real popular government."[60]

Taft read the accounts of Roosevelt's speeches less with interest than with concern. So did Elihu Root, who wrote to Taft concerning TR's criticism of the courts. "I shall be curious to know if he really meant that he would, if he could, deprive the Courts of the power to pass upon the constitutionality of laws. Of course I have always considered that the most valuable contribution of America to political science." Well familiar with TR's habits of rhetorical excess, Root added that "I don't suppose he really meant it, but was rather using an argumentative expression."[61] Taft wasn't so sure, although he agreed with Roosevelt in his specific criticism of *Lochner.*

The real problem in Roosevelt's remarks, Taft noted, was not his criticism of two High Court decisions, in which, as a matter of fact, both Taft and Root concurred. Rather, "it is that there is throughout the West, and especially in the insurgent ranks, to which Theodore was appealing, a bitterness of feeling against the Federal Courts that this attitude of his was calculated to stir up, and the regret which he certainly expressed that courts had the power to set aside statutes was an attack upon our system at the very point where I think it is the strongest." Indeed, "my fear is that in this regard he simply spoke the truth of his own views."[62] Moreover, TR's speeches "are fuller of the ego now than they ever were, and he allows himself to fall into a style that makes one think he considers himself still the President...." Further, "in most of these speeches he has utterly ignored me."[63]

It cannot be said that by August of 1910, TR had determined to seek the nomination in 1912. But it is clear that others were committed to his cause, and were pushing him in this direction. Pinchot, for example, wrote to TR on August 18th that "you can afford to be beaten after making a fight for Progressive issues, but you cannot afford not to make the fight. To do so ... would be to disappoint the faith of the whole people in you....I know ... that you are not going to disappoint them, and ... I sympathize more than I can easily say in the difficulties which you face just now. At the same time, I see only one way out."[64]

The fall campaign came and went. Taft prepared to deal with a lower house controlled by the Democrats.[65] By now, he realized that TR would try to wrest re-nomination from him. Yet the president had no intention of walking

---

[60] Theodore Roosevelt, "The Nation and the States," delivered before the Colorado Legislature, August 29, 1910, 41.

[61] Root Papers, LOC, October 14, 1910.

[62] Ibid., October 15, 1910.

[63] Pringle, 573.

[64] Pinchot Papers, Box 128, August 18, 1910.

[65] Garfield described the elections as "a sweeping [D]emocratic victory for the country.... This seems a stinging rebuke to Taft and the Standpatters. I am not in the least surprised." Garfield Diaries, November 8, 1910.

away from the White House voluntarily. To be sure, he found the presidential experience far from enjoyable, the White House too confining, and the functions of his office sometimes overwhelmed him. But Roosevelt's speeches in the Midwest had contained "wild ideas," and his comments in the New Nationalism address "frightened every lawyer in the United States." Indeed, "the thing of all others that I am not going to do is to step out of the way of Mr. Roosevelt...."[66]

Of course, Roosevelt's main contentions were anything but radical.[67] They were well located in past American legal history, as Leonard Levy and William Novack, among others, have demonstrated.[68] The fact that by the early twentieth century, changing assumptions concerning the police power had apparently lessened its contemporary significance in no way diminishes its primary importance.[69] Roosevelt's speeches were delivered during the ascendancy of a conservative interpretation of judicial power. To a former judge such as Taft, who had given up life tenure for government service, these assumptions seemed much more radical than they were in fact. When one considers that the Republicans had lost control of the House, and that the split between the insurgents and the so-called regulars had widened, Taft's conviction that TR had moved to the left is not unreasonable.

In the 1910 elections, Taft had predicted a new Democratic majority of approximately twenty-five seats.[70] In fact, the Democrats emerged with a fifty-vote margin. The president and his predecessor had cooperated in seeking Republican gains in New York, but to no avail. TR's choice for the governorship went down to defeat. A Democratic gubernatorial candidate even defeated a Republican in Taft's home state of Ohio. All in all, as Taft wrote to an old friend, "I shall not become a misanthrope or a pessimist, if, as is probable, my services as President shall be limited to one term." But writing in early November, Taft still found it difficult to accept the obvious, that TR was now his potential opponent. He predicted that Roosevelt's "coolness will wear away[,] and our old relations will be restored, I hope, in the course of a year. When a minister vacates his pulpit and recommends a successor, and then takes his place in a pew, his attitude towards the sermons of his successor

[66] Pringle, 572.

[67] In this context, his comments to Pinchot are of interest. "Remember that the extreme men on the Insurgent side are really working for defeat just as much as are the Cannon-Aldrich leaders. To go on behalf of the people much further than the people want is considerably worse than useless." Letters, vol. 7, August 17, 1910, 113.

[68] See Leonard W. Levy, *The Law of the Commonwealth and Chief Justice Shaw* (New York: Harper & Row, 1957), and William J. Novack, *The People's Welfare* (Chapel Hill: The University of North Carolina Press, 1996). To understand the significance of Roosevelt's contentions, the second half of Novak's book is particularly helpful.

[69] The best explanation of how this transformation occurred is found in William Wiecek's study of *The Lost World of Classical Legal Thought: Law and Ideology in America, 1886–1937* (New York: Oxford University Press, 1998).

[70] He wrote to Mabel Boardman that "everything is chaotic politically. I shall not be surprised by our general defeat." Boardman Papers, November 5, 1910.

is likely to be very critical for a while."[71] Perhaps Taft was more candid to Mabel Boardman, to whom he wrote on Christmas Day. Thanking her for a Christmas gift, he added that "I shall think of one whose confidences and sympathy have warmed me to courage and hope in the face of the cold blast of popular disfavor."[72]

Taft's observation about TR may well have reflected a belief on his part that it was the former president who had caused the growing tension between them, and not Will Taft. There is some validity to this view. For it was TR who had declined every invitation from Taft to visit the White House. It was TR who had continually welcomed a steady stream of Republican malcontents to Oyster Bay, all apparently united by the desire that he reenter national politics and Taft remove himself. And it was TR who had kept silent for so long about his successor that his disenchantment with Taft's performance thus far could be taken for granted. Yet, had Taft been given to more retrospection than he usually demonstrated, he might have seen that he had contributed in large measure to the expanding fractures in his relationship with Roosevelt, a process that had been going on since the start of his second term. Only on the surface, was all well between them.

In the first place, Taft had rebuffed TR several times on a nomination to the Supreme Court, and one suspects that he had not been very candid with TR as to why. The subtle but lasting antagonism between Nellie Taft and Edith Roosevelt cannot have helped matters. In the second place, the rapport between the two men had reached its height after 1904, when Taft moved with marked success into his role as a capable, loyal, competent, and always subordinate to Roosevelt. This is how TR came to view Taft as his second term wound down. Further, either because TR did not comprehend it, or else Taft chose not to so indicate, the two men in fact had very different views on the presidency as an institution. Far more experienced in administration than Roosevelt, Taft believed in organized channels of executive management, as well as clearly defined spheres of authority between Congress and the White House.

Thus, for example, Taft had observed with disapproval the informality with which Pinchot, TR, and James Garfield Jr. had cut corners – albeit with some success – as they fashioned conservation policies often in spite of rather than along with Congress. Taft found Pinchot's facility for ignoring his nominal superior, the secretary of agriculture, and going directly to TR, who welcomed the hero-worshiping camaraderie of Garfield and Pinchot, at odds with the way executive departments were expected to operate. Indeed, the primary reason Taft declined to retain Garfield as secretary of the interior concerned his doubts about Garfield's ability to exercise independent control over the Interior Department. But shortly after his election, Taft had indicated to TR that he intended to retain the entire cabinet. Instead, he replaced all but two

[71] Taft to Mrs. Aaron Perry, Pringle Papers, November 3, 1910.
[72] Boardman Papers, Christmas, 1910.

members, and had to be prompted by TR to inform the various secretaries of his decision. When TR offered to relay word of Taft's intentions so that his cabinet members could make alternative plans, Taft replied with a curt letter to the President unlike any of his prior communications to TR. This episode, early in 1909, may be described as the initial symptom of what ultimately became an irrevocable rupture.

TR, of course, found himself in an increasingly awkward dilemma as his second term drew to a close. He threw himself into Taft's campaign to such an extent that to some, the word "TAFT" actually meant "Take Advice From Theodore."[73] Further, he hated to leave the presidency, and may well have regretted making the statement late in 1904 that he would not seek elective office again. Such regret increased as TR realized that his chosen heir had a vastly different conception of the presidency. In 1908, Taft had kept silent as TR exercised his authority, and warred with Congress while doing so. TR may have assumed that Taft's silence implied consent, or at least tacit approval. But it did not. To his credit, Taft indicated early in his presidential tenure that he could not and indeed would not practice what had been the "presidential" norm for the last seven years. He had made the same point during the campaign.

Thus, as Taft entered the second half of his term in 1911, his relationship with TR was characterized by a virtual wall of silence between them. TR seems to have believed that Taft should have treated him as had been the case during his own second term. Taft seems to have believed that as president, he deserved the same type of support and loyalty he had given TR. Thus far, each commented to their circle of correspondents, rather than to each other. But in 1911–1912, this would soon change, and for the worse, with their rhetoric characterized by anger and vituperation.

[73] See htpp://elections.harpweek.com – commentary following the cartoon of October 10, 1908.

7

At the Brink, 1911

ECHOES OF BALLINGER

Although the official investigation of the Ballinger–Pinchot imbroglio had concluded by the spring of 1910, echoes of the incident reverberated through 1911. While the Republican majority on the investigating committee had forcefully exonerated Ballinger, the Democratic minority had with equal emphasis denounced his performance as secretary of the interior. There could be little doubt, however, that Ballinger's effectiveness as a cabinet member had been compromised. If not guilty of dishonesty, his lack of judgment in the Cunningham claims matter was obvious, except to the President. During the remainder of 1910, intimates close to Taft tried to have the beleaguered Ballinger eased out of office, but the president would not hear of it, and consistently defended Ballinger's honesty and integrity.

If anyone was at fault, according to Taft, it was the insurgents and/or their associates who rallied around Pinchot as the symbol of their cause. They had conspired against Ballinger, and as Taft wrote in May 1910, "If I were to turn Ballinger out, in view of his innocence and ... the conspiracy against him, I should be a white livered skunk. I don't care how it affects my administration.... He has been made the object of a despicable conspiracy, in which unscrupulous methods have been used that ought to bring shame to the face of everyone connected with it."[1]

But by January 1911, Taft realized that he could no longer afford to support Ballinger, who, to his credit, had offered to resign several times, only to have each offer soundly rejected by the president. Now Taft faced a House of Representatives controlled by the Democrats, looking forward with some eagerness to 1912. The Ballinger–Pinchot affair still lingered in the press, and Pinchot – as we have seen – had been far from quiescent since his dismissal. Taft finally had to confront the looming presence of TR, even though by the spring of 1911, and for a brief interval thereafter, a reasonably amicable

[1] Pringle, 473–474.

rapport had evolved between the two men since the debacle of the fall elections. For Taft, the Republican defeat had revealed growing dissatisfaction
with his presidency, while for TR, the defeat of the New York ticket for which
he campaigned with typical vigor indicated that, at least in parts of the East,
his great popularity was open to serious question.

Taft's old friend Otto Bannard, one of the very few acquaintances who
called the President "Bill," and who had known him since his college years in
New Haven, told him what needed to be done with the interior secretary, and
why. Obviously feeling no need to be tactful, Bannard was blunt. "Ballinger
should be excused March 4th. No matter how cruel the unproved charges,
business is business and religion is religion, and second mortgages are trouble-
some. You have stood by him to the limit, and now he should show his appreciation of your kindness. It is not fair for any man to insist upon encumbering
his party when he ceases to be useful. Politics is hell just like war, and there
is not much space to let for sentiment beyond a few weeks."[2] One cannot say
how much Bannard's missive influenced Taft. However, a few weeks later,
Ballinger offered to resign yet again, and this time Taft accepted, with yet
another vigorous denunciation of the treatment accorded his secretary of the
interior. His letter of acceptance is remarkable if only because of the deep
seated anger that the controversy – now well over a year past – still aroused
in the president.

Ballinger had been "the object of one of the most unscrupulous conspiracies for the defamation of character that history can show." Its perpetrators
"showered you with suspicion and by the most pettifogging methods exploited
to the public matters which had no relevancy to an issue of either corruption
or efficiency in office, but which ... served to blacken your character and to
obscure the proper issue of your honesty and effectiveness as a public servant.[3]
The result has been a cruel tragedy.... The conspirators who have not hesitated to [employ] the meanest methods ... plume themselves, like the Pharisees
of old.... Every fiber of my nature rebels against such hypocrisy and nerves me
to fight such a combination and such methods to the bitter end...."[4] For his
part, Ballinger concluded that the attacks against him came from "the malev-
olent political conspiracy aimed chiefly at our good President."[5]

Perhaps intending a gesture to his critics to demonstrate that he remained
at heart a supporter of "progressive conservatism [his phrase]," Taft selected a
close associate of Pinchot's, Chicago attorney Walter L. Fisher, as Ballinger's
replacement. The choice bothered the former secretary. The appointment of
"my successor ... in view of his attitude toward your enemies and my enemies

---

[2] Pringle Papers, January 28, 1911.
[3] Unfortunately for Taft, the "matters" to which he alluded involved his own misdating of a
presidential finding.
[4] Pringle, 731; Gould, 148.
[5] Ballinger to Mabel Boardman, Boardman Papers, April l3, 1911. Ballinger probably had both
Pinchot and James Garfield in mind when he wrote this comment.

was, I frankly confess, hard to bear, but not withstanding this I credited you, as I do now, with absolute sincerity."[6] Far less impressed, Garfield called the new appointment "just another one of Taft's incomprehensible actions displaying his absolute lack of political sagacity...."[7]

AGAIN THE TARIFF

But it was not just the lingering echoes of this controversy that roiled the White House waters in 1911. There was also the matter of the tariff. While Taft may well have mishandled what became the Payne–Aldrich tariff, at least he tried to do something about it, in stark contrast to Roosevelt, who had avoided and evaded tariff measures. Taft realized that popular resentment against the tariff had contributed to the Republican defeat in 1910. He also understood that while a Democratic majority in the House might ensure that there would be a number of attempts to pass further reduction measures, the Democrats lacked sufficient votes to override any presidential veto of tariff revisions. But the president did not see the tariff issue in such simple terms.

Although he was committed to tariff reduction and, of equal importance, believed that in its platform his party also had committed itself to such reduction, Taft still accepted the principle of protectionism, as did the dominant Eastern wing of his party. He never imagined that he would go against such a long-standing Republican tenet. It was one thing to remain a committed adherent to something the Republicans had endorsed for more than half a century. But it was quite another to be able to recognize the need for revision, and Taft did.

Further, in 1909, Taft endorsed creation of a tariff commission, also supported by Senate insurgents such as Beveridge and La Follette. Various business elements joined in pushing the commission as a means to "remove politics from the tariff."[8] Taft's endorsement is yet another instance of his tendency toward progressivism, a key tenet of which emphasized the use of expertise in solving problems of government. But while this idea appeared relatively uncomplicated, in fact it caused much contention between the insurgents and Republicans. The issue was not so much the necessity nor the validity of expertise as its relationship to traditional political practices.

For example, what were supposed to be the powers of a tariff commission? For a Congress, long accustomed to logrolling and dealmaking, this was a serious question. A panel to propose and advise might have some merit; but a panel that could adopt its own versions of tariff schedules – and have them carry the force of law – was a very different matter. In 1909, modern

---

[6] Bromley, 198.
[7] Gould, 148. "Poor Taft," wrote TR. "If two years ago he had done some of the things he has done now, he would probably have saved himself from nine tenths of the blunders he has made and is making." Letters, vol. 7, April 28, 1911, 246.
[8] Bromley, 146.

administrative law had not yet evolved to the point where Congress might be ready to take such a step. Further, Taft was concerned that disputes over implementation of a tariff commission might adversely affect the drive for a reduced tariff. Several months before his inauguration, he wrote that "the tariff commission business is of course one in which I sympathize with those who favor it," but "it is impractical, because Congress will never adopt it."[9]

Moreover, Taft added that "I should be the last to advocate a commission with any power to fix rates – if that were constitutional, as it would not be."[10] Instead, he sought a permanent tariff commission "which could make its investigations and report each year the facts in respect to the matter." It would serve as an advisory board to the president, exercising no power of its own. Congress declined even to go this far, although the final version of the tariff measure contained provision for the president "to engage expert assistants to advise him," and provided $75,000 in stipends. Although it did not concede the point, Congress had in fact authorized an advisory panel "consisting of experts who could actually bring forward accurate information on which future [tariff] revisions would be based."[11] For the first time, the Chief Executive could receive the results of expert research into the various rate schedules, and would be in a position to utilize it as the justification for minimum or maximum rates as mandated by the statute.

Politics of course, was never far from any congressional action, and the thought that Taft could possibly select a low-tariff advocate had troubled Speaker Cannon, who vainly sought a pledge from the president that this would not happen. Taft replied that "if the bill is passed I will appoint [them] without [his] assistance."[12] He promptly hired a committee of three, with a professor of economics from Yale as its chairman. Early in 1911, the group met, and its first chairman, Professor Henry Emory, recalled that Taft instructed his "advisors" to "find out as rapidly as possible all essential facts regarding the effect of the tariff without reference to any party, any theory, or any sectional interest." I shall never forget," added Emory "the emphasis with which he told us that he wanted the facts and nothing but the facts."[13]

By 1911, Taft's political context had shifted. The Democrats now controlled the House, and while pushing for further tariff reduction, had an additional goal of generating issues for the 1912 election, in which they sensed a major opportunity for success. Supporting a lower tariff would resonate among urban Democrats, especially upset about the high cost of living. Of course, it was obvious that even with support from the insurgents, the House Democrats lacked the votes for a presidential veto override. But if the House passed a reduced tariff measure, and Taft vetoed it, the Democrats could point both to his inconsistency as well as to his lack of sympathy for urban hardship.

[9] Ibid., 146.
[10] Ibid., 147.
[11] Pringle, 457
[12] Pringle, 457.
[13] Ibid., 599–600.

He had called for tariff reduction, yet when push came to shove, the president appeared unwilling to deliver.

Taft had requested his "Tariff Board" to research the ways in which the Payne–Aldrich tariff had operated on wool and cotton, areas of concern to both farmers and textile factory workers. The board was to report its findings no later than December, 1911, when the new "Congress would convene."[14] The Democrats saw no reason to wait, and when two reduction measures reached his desk, Taft saw no reason to wait, either. "I shall veto both," he wrote to Charles Taft, "no matter in which form they come to me; because the bills have been drawn without accurate knowledge".[15] One of the statutes dealt with the wool schedule, which formed a complicated and controversial part of the original tariff statute. Taft's position, that "I have not had time to hear from the Tariff Board, who are engaged in studying the wool question," while sound from the standpoint of the need for expertise, brought him no political benefit, something he readily conceded.[16]

"I am inclined to think that this is a clever move both on the part of the Insurgents and the Democrats[,] and that it will involve me in a loss of prestige.... It will be said that I criticized the wool schedule ... and yet when an opportunity is presented to modify it[,] I veto it." Delaying action "until we can get at the facts" meant that "I will have to take the burden[,] but I am ready to do so."[17] The president was more candid with Mabel Boardman. "This is a great and awful time, and the Democrats and insurgents think they have put me in a hole with respect to the tariff. Possibly they have, but there is only one thing for me to do and I am going to do it, let the consequences be what they may."[18]

Here, Taft endorsed the progressive thrust toward the use of expertise in governmental administration, even as he objected to the inconsistency of Congress's embodying it in the guise of the Tariff Board, only to refuse to facilitate its work, resorting instead to political opportunism. The resulting stalemate meant that any further tariff reform awaited the outcome of the 1912 election.

Taft apparently made a distinction – at least in his own mind – between insurgents and progressives. He found insurgents to be uncooperative nuisances. But he shared the goals of the progressives, if not the methods of reaching them. Such a distinction had been reflected in the Ballinger–Pinchot controversy. Taft's predecessor as chairman of the Philippine Commission, Cornell University President Jacob Schurman, observed that "the reactionary worships the past, the radical flouts the past, but the Progressive, while retaining all that is sound and valuable in the past, also vitalizes it with the living

[14] Ibid., 600.
[15] Ibid.
[16] Pringle Papers, July 28, 1911.
[17] Ibid.
[18] Boardman Papers, July 28, 1911.

ideas of the present and creates new institutions for our day and generation."[19] If one added to this description the obligation to make progress by incremental steps using the living law as the means of attainment, Schurman's statement is an apt description of Taft's worldview.

TAFT AND ANTITRUST

Unlike contemporaries such as Hughes or Root, or even his brother Henry and Henry's law partner George Wickersham – who served as Taft's attorney general during his entire term – the president had not experienced any great success as a practicing attorney. This may been due more to the lack of opportunity than to his ability. In fact, with the exception of a few years just after his admission to the Ohio Bar, he had not really practiced law at all. Rather, as his career evolved, he had administered the law in various guises: as a trial judge, solicitor general, circuit court jurist, Philippine Commission president, secretary of war, and ultimately TR's successor. Similarly, his view of corporate law remained narrowly circumscribed, and Henry Pringle is correct to note that the term "'corporation attorney' could never be placed upon him."[20]

But Taft's lack of interest in corporate matters was matched by a lack of respect for Wall Street, a lack that had emerged even before Taft returned to Washington to join TR's cabinet in 1903. Taft had strongly supported his chief when the Northern Securities case went before the Supreme Court. His opposition to what he considered the narrow-minded, myopic greed of Wall Street is reflected in a striking comment he made in 1910. "Wall Street," he wrote to his brother, "as an aggregation, is the biggest ass that I have ever run across."[21] Taft's hostility toward Wall Street was coupled, however, by strong support for enforcement of the Sherman Act, now twenty years old. This did not represent a change in heart for Taft. As discussed in Chapter 2, Taft as circuit judge had breathed new life into what appeared to be a moribund Sherman Act in the famous Addystone Pipe case of 1898.

Taft's strong support for the Sherman Act ultimately pointed to a major difference in philosophy with TR. Roosevelt liked to emphasize, as had Herbert Croly in his new book, *The Promise of American Life*, that bigness was here to stay, along with all the ramifications for corporate and industrial expansion that the term implied. It was futile, TR insisted, to attempt to break up all the trusts. What was needed, rather, was the ability to distinguish between good trusts and bad trusts, thus to gain the benefits of big business even as the government punished its abusers. As a loyal subordinate, Taft may

[19] Bromley, 294. "Day by day," observed *The New York Times*, "the President is revealing himself as the Progressive on old issues, rather than as the inventor of new issues." Ibid. The *Times's* editorial was called "Mr. Taft's Progressivism." Of course, keeping one eye on the past and the other on the future at the same time can be difficult.
[20] Pringle, 654.
[21] Ibid., 655.

have silently acquiesced in TR's efforts to separate the trusts. But as president, he did not concur.

Anticipating the position that Louis Brandeis would take with Woodrow Wilson a year later, Taft emphasized that size as well as corporate behavior was the issue. He denied "that an administration and president could discern genuine differences between a good trust and a bad trust."[22] But whatever the size of the trust, it was its conduct that most troubled him. He reiterated his lack of interest in trying to distinguish between the good and the bad. Rather, as Lewis Gould well notes, he looked for results from "the gentle but continuous prosecution of all these combinations until they learn better."[23]

Yet Taft conceded that the Sherman Act did not forbid "the accumulation of large capital in business enterprises," especially in those corporations "in which such a combination can secure reduced cost of production, sale and distribution." He insisted, however, that "every trust of any size that violates the statute will, before the end of this administration in 1913, be brought into court to meet and acquiesce in a degree of disintegration by which competition between its parts shall be restored and preserved."[24] Indeed, in four years, Taft's administration filed more antitrust suits than those initiated during the seven-plus years of the Roosevelt era.

The conservative wing of the Republican Party, the group most disaffected with TR toward the end of his term, did not welcome Taft's antitrust activities, all the more so as he appeared to mean what he said. Efforts to gain their support were not strengthened when, in September 1911, attorney general George Wickersham was quoted to the effect that "probably one hundred additional corporations would be called to account under the Sherman Act, that the guilty officials would go to jail," and that the largest corporation in the country, U.S. Steel, might well be included in this number.[25] Taft's military aide, Archie Butt, a prolific but not always profound chronicler of the Taft presidency, noted with some accuracy that Wickersham "has about as much political judgment as an ox."[26]

Both Wickersham and his chief approached the antitrust problem much as lawyers, with little interest and less instinct for the political consequences that might result from their actions. The Sherman Act had long since been enacted, its constitutionality had been affirmed and reaffirmed by the High Court, and all that remained was its consistent enforcement. Further, Taft disagreed with those conservative businessmen who claimed that the meaning of the statute was not clear. Such had been the complaint of some individuals typified by Henry Lee Higginson, a prominent Boston financier, better known perhaps as the founder and for more than thirty years the sole proprietor of the Boston

[22] Gould, 164–165.
[23] Ibid., 165.
[24] Pringle 668–669.
[25] Ibid.
[26] Bromley, 302.

Symphony Orchestra. Higginson maintained that "any well-trained business-man is wiser than the Congress and the Executive." Moreover, as Cleveland Amory noted, "he did not hesitate to correct such mere elected mortals as the temporary occupants of the White House."[27]

Early in January 1911, Higginson deferred participating in fund raising for Taft's reelection campaign. "We have decided not to try to get any money at present." Indeed, "I would much wish to be dropped out of the whole thing." In the antitrust attacks ordered by Taft and Wickersham, "my own belief is that Government is making a great mistake.... It is almost impossible to learn in Washington ... what a man may or may not do, or what a corporation may or may not do.... Is it wise to spend millions in law suits when private conversation will fetch the same result at no cost? It makes me laugh or weep."[28]

In a later letter to Higginson, Taft gave his views short shrift. "I confess that I don't see where the uncertainty arises in respect to future business. The decisions of the Supreme Court are easily interpreted and anyone can follow them if he is only willing to understand that ... combinations ... to suppress competition, to control prices and to establish a monopoly are unlawful in so far as they affect interstate trade."[29] To a close friend and erstwhile critic of his antitrust policies, Taft insisted that "the methods of business ought not to include combinations for the purpose of suppressing competition and driving other people out of business.... In other words, you seem to think that unfair competition is essential to progress in business[,] and I deny it, and I am strongly in sympathy with the principle of the anti-trust law that denies it."[30]

Critics of Taft's antitrust emphasis sometimes pointed to the number of lawyers whom he had selected for his cabinet. It will be recalled that as president-elect, Taft had stated that lawyers with experience in corporate law would be best qualified to deal with corporations when it came to adopting new regulatory statutes. As for Wickersham, who bore the brunt of criticism from Wall Street conservatives, Taft drafted a reply – part of which was deleted prior to publication – in which he defended his attorney general. "Now, I know something of professional ethics, and their first principle is a lawyer shall be loyal to his present client, regardless of whom he may have served in the past.

---

[27] Cleveland Amory, *The Proper Bostonians* (New York: E. P. Dutton & Co., 1947), 313.

[28] Higginson to A. P. Andrews, January 2, 1911, Boardman Papers. Higginson's final comments brings to mind the famous remark attributed to J. P. Morgan after Roosevelt had ordered that an antitrust suit be launched against Morgan's Northern Securities Company. "If we have done anything wrong, send your man to my man and they can fix it up." G. Wallace Chessman, *Theodore Roosevelt and the Politics of Power*, (Boston: Little, Brown & Co., 1969), 85.

[29] Pringle 655.

[30] Bromley 302. Written in June, 1912, Taft's views on antitrust remained consistent throughout his term. In 1911, he had insisted that "we did get along with competition; we can get along with it. We did get along without monopoly; we can get along without it; and the business men of this country must square themselves to that necessity." Ibid.

Wickersham has the government for his client now, and the tirades aimed at him are the most eloquent of tributes to his good faith."[31]

TR AND ANTI-TAFT

By the fall of 1911, Wickersham and Taft could claim at least two victories in their antitrust campaign. The Supreme Court had sustained the government's position in two major decisions involving the Standard Oil and American Tobacco trusts, not to mention a number of other cases. Now they turned their attention to U.S. Steel, one of the largest firms in the United States, and one that had previously involved president Theodore Roosevelt in an incident, the aftermath of which can be considered the final step along the path that sealed the ultimate break between him and Taft.

In 1907, as TR confronted the financial panic, he met with J. P. Morgan, who was speaking for a group of financiers. They advised the president that U.S. Steel had an opportunity to purchase stock in the Tennessee Coal, Iron and Railroad Company "at a price somewhat in excess of its true value,"[32] otherwise a major firm that held a majority of the Tennessee Coal securities faced possible financial collapse. Executives of U.S. Steel sought assurances from TR that he would not file an antitrust suit against them as he had against Morgan's Northern Securities Company. TR replied that "I felt it no public duty of mine to interpose any objections."[33] Given this positive statement, the purchase went forward, resulting in even greater monopolistic strength for U.S. Steel.

Almost immediately, TR was described as one who had been tricked by dubious methods so typical of Wall St. With characteristic emphasis, the president defended his action or, rather, inaction. "I would have shown myself a timid and unworthy public officer if I had not acted as I did. I never had any doubt of the wisdom of my action – not for a moment."[34] Roosevelt "had acted in the public interest during a moment of crisis." Although when they met with TR, the spokesmen for U.S. Steel gave the distinct impression that they had not wanted to purchase the stock, they had in fact come away with what one expert calls "the best bargain the Steel Corporation or any other concern or individual ever made in the purchase of a piece of property." The most recent study of the Taft presidency concludes that "the truth was, of course, that Roosevelt had been deceived in 1907." Messrs Frick and Gary "had not given him all the facts, and he had served their interests far more than the interests of the public."[35]

---

[31] Pringle, 656–657.
[32] Henry Pringle, *Theodore Roosevelt* (New York: Harvest Books, 1956), 310–311. The price was $45 million.
[33] Gould, 165.
[34] Pringle: Roosevelt, ibid.
[35] Ibid, Gould, 167.

During the next four years, TR was surely aware of all the comments, alleged facts, and interpretations concerning the US Steel incident. But never did he back away from his explanation, or concede that he might have been misinformed. Again, Lewis Gould is correct when he notes that "to question Roosevelt's probity on this subject thus meant not only impugning his record as president, but also doubting his personal honesty. When, TR testified before a congressional committee in 1911, and reiterated his views yet again, he considered the matter finished, and "to reopen the question of whether [he] had been misled was to risk an explosion from an angry former president."[36]

The assault against the trusts gathered steam in 1911, even as relations between TR and Taft improved at least to the level of semi-cordial correspondence. In January, for example, TR sent a ringing endorsement to Taft concerning the president's proposal for tariff reciprocity between the United States and Canada. "It seems to me, "he wrote, "that what you propose to do with Canada is admirable from every standpoint. I firmly believe in free trade with Canada for both economic and political reasons.... Whether Canada will accept such reciprocity I do not know, but it is greatly to your credit to make the effort." True, "it may damage the Republican Party for a while, but it will surely benefit the party in the end...."[37] Further, TR responded favorably when Taft sent him the text of his forthcoming message to Congress. In April, Roosevelt wrote to Taft, "Well, thank Heaven! I am coming to the end of the last speaking tour I shall ever make....and never again will I have to make a tour, or have to make more than an occasional speech."[38]

Although the earlier relationship between the two men could never be restored, Roosevelt in his private correspondence seems to have moderated, at least for the moment, his personal animus toward Taft. And his opposition to any possibility of his renomination remained very much in evidence. "Every friend of mine will show his friendship by seeing that there is no movement started to have me nominated."[39] Indeed, added TR, "I get almost as much disgusted with most of the progressives as with the standpat crowd." By mid-June, 1911, Roosevelt stated that Taft "is stronger than he was.... He is good-natured, kindly in a rather superficial fashion, and thoroughly well meaning...." He added that my "supporters" would very much resent my supporting him for the nomination, which is not necessary, and which I would

[36] Ibid.

[37] January 12, 1911, Boardman Papers. Although it took a special session of Congress, plus Democratic support to bring it about, Congress approved the reciprocity agreement, only to see Canada reject it in September. Taft's cause had not been aided by an inane comment from the new House Speaker James "Champ" Clark, who announced that "I look forward to the time when the American flag will fly over every square foot of British North America, up to the north pole." Bromley, 263.

[38] Pringle Papers, April 1, 1911. In a letter to Henry Wallace, TR noted that in 1910, "I have had to refuse between 3,600 and 4,000 requests to speak."

[39] Letters, vol. 7, May 31, 1911, 274; June 27, 1911, 300.

not do. But I think they will now for the most part follow me in supporting him after the nomination, which a year ago seemed problematical."⁴⁰

By August, TR reiterated that "I have been much disappointed in Taft," who "is a well meaning, honest man." But he "permitted his wife and brother ... to make him very jealous of me, and very anxious to emphasize the contrast between our administrations, and by sundering himself from my especial friends and followers.... In consequence he has frequently taken a reactionary attitude, and the progressives and radicals in the party, being left without any progressive leadership at all, have gone every which way, and have often been violent and foolish." Nevertheless, "Taft will be re-nominated, and I hope will be re-elected. I shall not interfere with the nomination."⁴¹ On the same day he wrote these lines, TR amplified his views on Taft for his oldest son. Now there is a tone of antagonism as well as regret.

"I do not care for Taft, indeed I think less of him as time goes on.... He is a flubdub with a streak of the second-rate and the common in him, and he has not the slightest idea of what is necessary if this country is to make social and industrial progress. He does not even know what the problems are that confront our civilization, not to speak of realizing their seriousness." On the other hand, "Gifford Pinchot is a dear, but he is a fanatic, with an element of hardness and narrowness in his temperament, and an extremist." Roosevelt found it an "awful pity" that "when the progressives were in control of the Republican Party," Taft "should have thrown over his chance and hurt the party and the country" by "identifying conservatism with reaction...."⁴² "I do not," TR wrote in September, "pretend to say that I like Taft, or approve of him, or enjoy supporting him...."⁴³

This atmosphere of growing dislike was the background in which the Taft administration launched the antitrust law suit against U.S. Steel on October 26, 1911. The filing of the bill did not in itself irritate Roosevelt, although as will be noted, he soon made public a proposed method for antitrust action that was very different from that of Taft and Wickersham. Rather it was a conclusion that during the recent financial panic, "the President [TR] was not made fully acquainted with the state of affairs," and thus was not "fully advised. If he had been, he would have understood the motives" of U.S. Steel.⁴⁴ Such statements contradicted Roosevelt's earlier testimony to a congressional committee, and implied ineptitude if not inaccuracy on his part. The president was out of Washington, traveling in the West as the lawsuit was filed, and

⁴⁰ Ibid., June 27, 1911, 297. TR commented further that Henry Cabot Lodge "does not care for Taft; he is not well contented with the Regulars, and loathes the Insurgents ... "

⁴¹ Ibid., August 22, 1911, 333.

⁴² Ibid., 336.000000 One suspects that Taft would have concurred with TR's assessment of Pinchot. On the other hand, at no time during the presidency of either man had the progressives ever controlled the Republican party.

⁴³ Ibid., 345.

⁴⁴ Gould, 167–168. On these pages, Gould has a perceptive interpretation of the event's significance for the road to rupture between Taft and TR.

although he fully approved it, Taft had not been informed of the references to TR embedded within the bill. For Roosevelt, the fact that Taft did not know about these references before they were made public irritated him even more. "My own conception of the office of President is that he is responsible for every action of importance that his subordinates take." Now, "it ill becomes [Taft] ... to act as he now acting....both he and Wickersham are playing small, mean and foolish politics in this matter."[45]

TR found the U.S. Steel lawsuit unacceptable for a second reason. For him, it typified what he considered to be the folly of the Taft approach to antitrust policy. Why should the government seek "to break up all combinations merely because they are large and successful?"[46] Taft's efforts to employ a series of lawsuits would in the long run be hopeless. TR proposed instead a new independent regulatory commission modeled after the Interstate Commerce Commission. This would provide effective government regulation.[47]

By this time, of course, the former president and his successor were no longer in communication with each other, but by late 1911, the Taft circle had received independent evidence that the Wickersham assault on U.S. Steel was generating resentment among Republicans, who normally would be firm supporters of Taft's. Such was reflected in a letter sent to Mabel Boardman by another Republican, Lawrence Hitchcock. He did not doubt the "great ability and high character that Mr. Taft has." More to the point was the conclusion that "there is a strong feeling against him by the business men of this country because they feel that his judicial training is enforcing him to interpret and carry out the Sherman Act as it stands and as the courts have interpreted it." Such a policy "means the breaking down of both good and bad corporations ... in a way that does not at all do away with the evils of these same corporations...." Instead of "using the law to annihilate the huge business interests in this country which I believe is very unpopular," Taft "should endeavor to get through some legislation controlling in a rational way by supervision all interstate business, much as Mr. Roosevelt writes of...." Like Boardman, Hitchcock has "been an admirer of Mr. Taft ... but I think that his whole attitude in this matter is wrong and not at all popular, but so unpopular that it will be a very strong factor against him in the next convention."[48]

For more than a year, Roosevelt had reiterated many times over that he did not want the nomination in 1912, and that it would be an unfortunate development not only for him but also for the country and for his party. He added that all friends of his could show their friendship by having nothing to do with any effort to mount any sort of campaign on his behalf. The consistency

[45] Letters, vol. 7, October 30, 1911, 430; October 31, 1911, 431.
[46] Ibid., 429.
[47] See Roosevelt's article "The Trusts, The People, and the Square Deal" in *The Outlook*, vol. 99, November 18, 1911, 654–655. "Either the Bureau of Corporations should be authorized, or some other governmental body similar to the Interstate Commerce Commission should be created to exercise this supervision, this authoritative control."
[48] Boardman Papers, November 25, 1911.

with which he maintained these positions is beyond dispute. But at the same time, and with similar consistency, TR absolutely refused to say that under no circumstances would he accept the nomination. Several possible explanations for this "consistent inconsistency" come to mind.

It can be argued that on the one hand, TR had never recovered from his surrender of the presidency, and yearned to regain it. Although he was sincere in his refusal to declare his candidacy, careful examination of the statements he typically used reveals that Roosevelt consistently hedged his bets. Saying that "the last thing I want is the nomination," or "I do not want to be nominated for any office" is not the same thing as an outright refusal to serve, and/or a rejection of a proffered nomination. In December 1911, after going into all the usual reasons as to why he did not wish to run, Roosevelt added, "that of course circumstances might conceivably arise when I should feel that there was a duty to the people which I could not shirk, and so would accept the nomination."[49] Long-term admirers of Roosevelt's, such as Pinchot or James Garfield, urged him not to utter any statement concerning a denial to run. Garfield stated that the pro-Roosevelt sentiment in Ohio "has not been instigated by any of us, but is the natural result of present conditions." The only way to stop it "would be a flat-footed final statement from you that under no circumstances would you accept the nomination, and such a statement I feel sure you ought not to make."[50]

The exact date on which TR reached his decision not only to accept the nomination but also to seek it out cannot be ascertained, but between November and December 1911, he moved in that direction. He also appeared much more radical than he had in 1909. "We are now suffering," TR informed Garfield, "as was to be expected, from the fact that the insolence of the reactionary plutocracy has tended to create a revulsion that helps the Socialist cause and gives the leadership of the progressive [cause] to the wild-eyed radicals."[51] Such sentiments indicate that Taft, when compared with Roosevelt, could only appear more conservative *without any change on his part.*[52] Instead of claiming that Taft moved more to the right, it might be more accurate to argue that he remained – at least in his mind – what he had always been, consistent in his commitment to a "progressive conservatism." Rather, it was TR who had shifted leftward.

As TR moved closer to a statement that he would accept the nomination, Taft had not been idle. Unique among presidents in his use of the automobile, while in office he made more cross-country tours than any of his predecessors. During one such eight-week Western swing starting in September 1911 and covering 17,000 miles, his secretary, Charles Hilles, worked assiduously

---

[49] Letters, vol. 7, December 5, 1911, 451–452. "On no other terms would I ever dream of accepting it." Unmentioned was TR's belief that by 1911, Taft had failed to carry out TR's policies.
[50] Garfield Papers, November 27, 1911.
[51] Ibid., November 10, 1911. One suspects that TR never wrote to Henry Cabot Lodge in this tone.
[52] Emphasis added.

FIGURE 7. President Taft (center), secretary Charles Hilles (Taft's right), and aide
Archie Butt (Taft's left) out for a stroll, 1910. Courtesy of Library of Congress Prints
and Photographs Collection

to make sure that local Republican delegates would support the incumbent.
In 1911, for example, the South was a solid Democratic bastion in terms of
national politics. But every state had a Republican presence, and every state
would send Republican delegates to the Convention in Chicago. Careful courting by Hilles (Figure 7) of these delegates when added to traditional Eastern
Republican delegate strength in 1911, had the potential for Taft operatives to
retain control of the nomination process some eight months later.

As 1911 came to an end, Taft still displayed optimism for what lay ahead. "It
is very difficult for me to escape the conclusion not only that I am to be renominated but also that I am to be reelected," and this in spite of a "somewhat

formidable conspiracy" that included a number of Midwest progressives."[53] One of them, James Garfield, had a very different perspective. Taft "has lost the confidence of the party and the country. I have yet to find anyone, who has carefully studied the situation, who will express the belief that Mr. Taft could be re-elected. If that be true, … what excuse can there be for his nomination? It is certainly not destructive of the party to try to find a Republican who can win the election."[54]

Hinting at what had become a characteristic of his administration, Taft added that "I have had to fight my battle alone almost[,] and it has been pretty hard. I hope it may be different in the coming campaign both as to papers and speakers." As to his predecessor, "Of course Roosevelt is willing to make everything as uncomfortable for me as possible[,] but I think he expects me to be renominated and beaten, a result which he will bear with Christian fortitude." Actually there had been similar private expressions from TR earlier, but by this date he had probably made up his mind to accept the nomination, and from that conclusion it was only a very short step to announce that "my hat is in the ring." TR would not only accept renomination, but also would fight to gain it.

[53] Boardman Papers, December 24, 1911.
[54] Copy in Taft Papers, December 11, 1911.

8

The Split, 1912

On January 2, 1912, *The New York Times* published what Taft already knew. The headline read: "Teddy Envoy to Taft Says He Won't Refuse to Run." The unsigned report added that "there is no gainsaying the fact that the Roosevelt movement, which is going on more or less openly, is the only stone in the path of the President to renomination." Regardless, the Taft administration sees "nothing in sight that in any way seriously menaces the prospects for success" at the forthcoming Convention.[1] For his part, Roosevelt still took what he considered to be the high road concerning the election in 1912.

Two weeks after *The Times* announcement, TR wrote to the publisher Frank Munsey that "I am not and shall not be a candidate. I shall not seek the nomination, nor would I accept it if it came to me as the result of an intrigue."[2] TR did not specify what type of intrigue he meant. He added, however, that "I will not tie my hands by a statement which would make it difficult or impossible for me to serve the public by undertaking a great task if the people as a whole seemed definitely to come to the conclusion that I ought to do that task." His verbiage to one side, again, Roosevelt failed to mention how he would assess when the "people" had so concluded, and he left himself plenty of latitude as to his future actions.

Roosevelt's guarded flexibility was not new, and perhaps it can better be described as political expediency. In 1906, he had written to Taft that "the great virtue of my radicalism lies in the fact that I am perfectly ready, if necessary, to be radical on the conservative side."[3] As the 1912 election campaign gained in intensity, TR reiterated a point that he had often emphasized during his presidency. "As you know," he noted, "I have always believed that wise progressivism and wise conservatism go hand in hand, and that the wise

---

[1] Clipping in the Garfield Papers, January, 1912.
[2] Letters, vol 7, January 16, 1912, 479.
[3] Anderson, 51.

conservative must be a progressive because otherwise he works only for that species of reaction which inevitably in the end produces an explosion."[4] It may well be, at least up to TR's speeches during the summer of 1912, culminating in his proposals for judicial recall, that Taft would have agreed with Roosevelt. Taft consistently referred to himself as a believer in progressive conservatism (Figure 8).

Nevertheless, Elihu Root, who knew and understood TR better than many of his more outspoken admirers, was troubled by the former president's stance. In the first place, he questioned "whether you can possibly stick to it. It is going to be very difficult, especially difficult because of your temperament.... No thirsty sinner ever took a pledge which was harder for him to keep than it will be for you to maintain this position."[5] More important, Root realized that if TR was saying "that if a nomination comes to you in the right way you will accept it," serious implications followed. "The moment you say that, you are a candidate." Because Roosevelt categorically refused to state that he would not run for the office under any circumstances, such a refusal concealed – but not very well – his possible availability. Finally, Root stated that "I can see no hope for the party whatever in the coming election. It may be that neither of you could be elected under any circumstances, for I am afraid that the feeling which led to such disastrous results in 1910 is not yet spent, and that we shall see its effects in November.... I hope you will sit tight...."[6]

TR would have done well to heed Root's observations. One suspects, however, that by mid-February, he was unable to accept the insight reflected in them. TR's ultimate course resulted in defeat for himself, Taft, and the Republican Party. By this time, however, he had orchestrated the request from a number of Midwestern governors that he declare himself, and had done so. "I am looking at this," he insisted, "purely from the standpoint of the interests of the people as a whole, from the standpoint of those who believe in the causes which I champion, which three years ago I had every reason to believe the President ardently championed, and which most reluctantly I have come to believe he either does not understand at all, or else is hostile to."[7] Of course, the technique by which TR emphasized these conclusions had been well honed during his presidency. "He managed to let his light shine before men so constantly that they could not forget him for a day.... The deaf read and blind heard about him and all his works. He reached all classes and conditions."[8]

Root was not the only one to see real danger for TR on his current course. Later in February, 1912, TR visited Boston, and his host, local attorney and Judge Robert Grant, recalled, "From my humble point of view that he has made a great mistake – an unnecessary and possibly fatal blunder,

[4] Letters, vol. 7, August 14, 1912, 597.
[5] Root Papers, February 12, 1912.
[6] Ibid.
[7] Letters, vol. 7, February 14, 1912, 504.
[8] Sidney M. Milkis, *Theodore Roosevelt, the Progressive Party, and the Transformation of American Democracy* (Lawrence: University Press of Kansas, 2009), 78.

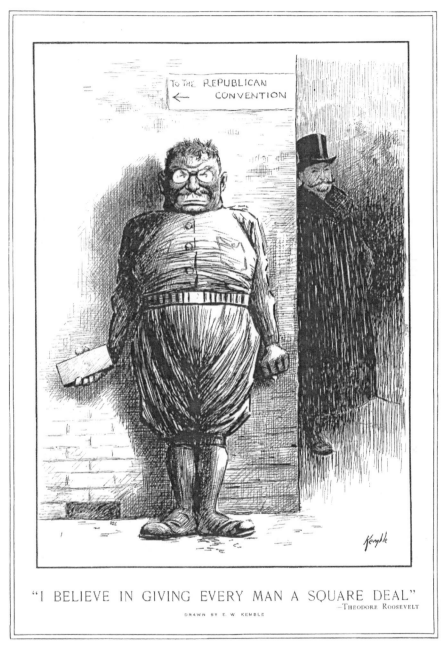

"I BELIEVE IN GIVING EVERY MAN A SQUARE DEAL"
—THEODORE ROOSEVELT

DRAWN BY E. W. KEMBLE

FIGURE 8. Cartoon from *Harper's Weekly*, March 9, 1912. The cartoonist ridicules the "fair play" aspect of TR's Square Deal by showing TR lying in wait to assault an unsuspecting President Taft. Reprinted by permission of HarpWeek, LIC.

which for the time being at any rate bids fair to destroy his value as a great national political asset. He might so easily have waited.... Curiously enough, the impression (whether logical or not) that he has not given Taft quite a square deal seems to have taken hold of the public mind.... Taft has become almost an idol, even in circles where a few months ago he was reviled. If he is [re]elected President, it will be on the crest of the wave of revolt from and denunciation of Roosevelt...." But Grant reiterated his belief that TR "had made an unnecessary mistake which promises to be his Waterloo."[9]

Supporters of Taft's were concerned but not surprised at Roosevelt's decision to "go public." Oswald Garrison Villard reflected his "doubt whether we shall ever make the country understand the real Roosevelt." Villard added that while he was not a partisan of Taft's, "it seems to us that no man was ever so abominably treated by a friend as he has been."[10] J. C. Hemphill did not "believe that the American people are fools enough to trust the administration of their affairs in the hands of the wild man who holds no friendship sacred; who makes no pledges he believes bound to keep. I am really sorry for him...."[11] Obviously referring to Roosevelt's very recent endorsement of public recall for judicial decisions, Hemphill added that "this latest demonstration of his proves beyond further question that he is crazy."

On the other hand, Taft's new secretary of war, Henry Stimson, was less concerned about TR's now open stance as a candidate than with what might happen, assuming he lost the nomination. "I think," Stimson wrote, "it is very important that matters should not be allowed to shape themselves as to provoke a bolt in case Mr. Taft is nominated."[12] TR had been a Republican regular since the 1884 Convention, and on his own probably would not join any third-party movement. "But he is now surrounded by men on whose advice he has acted in becoming a candidate, and who, I think, will jump at any excuse to initiate such a movement."[13] In particular, Stimson reminded Lloyd Griscom that TR's recent endorsement of judicial recall focused on an issue that was before state parties rather than focusing on the national Republican presence. "But I don't think that it will be the part of wisdom to follow Mr. Roosevelt into his side-track just for the sake of grappling with issues which are not before us, and on which issues Republicans ... have very widely varying convictions. Every slap that is thus taken at honest western Republicans increases the chance of a bolt."[14]

[9] Letters, vol. 8, March 22, 1912, 1460–1461, recalling TR's visit of February 25.
[10] Boardman Papers, January 30, 1912.
[11] Pringle Papers, February 25, 1912.
[12] Griscom Papers, March 24, 1912.
[13] The Pinchot brothers and James Garfield immediately come to mind.
[14] Ibid. Taft echoed Stimson's view concerning – at least for the moment – the limitation of the initiative, referendum, and recall to state rather than federal political forums. But in a letter to Cornell President Jacob Schurman, Taft observed that "I think I can be more effective possibly in pointing out the progressive nature of the present administration[,]and defending the independence of the judiciary...." Pringle Papers, February 29, 1912.

This correspondence took place as Taft and TR engaged in a series of primaries through the early spring of 1912. The results favored first Taft, and later in the spring, TR. But the real strength of the winner was not in the number of primaries he won, as much as with the majority of delegates selected in the state conventions. Here, Taft maintained consistent dominance. In retrospect, TR may have assumed that the pseudospontaneous announcement of his availability in February would create a dramatic outpouring of popular support for him. With a few exceptions, this did not happen.

Once TR had made his announcement of availability, Taft became more forthright in his attitude toward the former president, even if he avoided specific mention of his name. In a speech on February 12, 1912, for example, Taft mentioned "extremists" who, among other things, would have "the decisions of the courts ... depend on the momentary passions of a people necessarily indifferently informed as to the issues presented...." Such extremists, he added, "are not progressives – they are political emotionalists or neurotics – who have lost their sense of proportion...."[15] A few days later, Taft defended his choice of words to his brother, Horace. "I didn't intend to be severe in my speech, and perhaps ought to have left out the word 'neurotics' but it seemed to suit so many people that I know...."[16]

But Taft was "not very happy these days because I don't like the character of the contest. I hate to be at odds with Theodore Roosevelt, who made me President ... and towards whom I shall always feel a heavy debt of gratitude on that account. But, of course, he made me President and not deputy, and I have to be President; and I do not recognize any obligation growing out of my previous relations to step aside for him and let him become a candidate for a third term...." Moreover, "he is surrounded by so many sycophants and neurotics who feed his vanity and influence his judgment, that his normal good political sense is at fault in respect of the election."[17]

Until April, while TR had become more abusive in his comments about his successor, Taft still sought to keep the debate focused on issues rather than on invective. Early in March, he wrote to a friend that "the campaign is a very hard and sad one for me. Considering my close relations with Colonel Roosevelt, my admiration for him as a man, my gratitude to him as one who made me president, and my appreciation of him as chief with whom every relation was most delightful, it is hard for me now to be in opposition to him and feel that he is in bitter opposition to me. I do not mean to lend myself, in any way, to a personal controversy with him...."[18] One week later, Taft instructed one of his administration operatives to "utterly ignore the attacks" made by "Colonel Roosevelt upon me or the administration or on our friends...." Further, "I want to be consulted about every paragraph that goes out of a

[15] Pringle, 766.
[16] Taft Papers, February 15, 1912.
[17] Ibid.
[18] Ibid., March 5, 1912.

critical or hostile nature, and especially of a personal nature, with respect to Colonel Roosevelt or the canvass."[19]

By April, 1912, TR appeared to be on a winning streak for the primaries, and in a note to Mabel Boardman, Taft's tone reflected both discouragement and determination. "It is difficult, he wrote, "to tell where our lines may falter in view of these heavy defeats, but I believe we can still hold them so as to secure the nomination." True, he might lose, "but "when the forts of folly fall, they'll find our bodies near the wall."[20] Taft wrote this note on the night of April 15, awaiting the return from Europe of his military aide, Archie Butt, the capable, and diplomatic gentleman who had become as devoted to Taft as he had once been to TR, as well as personifying the one individual upon whom Taft relied with absolute confidence. Serving as the only remaining link between the Roosevelt and Taft households, even before he sailed for a badly needed vacation, Archie had already been warned that he could not serve two masters, at least not at the same time. While TR's circle made it clear that he was to return to them, Butt had already decided that his current president had a much greater need for his assistance. But Archie Butt sailed for America on board the *Titanic*, and never arrived.

Although not one to show his emotions readily, Taft found Butt's loss almost impossible to accept, even though as a jurist and lawyer he was well aware concerning the finality of proof. Again he wrote to Mabel Boardman. "It is hard to believe that he is gone. I expect to see him walk in at any moment. We don't realize what an exceptional character he had until we have lost him."[21] ... I cannot refrain from saying again that I miss him every minute, and that every house and every tree, and every person suggests him. Every walk I take somehow is lacking in his presence, and every door that opens seems to be his coming."[22] But in a public memorial tribute to Archie, Taft at last found closure and, it might be added, eloquence, a trait that rarely appeared in his speeches and writing: But when it did, it was unmistakable. "He was on the deck of the Titanic exactly what he was everywhere. He leaves a void with those who loved him, but the circumstances of his going are all what we would have had, and, while the tears fill the eyes and the voice is choked, we are felicitated by the memory of what he was."[23]

OPEN BATTLE

For Taft, the loss of Archie Butt was more significant than just as an example of the inevitable shock of unmitigated tragedy. It steeled the president, now

[19] Ibid., March 12, 1912.
[20] Boardman Papers, April 15, 1912.
[21] Ibid., April 19, 1912.
[22] Ibid., April 22, 1912. It must be understood that Butt had accompanied the president on virtually every trip, tour, visit, or outing, be it to the golf course, ball park, political event, or on the campaign hustings.
[23] Bromley, 330.

alone as he had not been earlier in his term, to become more outspoken and aggressive in his criticism of TR. Barely ten days later, Taft journeyed up to Boston, and demonstrated his newfound attack mode. TR "says that I am not a progressive, but a reactionary; that I was nominated by progressives....he intimates that I have not the spirit of the progressive...." Taft focused further on some legislative measures enacted during his term that might indeed be called progressive. These could include a postal savings bank, greater attention to antitrust enforcement, and budgetary reforms within the executive branch. Then he turned to the issue of a third term for TR.

Roosevelt, Taft emphasized correctly, had often spoke of his utter lack of personal desire to run again. Rather it was predicated upon his desire "to sacrifice his personal comfort" to the public good. Of course, "there is not the slightest reason why, if he secures a third term, and the limitation of the Washington, Jefferson and Jackson tradition is broken down, he would not have as many terms as his natural life will permit. If he is necessary now to the government, why not later?"[24] At this point, Taft articulated his prime concern with TR, a fear that he reiterated for as long as the campaign continued. "One who so lightly regards constitutional principles, and especially, the independence of the judiciary, one who is so naturally impatient of legal restraints, and of due legal procedure, and who has so misunderstood what liberty regulated by law is, could not safely be intrusted [sic] with successive presidential terms. I say this sorrowfully, but I say it with the full conviction of truth."[25] Further, Taft added, "I represent a cause ... the commitment of the Republican Party to 'wise progress ... to the progress of the people in pursuit of happiness under constitutional government.'"[26]

Here Taft linked two main threads of his campaign: ordered progress and its location in the context of an independent judiciary responsible to the constitution and not to the electorate.[27] Although one would not know it during the bitter fight between them, Taft in fact had viewed "himself as Roosevelt's heir apparent" and had "supported and extended the pragmatic progressive program that was the legacy" of TR. Under his leadership, Congress had enacted what Sidney Milkis correctly describes as "moderate industrial reform."[28] It bears reiterating that Taft considered himself to be a believer in

---

[24] Pringle, 799–780.

[25] Ibid., 781. In the not too distant future, another Roosevelt would win not three but four consecutive terms as president. In response, the American electorate amended the Constitution to provide that future presidents could serve only two consecutive terms.

[26] Milkis, 86.

[27] It might be noted that to the present day, federal judges appointed under Article III of the Constitution still retain their posts either for life or on good behavior, exactly as Taft experienced in his lifetime. While some states do indeed elect their judges, many have provided some sort of tenure for them. The fact that during his life and thereafter there has never been serious interest in amending the Constitution to provide for elected federal judges without life tenure is an indication perhaps that the values Taft espoused concerning an independent federal judiciary still hold.

[28] Milkis, 87.

progressive conservatism [his phrase]. In the spring of 1912, in the midst of the primary contests between himself and TR, he set down what he thought the Republican Party endorsed. His statement included some fifteen positions, and examination of several of them indicates why his self-description as a progressive conservative is apt.

After a preface that "to my mind, the Republican party stands for....," Taft endorsed the establishment and continuance of postal savings banks, a measure duly enacted by Congress and supported by the insurgents. He also called for the establishment of parcel post within the post office. Taft insisted upon the continued "integrity and independence of the judiciary." He pressed for "conserving the public health by the enforcement of the Pure Food and Drugs Act." He proposed "an old-age retirement bill for Government clerks" and passage of a "Workingmen's compensation law." It might be noted here that Taft did not mention labor's right to organize. He may not have felt it necessary, as his sympathy for both the right to organize and the right to strike was well known by 1912. It was labor's conduct during a strike such as the secondary boycott that he found improper.

Taft urged Congress to enact a "national incorporation bureau for regulation and control" of "industrial enterprises doing interstate commerce." Of course he remained committed to a protective tariff, but his position was not an example of doctrinal rigidity. Rather, he desired "revision of the tariff from time to time, schedule by schedule, on scientific principles, based on the reports of a nonpartisan board of experts; and maintaining needed protection equal to the difference between cost of production here and abroad."[29] Finally, the president urged adoption of "arbitration treaties with other powers and ultimately the creation of a general arbitral [sic] court in which to settle international disputes without resort to bloodshed."[30] All in all, his proposals represented an intriguing mix of traditional Republican political values, along with several suggestions for added federal regulation that had a distinct progressive tone.

As the primary season drew to a close, Taft sought help from some of his old associates, especially Elihu Root, who had served along with Taft in Roosevelt's cabinet, and whose resignation as secretary of war had created the vacancy Taft filled upon his return to Washington in 1904. But Root, although he supported Taft's renomination, declined to campaign for the

[29] During the 1912 campaign, the progressive platform position on the tariff was virtually identical with this position taken by Taft. See Letters, vol. 7, August 3, 1912, 593. On the use of experts, see the perceptive comments of Michael Bernstein, who reminds us that "expert knowledge and its utilization are immensely complicated historical problems – puzzles that require a great deal of analysis to appreciate the manner in which appeals to 'expertness' are often overt efforts to eliminate certain points of view from debate in matters of profound political significance." Michael A. Bernstein, "Tocqueville versus Weber," 28 *Law and History Review*, 2010, 238. His point has significance when applied to the debates over the tariff.

[30] Taft Papers, March 25, 1912.

president. Like his colleague Henry Cabot Lodge, he disapproved of TR's course, but could not bring himself to speak out against the former president.[31] Root assured Taft that "I consider you to be entitled to a renomination ... and that I am in favor of [it], and so far as using all my influence as Senator or otherwise to secure the adherence of my State to that view, I have had no doubt or difficulty."[32] But while TR had made his antagonism toward Taft very clear, "he has not attacked me."[33] Further, Root reminded Taft that he had served in TR's cabinet as an influential and trusted advisor. He did not feel comfortable in open opposition to him. "This, of course, makes no difference whatever in my attitude towards the nomination or in the firmness of my adherence to your candidacy or in the distinctness and certainty of my declaration ... in favor of that candidacy. It merely affects the kind of service which I feel at liberty to render and leads me to the conclusion that I cannot be of any use whatever in Ohio."[34]

Taft realized that the attitudes typified by Lodge and Stimson, while apparently pledging some sort of neutrality, in fact helped Wilson rather than TR or himself. By the late spring of 1912, he was philosophical about what he saw as his diminishing chances to beat Roosevelt at the forthcoming Republican Convention. "I don't expect to be successful," Taft wrote. Further, many more Republicans would "turn to [Roosevelt] when it becomes apparent, as it may and probably will ... that I cannot win."[35] Anger, resignation, and at the same time a new found determination to stay the course are reflected in his correspondence as the Convention loomed.

Taft was troubled by TR's constant harping on the link between Taft and leaders of the regular Republican Party in such states as Pennsylvania, New York, and Ohio. Claiming that Taft's association with these men reeked of corruption, especially when Taft won the primary, as was true in New York, Roosevelt struck a tone of self-righteousness that the president found irritating. Pringle observes that for TR, "the only honest primary, it would seem, was a contest in which Roosevelt won."[36] All others were open to question. Pointing to the evidence of the extent to which machine elements had aided Roosevelt, the inconsistency seemed obvious to Taft.

---

[31] "I am opposed," Lodge wrote, "to the constitutional changes advocated by Colonel Roosevelt ... but I cannot personally oppose him who has been my lifelong friend, and for this reason I take no part whatever in the campaign for the presidential nomination." Letters, vol. 7, 512. Henry Stimson, Taft's Secretary of War, took a similar position. Of TR he wrote, "And I now remain his sincere friend. But I believe that those who are forcing him, contrary to his original intention, into the arena against Mr. Taft are jeopardizing ... the real cause of progress in the Nation." Ibid., 520.

[32] Root Papers, May 15, 1912.

[33] See, for example, Roosevelt's observation to Garfield that "Taft comes pretty near being a skunk." Garfield Papers, April 30, 1912.

[34] Root, ibid.

[35] Pringle, 785.

[36] Ibid., 783.

Writing to his brother, the president noted of the bosses that "association with them when it is by and for Roosevelt has nothing of evil in it. It is only when they support me that bosses are wicked. Considering the use which Roosevelt made of bosses in the past, one would think the hypocrisy of such attacks would be seen...." Indeed, "the expenditure of money on Roosevelt's behalf has been extraordinary."[37] On his part, Taft freely admitted that "I have had the bosses with me."

Composing his letter in April, 1912, two months before the Convention, Taft said that he did not believe that TR "can or will be nominated." But "I shall not withdraw under any conditions. I represent a cause that would make it cowardly for me to withdraw now. It seems to me that I am the only hope against radicalism and demagogy, and that even if I go down to defeat, it is my duty to secure the nomination if I can ... in spite of all threats to bolt or establish a third party." Thus. Taft wrote on the day the *Titanic* sank that relying on the established nucleus of the party was vital "for the maintenance of true constitutional principles." If, in the event of a Democratic success, "it is important that [the resulting Republican] opposition should not be Rooseveltian and wildly radical."[38]

By May, Taft had accepted two key points central to the last months of his campaign for renomination.[39] In the first place, he became much more aggressive in his treatment of TR. "I have thrown away the scabbard and I am going to do the best I can," and "if I am defeated, I hope somebody will recognize the agony of spirit I have undergone in apparently lowering the dignity of my office when I thought it essential to the ultimate and righteous cause that I am defending and representing."[40] Moreover, Taft now recognized that "I have to do it nearly all myself. Men do not seem willing to come forward, even those who recognize the crisis." Even Root "has failed me. He is bitterly against Roosevelt, he tells me, but he will not come out to Ohio to help me." So too did other Republicans such as Henry Stimson, Taft's new secretary of war, "hang back. They are afraid of TR." And "so are many of the congressmen and senators."[41]

[37] Taft Papers, April 14, 1912.

[38] Ibid.

[39] It might be noted that Taft appears to have been the first incumbent to actively campaign and travel as he sought renomination.

[40] Ibid., May 10, 1912. A week earlier, Taft had written to an old friend in Cincinnati that "I greatly deprecate having to trail the office of the President in the mire of politics, but I can not help it. I am fighting for a cause, and I have got to win, not for myself, but to prevent this attack on the independence of the judiciary and to prevent the triumph of the dangerous demagogue." Pringle Papers, May 3, 1912.

[41] Pringle, 785. Throughout the fall, Taft suffered from an inability to rouse his cabinet to vigorous campaign activity on his behalf. In June, he complained to Nellie that "I find ... my cabinet, and especially Wickersham and Fisher, are not sufficiently sympathetic with me in an effort to help me out politically." Taft Papers, July 14, 1912.

In May, Taft wrote a candid letter to his mother's surviving sister, one that reflected acceptance and anger. His present situation "is about as painful for me as it possibly could be." Anticipating his possible defeat by TR at the forthcoming Convention, he noted that "if it is to be settled against me, it will be finally settled: and then I can retire to a quiet that will be restful." Further, "if now, fortune is to desert me for a time or permanently, it is my business to stand it...."[42] But Taft admitted that he had a "sense of wrong" in TR's attitude toward me "which I doubt if I can ever get over. The fact is that I do not think I ought ever to get over it." In the end, however, Taft predicted that "the hypocrisy, the insincerity, the selfishness, the monumental egotism, and almost the insanity of megalomania that possesses Theodore Roosevelt will make themselves known to the American people in such a way that his place in history will be accurately defined."[43]

Before assessing to what extent Taft's prediction may be considered accurate, it should be noted that he was not alone in applying such sentiments to Roosevelt. After the Convention, James Garfield, who was one of TR's most enthusiastic boosters, received a letter from a New York Republican, George Bishop. Bishop appreciated "how difficult it is for the Colonel to realize that in his own State he has become discredited; that his assumptions, his exaggeration of the Ego, his hallucinations, are understood here as nowhere else."[44] Sounding more like TR than himself, Taft informed an old friend in May that by the time of the Convention, his supporters would have sufficient delegates for the nomination, and "we don't propose to be defrauded or bulldozed out of it."[45]

"Isn't it amazing," asked a correspondent of Mabel Boardman's, "that *any* body should be left to support [TR] when one remembers the blustering bullying, prize-fighting sort of campaign he has made....? Do they actually *prefer* that one should be a brutal bragging swashbuckler....? What I should fear would be that all the conservatives in both parties would vote for the Democrat, radical though he might be, to make sure of beating Roosevelt." Indeed, added Charles Scott, "I very much fear that might happen even if Taft were the regular Republican nominee and TR should take a bolting nomination."[46] *The New York Times* concluded that TR's successful primaries meant that the United States "is not yet secure against the chief peril that besets democracies – the ambitious, plausible, selfish, and even conscientious demagogue."[47]

---

[42] Pringle Papers, May 12, 1912. Unlike with TR, it apparently never occurred to Taft to consider a bolt from his party if he did not gain the nomination.

[43] Ibid.

[44] Garfield Papers, June 27. 1912. "Here there is an underlying sense of fitness, of sanity, of poise, which revolts at the vagaries he has exhibited, in his mad struggle for a return to power."

[45] Gould, 178.

[46] Boardman Papers, May 26, 1912, emphasis in original. Scott's prescience might be noted.

[47] Milkis, 85.

ARMAGEDDON AND BEYOND

As the GOP faithful arrived in Chicago in June, reports of delegate strengths varied. It would appear, however, that based only upon the various primary contests, the results indicated an inconclusive lead for Taft. Yet such a lead was insignificant. Somewhat more important were the votes of those delegates who were already committed, and among this number TR had more than twice the votes of Taft, 411 to 201. But this figure, even when added to the primary results, was not sufficient for TR to claim victory. The New York delegation, which TR had wooed with financial support, emotional rhetoric, and minimal success, contained a majority of more than 160 uninstructed delegates. Well organized by the regular GOP machine, the great majority of them supported Taft.[48] But even this addition did not yet ensure victory for the president.

Rather, it was some 250 delegates drawn largely from the South who were pivotal, and whose votes might enhance Taft's totals, but were indispensable to TR – and both men knew it. This is why Roosevelt's managers had contested the votes of those 250, which would mean that the National Committee would have to consider each one before the Convention could get down to the business of selecting its nominee. But this committee, which consisted of some 53 Republicans, was dominated by regulars. William McKinley, Taft's erstwhile campaign operative, "had been busy since early February building up a political organization below the Mason-Dixon Line that would be impervious to insurgent appeals."[49] Indeed, TR had found much the same result when he was orchestrating Taft's nomination in 1908. No other candidate had had any real chance of success, and now – four years later – the math indicated the same fate for TR. If he was to have any chance at all, there would need to be a chairman who was sympathetic to TR's efforts – and again, both men knew it.

If Taft had been unable to persuade Elihu Root to campaign openly on his behalf during the primary season, he gained a much more significant result when Root agreed to accept nomination as the temporary chairman of the forthcoming Convention. Of course, Root had to be elected by the delegates, but to many, the diminutive lawyer and senator from New York was "Mr. Republican." Whoever filled this post would be in a position to make key rulings concerning the seating of disputed delegates. All involved realized how high the stakes were here. The candidate who received the great majority of these 250 votes would gain the nomination. Although fond of Taft (Root and Taft had sat next to each other during cabinet meetings), earlier as secretary of war, Root he had been an intimate advisor and mentor to Taft while Taft was in the Philippines. Root's relationship to TR had been especially close. Alone among Taft's advisors, Root had not only enjoyed his ties to TR,

48 Gould, 178.
49 Milkis, 81.

but also relished his ability to employ the presidential putdown, as noted in Chapter 3. Above all, Root was devoted to the Republican party as a political institution. From his perspective, Roosevelt's chosen course of action represented a selfish maneuver that could only damage it.

Before turning to the business of the Convention, the Republican National Committee had to deal with the Roosevelt claims of fraud and corrupt patronage concerning the disputed delegations. Early in June, it met to consider these allegations, and by a strong majority (39–14), the committee rejected TR's accusations. Indeed, among the disputed votes, it gave Taft 235, with only 19 going to the former president.[50] Already in the campaign, precedents had been ignored. By tradition, an incumbent remained in Washington, leaving the campaigning to party regulars. But during the spring campaign, Taft had broken with this tradition, realizing – correctly – that he had no choice. Never had an incumbent faced a season of primaries, many won by his predecessor. "I regret the necessity which brings me out." Taft felt "humiliated that I, as President ... am the first one that has had to depart from the tradition that keeps the President at home during political controversy."[51] Now another precedent was to be shattered.

It was the well-established custom that presidential candidates stayed away from their party conventions. Indeed, Taft never appeared in Chicago, although he was in constant phone contact with his managers. Faced with the Republican National Committee's rebuff, however, Roosevelt broke with tradition, having already separated himself from the president. He traveled to Chicago, and received a tumultuous welcome from his supporters.[52] As the opening of the Convention drew nigh, TR proclaimed to his followers that they stood at Armageddon, "where we battle for the Lord."[53] In speaking first, he "could upstage the party and by planting the idea that the convention was about to [endorse] a swindle, he could pave the first mile for his bolt."[54] His speech more symbolic than significant, TR probably gained little practical benefit from his eloquence. For no delegates were to be found at Armageddon, and Taft already claimed more than he needed, while TR was short by about 80 votes.[55] Unless the delegates reversed the decision of the National Committee, Roosevelt could not gain the nomination.

---

[50] Milkis, 108.

[51] Milkis, 86.

[52] *The New York Times* found TR's trip more flamboyant than fruitful. "This vain, wrong headed, impetuous man in his mood of shameless self-glorification has gone to the convention city to browbeat his opponents. Nothing like it, nothing so destructive to the dignity of our institutions, was ever dreamed of in the uncouth early days of our Republic." Milkis, 110. In October, *The Houston Post* described TR as " the first president whose chief personal characteristic was mendacity, the first to glory in duplicity, the first braggart, the first bully." See Kathleen Dalton, *Theodore Roosevelt: A Strenuous Life* (New York: Vintage Books, 2004), 398.

[53] Ibid., 112; Pringle, 802.

[54] Milkis, 111.

[55] Pringle, 803.

Thus, again, the position of temporary chairman assumed greater importance than usual at this Republican Convention, and Taft's managers had gotten the jump on TR by gaining Root's agreement to run. The former president's supporters nominated the Governor of Wisconsin, Francis McGovern, in the hope that he might be attractive to the delegates backing Wisconsin Senator Robert La Follette. But La Follette's followers viewed the campaign for the leadership of the nascent progressive movement as more fundamental than the issue of a presidential nominee. As a result, they refused to join TR's opposition to Taft. The ultimate split between the two progressive factions ensured Root's election as Convention chairman, much as the forthcoming division between Taft and TR ensured Wilson's victory in November. Root received 558 votes to McGovern's 501, figures that illustrate the depth of the division within the Republican ranks. Roosevelt's sole remaining hope was that the Convention might yet sustain his claims of irregularities concerning some 70 or 80 contested delegates.

In his keynote address, which was perhaps a preview of what was soon to come, Root focused less on the Democrats than on the accomplishments of his party. But he implied that Roosevelt's chosen course of action could only damage party unity and cohesion. Root concluded with several pledges that did not mention TR but were clearly aimed at his recent support for judicial recall. Root reminded the delegates of the GOP platform in 1908, which included the promise that the party "will uphold at all times the authority and integrity of the courts ... and will ever insist that their powers ... shall be preserved inviolate." Now, "we must be true to that pledge, for ... the limitations upon arbitrary power ... cannot be enforced except through the determinations of an independent and courageous judiciary." As he concluded, Root repeated his statement yet again. "We shall be true to the Republican pledge. The great courts in which Marshall and Story ... sat will not be degraded from their high office ... The keystone of this balanced and able structure of government, established by our fathers, will not be shattered by Republican hands...."[56]

TR's supporters now sought to substitute TR's delegates for those of Taft, a move that was defeated by a vote of 567 to 507. As to the 70 or so delegates still in dispute, Root, citing a rule of the House of Representatives, held that these delegates, though not able to vote on a challenge to their own seats, could still vote on the remainder, a decision that ensured Taft's nomination. Indeed, Taft was renominated on the first ballot by a vote of 561 to TR's 107. However, following Roosevelt's instructions, more than 300 of his delegates refused to vote at all.[57] No longer a prospect, the split was now a fact.

---

[56] Elihu Root, *The United States and the War, the Mission to Russia, Political Addresses,* (Cambridge, MA: Harvard University Press, 1918), 294.

[57] On June 10, William Parks had written to Garfield that "the purpose of the National Committee ... is to effectually *stack* [emphasis in original] the convention against Mr. Roosevelt....If Mr. Taft is re-nominated he would be beaten worse than Mr. Harrison was in 1892." Garfield Papers, June 10, 1912. Parks was correct on both points.

In spite of his victory, to numerous Taft supporters in Chicago his nomination left little to cheer about. One observer noted that "the only question now is which corpse gets the most flowers."[58] But Taft believed that his win in Chicago had ensured an even greater gain. He wrote to Mabel Boardman that regardless of what would happen in November – and Taft held few illusions on that score – "we have achieved the most important end and that is that [TR] can not be president or the [leader] of the Republican party. This result was a just judgment against such an unprecedented exploitation of coarse selfish ambition, attempting to cloak itself under the guise of an unselfish and disinterested desire to serve and help the people by sacrifice."[59] Two days later, Taft wrote that "we are all very happy over the result at Chicago, and we don't care what happens in November – at least we don't care enough to minimize the pleasure we have in the accomplishment of so great a result as the suppression of such an evil as Roosevelt."[60] Taft restated this position even as the campaign wound down and became a race between Wilson and TR, with Taft reduced to watching from the White House. Commenting to Gus Karger, Taft observed that "I will probably be defeated in November, but I am content. My victory came in June when I was renominated ... and no matter what happens, Roosevelt cannot be elected. I draw my consolation and satisfaction from that."[61]

It might be noted that even as he pursued his chosen course, TR also sensed the inevitable. "I think it probable ... that Wilson will win ... He will take the majority of the progressive Democrats, and he will keep not only all the reactionary Democrats, but he will take some reactionary Republicans when they find, as I believe they will find, that Taft cannot be elected." Possibly reflecting the driving ego noted earlier by Taft, TR added that "however, win or lose, the fight had to be made, and it happened that no human being could make it except myself."[62] Indeed, one correspondent of Root's went so far as to claim that between TR and Taft, "the issue is really a personal one. Col. Roosevelt sought from the date of President Taft's election to undermine him."[63]

---

[58] Pringle, 809, quoting Chauncey M. Depew.

[59] Boardman Papers, June 23, 1912. "Whether he will be completely [revealed] to all by November, we can hardly say – I doubt it." Taft consistently maintained this position even after he and TR had affected a sort of quasi-reconciliation, several years later. An alternative perspective is seen in TR's former Attorney General, Charles Bonaparte, who had noted in May "the plain truth [is] that the people did not want Taft in 1908 and after more than three years trial they want him so much less now than they did then[.] that they won't have him at any price in 1912. If they cannot get Roosevelt, mark my words, they will take a Democrat." Taft Papers, transcript of Baltimore meeting, May 3, 1912, 3–4.

[60] Ibid., June 25, 1912.

[61] Taft to Karger, September 7, 1912, Taft–Karger Correspondence, Folder 9, Cincinnati Museum Center. "His reference to Roosevelt was extremely bitter."

[62] Letters, vol. 7, August 3, 1912, 593. See also ibid., August 14, 1912, 598. Concerning the campaign battle as it stood then, TR wrote of Wilson, "My judgment is that he will win, and that I will do better than Taft." TR was correct on both points.

[63] Root Papers, June 26, 1912.

With the GOP Convention over, Taft awaited formal notification of his nomination. In the meantime, with pardonable cynicism, he predicted to Mabel Boardman that TR's "Bull Moose convention will doubtless be advertised as a success, and I think it was[,] in bringing together 1st. serious friends of Roosevelt ... 2nd. Student and professional disciples of every new governmental and political fad including woman suffragists. 3rd. Minor officeholders who wish to hold other offices. 4th. The discontented in politics who long for office in vain. 5th. The discontented in life who attribute their failure not to their own shiftlessness but to the 'system.' But it does not include the negroes for he seems to have driven them away."[64] Moreover, "If I can not win[,] I hope Wilson will, and Roosevelt feels that if he can not win, he hopes Wilson will."[65] Alone in the White House during the mid-summer heat, Taft had struggled to compose his acceptance speech, writing to Nellie daily – and sometimes more than daily – about his progress. Both the President and his secretary – soon to be the head of his reelection bid – "are sane, I think, and [we] look at the situation from the same sensible standpoint. If the election were to be taken today, I have no doubt we should be badly defeated. Whether matters will shape up so as to give us a chance, only the future can decide." However, given the "third party that may play a good deal of havoc with us....a defeat by the Democrats would not be a bad thing for the Republican party, and certainly we can stand it if anybody can."[66]

On August 1, 1912, Taft listened as Root delivered his formal notification that on June 22, "you were regularly and duly nominated by the national convention of the Republican party...." He did not mention Roosevelt by name, but stated that "neither in the facts and arguments produced before the national committee, the committee on credentials and the convention itself, nor otherwise, does there appear just ground for impeaching the honesty and good faith of the committee's decisions." In fact, Root concluded, "your title to the nomination is as clear and unimpeachable as the title of any candidate of any party since political conventions began."[67]

Taft delivered his acceptance address immediately after Root concluded his brief message of notification. Compared with his remarks in 1908, Taft's address both defended the accomplishments of his administration and warned

---

[64] Boardman Papers, August 7, 1912. Taft later noted that "if there is any vagary, crank or ism that Roosevelt has not embraced and adopted in his platform and speech, I am unable to state it." Taft Papers, August 9, 1912.

[65] Taft Papers, July 21, 1912. "I seem to think that we have won what there was to fight about, and that which follows is less important." Ibid., July 23, 1912.

[66] Ibid., July 14, 1912.

[67] Elihu Root, *The United States and the War, the Mission to Russia, and Political Addresses* (Cambridge, MA: Harvard University Press, 1918), 297–298. Root went on to extol Taft's values. "You believe in preserving the constitutional government of the United States. You believe in the rule of law rather than the rule of men.... You know that the great declarations of principle in our Constitution cannot be made an effectual guide to conduct in any other way than by judicial judgment ... and you maintain the independence, dignity and authority of the courts of the United States."

of the dangers inherent in the political ambitions of the man who had brought him to this place, even as he acknowledged that TR had been among the "great Presidents and great Republicans." Like his predecessors, "I have kept the faith." Perhaps because his party insisted upon "liberty under the law," it is "least willing to experiment with those innovations which would jeopard[ize] the integrity of our judiciary, which for more than a century has been the bulwark of liberty, the protection of the weak against the strong and the safeguard of the rights of the minority...."[68]

If he declared anew his allegiance to the rule of law, Taft also denounced what he considered inappropriate tariff bills, no doubt including those he planned to veto even as he spoke. He disapproved them "because they constituted a menace to the welfare of the American workmen, having been conceived in insincerity, drafted in ignorance[,] and passed with reckless disregard for millions dependent for a livelihood on the prosperity of the industries which they would have undermined."[69] But Taft took credit for more than just an insistence that tariff measures be based on expert knowledge instead of mere politics.

He mentioned the sequel to the Hepburn Act, which expanded the authority of the Interstate Commerce Commission. Now the ICC possessed regulatory authority over "express companies and telegraph, telephone and cable lines." Further, a new Commerce Court had been established. Taft singled out his railroad reform for special attention as prime examples of his "progressive legislation." He pointed to the statute restricting the "hours of labor of trainmen and telegraph operators," more rigorous inspection, and safety requirements. He cited establishment of the Children's Bureau, and reminded his listeners that the workman's compensation statute had passed the Senate but was stalled up in the Democratically controlled House, seeking to bar credit to Taft for a "wise and progressive measure on the eve of a national election."

Taft characterized the trust policy of his administration as "firm, consistent and effective." Moreover, "no discrimination has been shown towards friend or foe." During the "seven and a half years preceding this administration[,] 44 cases against trusts were instituted. During the less than four years of this administration 22 civil suits and 45 criminal indictments have been brought under the antitrust law." Such statistics were possible because the independence of the American judiciary. "Unfortunately, hostility to the judiciary and measures to take away its power and independence constitute the chief definite plans of that class of politicians and reformers from which the Republican party escaped at Chicago ... and I use the word "escaped" advisedly."[70] Change

---

[68] Taft Papers, undated draft of acceptance address, delivered on August 1, 1912.

[69] Ibid. On Agust 3, Taft received a letter from Yale Professor Henry C. Emery, his chairman of the Tariff Board. "No one knows more than I do," Emery wrote, "how sincerely you wish to bring about a real reform of the tariff, – and you know that actual legislation as the result of the Tariff Board's labors is my chief desire. But we prefer to remain childless rather than to beget bastards." Pringle Papers, August 3, 1912.

[70] Ibid.

was, of course, inevitable, but the "Republican party has always stood for the Constitution as it is, with such amendments adopted ... as new conditions, thoroughly understood may require, and this is the supreme issue of this campaign." Further, Taft embraced the view that "the day had passed when it was clearly obvious that the least government was the best government. The duty of government to protect the weaker classes by 'positive law' was now recognized."[71]

Taft's acceptance speech breathed rigid defiance, but inwardly Taft had doubted his chances of success even before he accepted the nomination. "Sometimes," he had written to Nellie, only a couple of weeks before his acceptance, "I think I might as well give up so far as being a candidate is concerned. There are so many people in the country who don't like me.... There are other and better things than being exceedingly popular." Indeed, "I have held the office of President once and that is more than most men have, so I am content to retire with a consciousness that I have done the best I could.... It is a very humdrum, uninteresting administration, and it does not attract the attention or enthusiasm of anybody...."[72] Taft was accurate in part because he refused to do any major campaigning for reelection, but rather left the bulk of it to the Republican Committee, which demonstrated a similar lack of enthusiasm. Nor did Taft's cabinet offer vigorous, sustained support. It wasn't just the depth of the TR–Taft split as much as the fact that the rupture made Wilson's election a virtual certainty, so why campaign against the inevitable?

As far as can be seen from his own papers, Root's campaign efforts on behalf of Taft appear to have been minimal. Root did promise to deliver one address, but there is also an undated and unsigned manuscript in his papers. Whether it was a speech or some sort of essay rebutting TR's strident claims about delegate theft, it is an interesting document because it says virtually nothing about the incumbent. Rather it focuses on TR's conduct during and after the convention. Perhaps Root never forgot TR's efforts to displace him, because this rebuttal denounces Roosevelt's tactics to a remarkable extent.[73] Whoever the author may have been, the tone is icy, and a sense of outrage is unmistakable.

The document begins by noting that "when an ambitious and unscrupulous man meets defeat where he anticipated victory, he naturally seeks to lay the blame upon other causes than himself." So it was in this instance. "Theodore Roosevelt, an unsuccessful candidate for a presidential third term, would divert attention from his own defeat, his own violation of his anti-third term pledges, his radical and unsafe doctrines ... by abusive repudiation of the

---

[71] Pringle, 832.

[72] Taft Papers, July 22, 1912.

[73] The essay has the title "Why Theodore Roosevelt Charges 'Theft' and 'Robbery.'" While it reflects Root's style of writing, on the other hand, Richard Leopold notes that Root consistently refused to engage in personal recrimination against an old friend. Leopold, 89. Regardless of the authorship, however, Root surely subscribed to the sentiments reflected in it.

decisions reached at the recent GOP convention." But "no one knows better than Theodore Roosevelt that a lie will travel seven leagues while truth is still putting on its boots. With malicious intent, therefore, he fills the air with charges of stolen delegates in order that many may hear the accusation ere the truth can reach them...." Indeed, "like all of Mr. Roosevelt's impulsive, erratic and false accusations, this particular charge is uttered without either the submission or offer of proof." In short, Roosevelt "charges theft and robbery because he is stung by the bitterness of defeat; because he has no other excuse to offer for failure; and because he knows that wild condemnation will always find some ears willing to listen."[74]

The bitter tone reflected in this document was echoed in the fall campaign. Taft engaged in only desultory stumping, and a sense of lassitude characterized the Republican effort as a whole. He realized that the real contest was between Roosevelt and Wilson. Yet Taft retained the hope that he might at least match if not exceed TR's popular vote totals. But Taft came in third, well behind Wilson, and almost 700,000 votes behind the former president.[75] He carried only two states, and recorded 8 electoral votes, while Roosevelt garnered 88, far behind Wilson, who received 435 electoral votes. Lewis Gould described the outcome "as thorough a repudiation of Taft and his administration as anyone could have predicted."[76] But contemporary observers were not so sure.

AFTERMATH

Shortly after the election, *The New York Sun* noted that "the name of President Taft will stand in the list of those Presidents ... who served this country far better and more wisely than the people could see...." As for Roosevelt, "the cruel and utterly undeserved punishment of a friend – the brutal wrecking of the party to which he owed all his honors in the past – do these really seem small and negligible besides the passing gratification of ruthless and selfish ambition?" *The New York Times* concluded that "he did not deserve it. These are the words that are on the lips of multitudes who were opposed to Mr. Taft's election.... His defeat under any possible conditions in his own party could hardly have been avoided, but his pitiful showing in the Electoral College is the result of forces that are not to his discredit – quite the contrary. Chief of these is the vindictive and treacherous enmity of Mr. Roosevelt ... When [Taft] refused to consult solely the wishes of the ex-President he aroused in the mind of that domineering gentleman sentiments of jealousy, wounded vanity, and implacable hostility. ... "

The New York World observed that Taft "has not awakened much enthusiasm[,] but he has created little antagonism...." But TR "passes from a

---

[74] Root Papers, 1912.

[75] Gould, 107

[76] Ibid. Again in 1936, another Republican presidential candidate would carry only two states.

retirement of peace to a career of turbulence. And to no purpose." Indeed, "Mr. Roosevelt might easily have saved his party in Chicago ... by subordinating himself. He chose to wreck the organization. He preferred the applause of the day to the veneration of the centuries." A day later, the *World* concluded that "history will deal much more sympathetically with Mr. Taft than did the popular majority at the polls ... Blameworthy as he has been in some respects, the fate that has overtaken him was not deserved. There will be a revision of the popular judgment as to him and it will be tempered by knowledge and sympathy...." Here, in short, "is a president who has met unmerited humiliation. Defeat was necessary and inevitable, but only by treachery and ingratitude could it be made so overwhelming."[77]

For his part, Taft had probably expected defeat, but perhaps not as much of a loss as that which he sustained. With rejection might come a respite from unwanted political tensions. "I am not greatly disappointed," he wrote a few days after the election, "and I am quite ready to leave the White House."[78] But if he lost, so had Roosevelt, and Taft found solace in this reality. Indeed, he hoped that "we may end the Rooseveltian menace to our Government and keep him harmless." In fact, "he is today the most dangerous element we have, and it is our business to make the Republican Party independent of him[,] and able to defeat his purposes." Moreover, Roosevelt's platform was not necessarily the only program synonymous with progress. As Taft emphasized in the closest thing to a brief concession speech, Republicans "favor every step of progress toward more perfect equality of opportunity and ... ridding society of injustice. But we know that all progress worth making is possible with our present form of government...."[79]

Taft assumed that upon leaving office, "I am perforce obliged to practice law, because I have not enough to live on without it." But he would "give certainly half of my time" first to keeping the GOP free from "Rooseveltism," and second, "to the preservation of the constitutional structure which we value so highly." He believed that other Republicans would welcome his assistance, because "there is nothing that can come to me higher than that which

[77] These quotations are taken from a printed text in Root's papers for 1912, with the title "The Metropolitan Press on President Taft after Election."

[78] Pringle Papers, November 8, 1912. Not all Republicans accepted Taft's defeat with the poise demonstrated here. One Taft supporter sent a telegram to TR: "Having accomplished your purpose animated by a feeling of crazy jealousy and desire for revenge[,] and standing as the most colossal liar of the time[,] many former admirers are now trusting you will subside." Ibid., November 5, 1912.

[79] Ibid., November 5, 1912. A few weeks later, Taft reiterated that he had no objection to the states' implementing the initiative, referendum, and recall, "if they so desire." But "the real menace to our institutions is the disposition of the Bull Moosers to dispense with the constitution altogether and to transfer the power to the legislature." Popular efforts "to recall the judiciary would take away the chief instrument by which the rights of the minority and the individual are protected." Ibid, November 20, 1912.

I have had, and therefore I hope to be acquitted of personal ambition...."[80] In some respects, Taft was not a good prognosticator concerning his future.

He had not practiced law for more thirty years, and contrary to his assumption in 1912, in fact he never returned to it. Yet his relationship to legal activities was far from over. On the other hand, during the remaining eighteen years of his life, he neither sought nor served in elected office again. Nevertheless, in a real sense, the future brought a sort of ultimate redemption for Taft, but bitterness, defeat, and personal tragedy for both Roosevelt and Wilson.[81]

[80] Ibid, November 8, 1912.
[81] Gould, *Four Hats in the Ring*, 184.

9

Relief and Renewal, 1913–1921

Departing presidents have reflected a variety of sentiments as they left the White House. Andrew Johnson had little to say as he made way for Ulysses S. Grant, the former commander of the Union Army, while Theodore Roosevelt made it clear that he alone had decided not to seek a second full term. His disappointment at surrendering the office he loved, however, was palpable to all who knew him. Taft, on the contrary, welcomed his forced exit with obvious relief. In a perverse way, he considered that by blocking TR from election, he had actually attained a goal far more important than simply retaining his office. Now, the prospect of reemphasizing the dangers of 'Rooseveltism' to all who would listen seemed very attractive to him.

And what better forum in which to do this than at Yale University as a professor of law? Taft had frequently emphasized that as a young lawyer in Ohio, he always seemed be in the right place when the jobs were falling all around him. It happened once again early in 1913, when he accepted such an appointment from the university. The position obligated him to give lectures to the Yale undergraduates as well as to law students. Thus Taft foresaw a great opportunity where he could "proclaim the evangel [sic] of constitutionalism and international peace – the two objects that I have been anxious to use the rest of my life so that someday we shall secure that advantage which we lost during my administration."[1]

Taft found law school and undergraduate lecturing fulfilling but challenging. He welcomed the opportunity "to take little excursions into various new

---

[1] Pringle, 851. "For there is nothing in life," Taft added, "quite equal to the thought of being useful." Ibid. Within a few months, Yale also offered Taft the deanship, "but I declined it. It would require me to devote a great deal of attention to executive details that other men can perform better than I can...." Boardman Papers, September 23, 1913. Soon, Taft assisted in the quest for funds to rebuild Yale Medical School, and concluded that Andrew "Carnegie is a doddering old chunk of vanity and obstinate views, and I don't know that I can do anything with him." Ibid, April 14, 1914.

fields of knowledge," resulting in "the increased humility one has in regard to his own ignorance[,] and the wisdom of tentative conclusions on all subjects rather than a complete certainty." But in his own fields of municipal and constitutional law, his background and experiences "furnishes a reason for considering certainty as to what changes ought not to be made in our present structure." There remained, "of course ... a very large sphere for change and reform and experiment. I wish to avoid as far as I can dogmatism and rigid conservatism, but history teaches so certainly some truths that a man who does not accept them is blind."[2]

The former president's emphasis on constitutionalism, replete with both its potential and limitations, seemed even more important to him in the wake of TR's defeat. He noted to Mabel Boardman that the Republicans were talking of changing the basis of representation for the next convention, a move he supported because "the Southern end of the party has had much too great influence[,] and that it has always been a scandal." However, "it enabled us to beat Roosevelt, for which we perhaps ought to be chary of too much condemnation.... I am inclined to think that, as the years go on, and people look back, they will find no more satisfactory occasion for gratitude to me than for beating him in ... Chicago." If TR had been nominated, Taft added, he probably would have been elected, for Taft would never have bolted the party, and thus there would have been no one opposing TR on the Republican ticket. And "if he had been elected, I don't think anybody could measure the damage he would have done."[3]

While Taft's feeling of outrage receded, the lingering bitterness over Roosevelt's turn after 1910 toward what Taft considered socialism remained, even after some sort of rapprochement restored civility if not cordiality to their correspondence in 1918. And in an age of change, the rapidity with which that change had occurred not only made TR seem much more radical than in fact he was, but also made Taft appear more conservative than was actually the case. He wrote to Elihu Root that "the disquisitions of modern sociological jurists ... and economists ... excite my indignation, and with their assumption of omniscience shake the foundations of law as I have been trained to know them."[4] In reply, Root wrote that "you are in good luck to be out of all this. I wish I were out."[5] Taft responded with an observation that "of all the fools that I have run across, I think the Professors of Political Economy and ... indeed some of law – now at large in the University field, take the cake." He then commented on Charles Beard's newly published book dealing with an economic interpretation of the Constitution. Far from impressed, Taft wrote, "I suppose that he thinks the instrument would have been better if he could have demonstrated that the members of the Constitutional Convention were not men of substance but were dead bodies, out-at-the-elbows demagogues,

[2] Boardman Papers, January 6, 1914.
[3] Ibid., May 27, 1913.
[4] Root Papers, May 1, 1913.
[5] Ibid., May 3, 1913.

cranks who never had any money, and representatives of the purlieus [outsiders] of the population"[6]

Although Taft had welcomed Wilson's election, considering the alternatives he soon found more cause for criticism than congratulation. He did not hesitate, however, to acknowledge his own shortcomings by comparison with the new president. "I don't like to seem invidious in my reference to my successor, and I greatly admire his power which I never possessed, of using every means at hand to coerce men to follow his lead, for I like to see these independent Democrats, who were so courageous under other conditions, groveling before the man who carries the schoolmaster's rod...." Moreover, "the use of the Washington correspondents by this Administration for the presenting of its views has been masterly." Wilson's performance "moves me to say that Theodore is not the only pebble on the beach in the use of the press. It shows a keenness of the use of political instruments and an ability in this direction that[a]rouses my very great admiration."[7]

Taft's negative feelings toward TR included his conviction that Roosevelt would do all he could to gain the 1916 nomination. Although he was not privy to Roosevelt's correspondence, he was absolutely correct in this assumption. Again, TR indulged in all the mental machinations he had demonstrated in 1911–1912. In 1914, he wrote that "the people as a whole have had enough of all reformers and especially of me."[8] A few months later, he observed that "Taft is backing up Wilson," and that "one is as bad as the other."[9] As in 1912, TR once again steadfastly refused to state that under no conditions would he accept the Republican nomination.[10] Instead, he issued more evasive pronouncements such as, "If the country is not determined to put honor and duty ahead of safety, then the people most emphatically do not wish me for President."[11] Indeed, "they would only nominate me if they felt that public sentiment in my favor was overwhelming, and I do not see the slightest

---

[6] Ibid., May 5, 1913. "I beg you to get the book." Interestingly, in due course, Charles Beard reviewed Henry Pringle's biography of Taft for the *Columbia Law Review*, and wrote that Pringle's work "corrects the popular judgment that Taft was a do-nothing conservative," a conclusion that "well deserves to be spread upon the record. Indeed, placed against the background of good, old Republicanism, Mr. Taft was an almost dangerous 'progressive[,]' and his actual achievements in that line outweigh those of his rival of 1912...." Clipping in the Gifford Pinchot Papers, LOC, Box 347. Beard's insights remain noteworthy.

[7] Ibid. Taft knew whereof he spoke concerning the Washington correspondents and Wilson. One of the most knowledgeable of them was Gus Karger, the correspondent for Charles Taft's newspaper, *The Cincinnati Times-Star*, and a close friend/confidante of the former president's.

[8] Letters, vol. 8, November 19, 1914, 844.

[9] Ibid., February 22, 1915, 894.

[10] His contempt for the Regulars was unabated. "As for the Republican party, at the moment the dog has returned to its vomit." Ibid., November 7, 1914, 839.

[11] Ibid., February 4, 1916, 1014. "It would be an entirely unwise thing to nominate me, unless this country is in something of the heroic mood that it was in the time of the Revolution...." Ibid., February 8, 1915, 1016.

sign of such a condition of things."[12] Such sentiment was not very prevalent, and the editor of the Roosevelt Letters was accurate when he wrote that "the Republicans ... were determined to nominate anyone – and most probably [Charles Evans] Hughes – instead of Roosevelt."[13]

But early in 1915, Taft still had his doubts as to whether or not Charles Evans Hughes would accept the nomination. However, "our friend Theodore is trying to go in the game and indicate whom he will support and whom he will not.... If he will support Root, I think we ought to nominate Root, just to give him [TR] the pleasure of eating crow."[14] Yet by September 21, Taft had no doubt of TR's inability "to capture the Rep [sic] Convention.... He can't carry the primary States but if he could, he couldn't carry the rest of the country. He is dead[,] my dear Gus...."[15]

So Taft settled into a comfortable post-presidential career at Yale, one that lasted for eight years. But at the same time, he managed to build a side occupation as a lecturer to numerous clubs and organizations. Even if he had not been highly regarded in the White House, once outside of it, his attractiveness as a speaker was marked by great success. Indeed, he traveled again all over the country, and for fees ranging up to $1,000 per appearance. This was in addition to articles that he frequently produced for the more popular journals of the day. Invariably, he repeated the same lecture many times over, commenting on political trends of the times, always through the lens of one suspicious of Rooseveltian doctrine. Pringle does not exaggerate when he notes that Taft "was away from New Haven as much as he was there."

One of Taft's most popular lectures was called "The Signs of the Times." In it, Taft focused on Roosevelt's proposed popular recall of judicial decisions, and he loved to quote the well-known British historian Lord Acton, who had written that "government by the whole people being the government of the most numerous and most powerful class, is an evil of the same nature as unmixed monarchy, and requires for nearly the same reasons, institutions that shall protect it against itself, and shall uphold the permanent reign of law against arbitrary revolutions of opinion."[16] Another "and most dangerous result of this direct ... judicial decision by the people," Taft added, "is [that] it takes away all the security we have in the constitutional guaranty of personal rights. The constitution loses altogether its function as a restraint self-imposed by the people upon the temporary action of the electorate."[17]

[12] Letters, May 4, 1916, 1037.

[13] Ibid., vol. 8, n.1, 1052.

[14] Taft to Karger, April 1, 1915, Taft–Karger Correspondence, Mss qT1241k, Box 1, Folder 25, Cincinnati Museum Center. Hereafter cited as Taft–Karger Correspondence, followed by date ands folder number.

[15] Ibid., September 21, 1915, Folder 28.

[16] Boardman Papers, "The Signs of the Times," lecture delivered on September 6, 1913, p, 17.

[17] Ibid., 21. On the other hand, by 1916, in what turned out to be a futile attempt to reingratiate himself with Republicans, TR had backed away from the Initiative, Referendum, and Recall. Shortly before the Republican Convention, he wrote that "I never took any very strong ground about the Initiative, Referendum and Recall. I always said that they were pure pieces

Late in 1913, Taft's old friend and mentor Elihu Root received the Nobel Peace Prize. "I love you, old man," Taft wrote, "and nothing has done me so much good as [this] award ... to you." Perhaps thinking of his own past presidency, Taft added that "every once in a while, after one is discouraged at the lack of a sense of justice in the world, and the working out of proper rewards, something happens to convince you that after all, just compensation does come, and no recognition was ever more properly shown than in this last Nobel award. It makes me very happy."[18] For his part, Root continued to view Taft with a sardonic sense of warm regard. Noting the Taft habit of summering for as long as possible in Canada, Root wrote in 1914 that "I had begun to fear that you had been pressed into the Canadian contingent for the war in Europe and I thought we should never see you again, because if you ever got on the firing line it would be just about impossible for the Germans to miss you."[19]

EXTERNAL ISSUES

Replete with his professorial functions, his writing, and his public appearances, Taft kept an eye on his successor. During his first term, Wilson had three opportunities to nominate a new Supreme Court Justice. In July 1914, the death of Justice Lurton, according to Gus Karger, "once more brought your name forward. I think the reference, although intended as a compliment and a mark of respect to you, is entirely gratuitous."[20] Karger further informed Taft that Wilson intended to nominate his attorney general, James McReynolds, to the High Court. Taft replied that "I have not been at all excited by the suggestion of my name for the Supreme Court, nor have I ever been of the opinion that Wilson could rise to the point of generosity and broad view required to make an offer" to one such as himself." Indeed, "Wilson would no more think of offering me the appointment than he would of flying."[21] Already Taft had had one run in with McReynolds concerning an issue beyond the scope of this study, and he was not impressed with the man.[22]

of machinery. I still think they can be usefully employed in certain states at certain times. In other words, I was never ardent for them." Letters, vol. 8, May 16, 1916, 1043.

[18] Root Papers, December 12, 1913. Of course, Roosevelt had a very different perspective on Root, "who shared Taft's guilt four years ago. Indeed, if there must be a choice between them, I think that Root's offense was as rank as Taft's and more wanton." Letters, vol. 8, September 28, 1916, 1118.

[19] Ibid., September 12, 1914. Less than two months later, Root nominated Taft for membership in the Century Association, "not because he has been President, but because he is a delightful fellow, a most agreeable companion of very great ability.... His judicial opinions, his state papers, and his public addresses are all of a very high order. The very qualities which made him a poor politician made him a good judge. ... " Ibid, November 6, 1914.

[20] Karger to Taft, July 17, 1914, Taft–Karger Correspondence, Folder 22, Cincinnati Museum Center.

[21] Boardman Papers, July 15, 1914.

[22] The matter concerned the decision of the Lincoln Memorial Commission, on which Taft sat as chairman. The Commission had proposed that the new monument be built with Colorado

"McReynolds would not make a good no[r] a great judge. He is very narrow-minded, [and an] intense partisan, full of the wind of rhetoric, and of limited vision generally."[23] Taft's prescience concerning McReynolds is of interest if only because he was so accurate in his assessment. Uniformly regarded as one of the worst justices in the Supreme Court's history, in addition to having the flaws noted by Taft, McReynolds was disagreeable, bigoted in personality, and rude to members of the Court staff. In 1914, Taft could not foresee that when he finally took his seat on the Court as Chief Justice, McReynolds would have already been on the bench for seven years, and he would be there for another ten years after Taft resigned in February of 1930.

Partisan though he might be when commenting on Wilson's domestic agenda, in terms of foreign policy – especially during the early stages of World War I – Taft strongly supported his president. Alone among prominent Republican leaders, he endorsed Wilson's efforts at neutrality once the long-delayed conflict became a reality. Indeed, in the wake of the *Lusitania* sinking, Taft wrote a private letter to his successor. "War," he noted, "is a dreadful thing, [and] would involve such enormous cost of life and treasure for us that if it can now be avoided, in a manner consistent with the dignity and honor of our country, we should make every effort to this end. ... it would be most gratifying to have our nation take the position in favor of a peaceful mode of settling difficulties in the midst of war." Suggesting that Wilson might consider the breaking of diplomatic relations with Germany – a step that Wilson did take early in 1917 – Taft separated himself from TR's strident jingoism. "I am glad to have the opportunity of expressing to you my confidence that you will take the wise and patriotic course and that you will avoid war, if it is possible." But if Wilson saw no other way except "to summon Congress and declare war, of course the whole people will be with you without regard to party. With earnest prayer that you may good deliverance make," Taft signed this heartfelt letter to Wilson, who promptly acknowledged it with "the deepest appreciation."[24]

Of course, there was always politics, and late in December 1917, Taft observed that "the dead Progressive Party is like the legs of a frog after its head is cut off. The twitchings are seen in the string of Progressive ... correspondents that continue to distill the old virus ... that there is still a very great probability that [TR] may be called to the head of the ticket. This bogey continues to frighten regular Republicans" such as Senator Frank Brandegee, who wrote to Taft, urging after much backing and filling that he not attend the

marble. Southern Democrats in Congress objected, and launched a campaign to overrule the Commission's recommendation. Himself a conservative southern Democrat, McReynolds originally ruled against Taft's Commission. Ultimately, the memorial *was* built with Colorado marble, but the huge statue of Lincoln inside the structure was carved from Georgia marble. See the Root Papers for 1913–1914.

[23] Taft to Karger, July 20, 1914, Taft–Karger Correspondence, Folder 22, Cincinnati Museum Center.

[24] Ibid., May 10, 13, 1915, Folder 26, Cincinnati Museum Center.

forthcoming Republican Convention for fear of exacerbating old frictions.[25] Taft replied with a letter that bristled with candor:

"I rather think it has come ... to a pretty pass if a regular Republican with some standing in the party, cannot propose to go to a National Convention without arousing the fears of ... those who claim to be Republicans, and who are now coming back into the party.... One would think that a man who had led the party even to defeat might at least be allowed a seat in a convention of some 600 or 700 delegates, even at the risk of hurting somebody's feelings who had attempted to kill the party at the last election.... One of the difficulties with you gentlemen who live in Washington, and pick up your political information from the cloakrooms, is that ... the country moves on and that you ride with your backs to the engine. ... " Taft predicted that "there won't be any bolt at all, no matter who is nominated," and this included "the ridiculous proposal that Roosevelt may be the nominee...." What was wrong, he wondered, with having "everybody understand that we are a Republican and not a Progressive party, that we are not apologizing for Republican principles or Republican delegates."[26]

Taft's confident tone as well as his accurate assessment concerning TR, who like himself would never again hold elective office, was based in part on his willing acceptance of the fact that he was "out of politics." Even more than usual, he could afford to be candid. Regarding his comments to Brandegee, "I feel so out of it myself in every way that I think I can tell the cold truth ... for at least one Senator" about the "pusillanimous course that they allow to be put out as the judgment of Republicans in Congress." Taft predicted – correctly – to Gus Karger that the eventual nominee would be drawn from several possible candidates, including Charles Evans Hughes and Elihu Root.[27]

AGAIN LOUIS BRANDEIS

Before the Republican Convention was held, it fell to Wilson to replace yet another of Taft's Supreme Court selections, as Justice Joseph Lamar had died on January 2, 1916. Again Taft's name was mentioned, but the idea that Wilson would appoint Taft "only amuses me." Taft pointed out to Karger that with two Democrats on a nine-member bench, "it is more than human nature to expect that Democratic partisans would be willing to have a Republican appointed. Indeed, "they would not be willing ... even if there were eight Democrats on the Bench." For "the Democrats are quite willing to have

---

[25] Ibid., December 16, 1915, Folder 29, Cincinnati Museum Center.
[26] Ibid., December 27, 1915. Taft could not resist reminding Brandegee, a Republican "Old Guard" Senator from Connecticut, "that I hope the delegates to the next national Republican Convention will have more courage ... than the present representatives of that party in both Houses of Congress."
[27] Ibid.

non-partisan appointments made when they are out of office, but never when they are in."[28]

But if Taft found the nomination of McReynolds somewhat unappealing, he found Wilson's second choice singularly appalling. According to Karger, upon receiving official notification that Louis Brandeis had been nominated, "the Senate simply gasped."[29] Calling Wilson's choice a move of "devilish ingenuity," Taft described it as "one of the deepest wounds that I have had as an American and a lover of the Constitution and a believer in progressive conservatism." Moreover, Wilson had selected "a muckraker, an emotionalist ... a hypocrite, a man who has certain high ideals in his imagination, but who is utterly unscrupulous in method in reaching them, a man of infinite cunning ... and, in my judgment, of much power for evil."[30] Taft paid grudging tribute to Wilson's political skill in selecting a nominee who was completely unacceptable to the Senior Senator from Massachusetts – Henry Cabot Lodge. "When I consider the heartfelt indignation of Lodge and [Massachusetts Junior Senator, John] Weeks at having to alienate the Jews of Massachusetts with their candidacies just before them, I derive some wicked amusement."[31]

The president has "projected a fight, which with master art he will give the color of a contest, on one side of which will be ranged the opposition of corporate wealth and racial prejudice, and on the other side the down trodden, the oppressed, the uplifters [sic], the Labor unions, and all the elements which are supposed to have votes in the election." Wilson will win with Brandeis, Taft predicted, "because of the white livered Senators we now have. The Senate has been LaFolletized and Gomperized so that it has ceased to be the conservative body it was."[32] This appointment, he added, "will be remembered long after the excitement of the confirmation has passed away...."[33]

---

[28] Ibid., January 11, 1916, Folder 29, Cincinnati Museum Center.

[29] Ibid., Karger to Taft, January 29, 1916, Folder 30, Cincinnati Museum Center.

[30] Ibid., Taft to Karger, January 31, 1916. Among the papers of Brandeis biographer Lewis J. Paper is a letter to Paper from Arthur Schlesinger Jr. Schlesinger wrote that Brandeis "had the highest standards, but also the righteousness, or self-righteousness, that permitted him to violate standards he would insist on for others." Lewis J. Paper Papers, Harvard Law Library, Box 9, April 8, 1980. [Cited with permission.].

[31] Fully aware that in 1916, for the first time in his extended senatorial career, he would have to face the electorate in seeking to retain his Senate seat, Lodge knew only too well of Brandeis's great popularity as a reformer in a rapidly changing urban environment. He did not want to risk taking a lead in bringing about Brandeis's rejection, only to face a possible prospect of a contest with him for his long-held Senate seat. See A. L. Todd, *Justice on Trial: The Case of Louis D, Brandeis* (Chicago: University of Chicago Press, 1964), 82–85. Lodge left it to others to lead the ultimately unsuccessful efforts to reject the nomination.

[32] Taft to Karger, January 31, 1916, Taft–Karger Correspondence, Folder 30, Cincinnati Museum Center.

[33] Ibid. One might note Taft's accuracy, even if for the wrong reason! Taft's anger at Wilson lingered. Late in February, he thought that "the Jews have a right to complain that the first man selected from among them for the Bench should be of such a character." Ibid., February 20, 1916, Folder 30.

The lengthy Senate consideration of the Brandeis nomination should be seen in the context of issues such as Wilson's campaign for a second term, military preparedness, and the growing support for the Allied cause [in World War I]. Yet Taft continued to distance himself from the strident anti-German rhetoric that came from Lodge, TR, and even Elihu Root. Ever the lawyer, Taft consistently reflected his legal background. "No one has a stronger feeling of disgust towards the President that I have, but we ought to measure our words and select the proper grounds for attack[,] and make that attack forcible, less by the use of expletives than by the statement of facts."[34] Such would be the approach taken by Justice Charles Evans Hughes, who as early as January 1916 had received Taft's strong support for the presidential nomination.

"I will be very much gratified to have him nominated," all the more so as "Roosevelt could not afford to oppose him. He would merely put himself in a ridiculous position, and no one appreciates that more than" Roosevelt himself. "The consequence is that if Hughes is nominated[,] [TR] will take a good running jump right back into the Republican party and will be a perennial candidate."[35] Indeed, he will "jump into the campaign and call names and seek to make himself the leader of it – a situation which will make Hughes, with his judicial temperament, nervous and impatient, to a point where he will call out 'save me from my friends.'"[36] Moreover, "Hughes is the logical candidate, in the sense that he does not represent any of the bitterness of the issue of 1912. He was on the Bench at the time and could take no part in it."[37] Indeed, "if Hughes could be sure that Roosevelt would not run against him, as he certainly would not, I think he would accept the Republican nomination, and that is the way events are tending."[38]

As the presidential campaign wound down, Taft found himself strongly against Wilson's domestic policies. But the European war remained a very different matter, and "while I am pro-ally in my sympathies ... I am utterly opposed to the view that we now have a responsibility in respect to world matters that should carry us into this war ... I am utterly out of patience with any such view." Indeed, "while Wilson has not been as prompt and has been satisfied with phrases in his notes ... I sympathize with his desire to avoid war."[39] But such sympathy, while genuine, could not overcome Taft's great dislike for the president.

"It will be very hard for me to bear another administration of Wilson," Taft wrote just before the election. "I despise him so because of his hypocrisy."

[34] Ibid.
[35] Boardman Papers, January 18, March 28, 1916.
[36] Ibid., January 18, 1916.
[37] Ibid., February 20, 1916. "Roosevelt of course does not want Hughes, because he does not want anybody except Roosevelt, but I think the nomination of Hughes would be more agreeable to him than that of any other regular Republican, because he could save his face."
[38] Ibid., April 4, 1916. Earlier, Taft had noted that TR "is going to have political ambition[,] and be a candidate for the Presidency as long as he lives." Ibid., March 27, 1916.
[39] Ibid.

Perhaps with Wilson's nomination of Brandeis in mind, Taft added that "he will go far toward wrecking our system of government."[40] Taft also believed that the shrillness of TR's calls for preparedness had not helped the Republican cause. Even worse, TR was planning ahead for the 1920 campaign. TR "is like an old man of the sea on the back of the Republican party."[41] But Taft's resentment of Wilson was temporarily muted, for less than two months after his inaugural, Wilson asked for and received a declaration of war against Germany.

Taft watched with amusement rather than sympathy as TR vainly sought to raise a division of volunteers to fight in France, as his famous Rough Riders had done in Cuba, almost twenty years before in 1898. But neither the Secretary of War Newton Baker nor Wilson himself approved TR's request. Taft agreed, noting that "it would involve great risk to entrust 25,000 men to a commander so lacking in real military experience and so utterly insubordinate in his nature."[42] Moreover, the "splendid little war" to which TR had thrilled was now symbolic of a bygone era. In its place had come trenches, tanks, machine guns, barbed wire, airplane dogfights, and poison gas. A man in poor health, almost sixty years old, unfit to confront such an environment, "Roosevelt has been yelling himself hoarse for compulsory service, but when it works against him, it may not strike him [as] quite so favorable."[43]

By May 1918, TR and Taft had resumed a relationship of superficial cordiality, united by their mutual dislike and distrust of the president. Taft saw no political significance in the new rapprochement. Rather, "life is too short to preserve these personal attitudes of enmity, and I am glad to have the normal status resumed."[44] The immediate aim for both former presidents was the election of a Republican Congress in 1918. By the midpoint of his second term, Wilson had already displayed several examples of poor political judgment, not the least of which was his ill-conceived plea to the country that it elect a Democratic Congress, and this after repeated references to the need for Republicans and Democrats alike to work together in support of the war effort. Taft believed Wilson's move to be "an incredible blunder," and "one of those surprises ... which comes from his losing his bearings...."[45] In a similar vein, Taft felt that "Wilson is opening a Pandora's box by his trip[s] to Europe ... Certainly it is not wise politically."[46]

[40] Pringle, 899.
[41] Ibid.
[42] Taft to Karger, April 7, 1917, Taft–Karger Correspondence, Folder 38, Cincinnati Museum Center.
[43] Ibid. Denied his request to serve, Roosevelt's four sons all fought in the war. One of them was killed in 1918. TR never got over the loss of Quentin – his youngest son – and it probably contributed in part to his own death early in January 1919.
[44] Pringle, 911.
[45] Ibid., 913.
[46] Taft to Karger, Taft–Karger Correspondence, November 28, 1918, Folder 48, Cincinnati Museum Center.

In addition to his ongoing support for Wilson's efforts to bring about a League of Nations, Taft also agreed to serve as the cochairman of the National War Labor Board (NWLB), a position he held for some fourteen months, beginning on April 8, 1918. The Board included an equal number of representatives from employer groups, and organized labor, along with two cochairmen. Possibly because strikes and lockouts were deemed inimical to the war effort, Taft hoped "to arrange a truce between labor and capital in this country."[47] For more than a year, the Board did just that, and what is remarkable about Taft's accomplishment is the great extent to which he sided with labor against his own kind. "I had," he recalled, "to read the riot act to my people once or twice," but he "came into curiously agreeable relations with the labor men," and he demonstrated impressive doctrinal flexibility.[48] Taft's accomplishment is all the more surprising because he had "gone into this Labor Commission business not because I have been optimistic as to the business of our Conference … but because discouraging as the prospect is, I feel I have no right not to help to make an effort to secure some basis upon which labor and capital may be kept loyal during the war…." Capitalism, he added, "can be restrained by taxation and otherwise."[49]

Among the principles that Taft endorsed was the commitment to "a living wage," which "is to insure the subsistence of the worker and his family in health and reasonable comfort." Further, the employee rights to unionize and bargain collectively "are affirmed and may not be denied, abridged, or interfered with by the employers in any manner whatsoever," at least for the duration of the war. Taft even rejected "yellow dog contracts," which compelled workers not to join a union, with dismissal the inevitable result of violation. His refusal to enforce them is all the more striking because a divided Supreme Court had upheld such agreements in 1917.[50] The exigencies of war apparently overrode any constitutional scruples Taft may have had. His experience on the NWLB was yet another indication of what might be called his progressive flexibility. Indeed, no less a progressive than Justice Louis Brandeis told Taft "of the great service he had rendered the country by his action on the Labor Board."[51]

---

[47] Pringle, 916.

[48] Ibid., 917.

[49] Root Papers, March 12, 1918.

[50] Pringle, 920. The case is *Hitchman Coal and Coke Co. v. Mitchell*, 245 U.S. 229 (1917). Taft's attitude brings to mind the comments by Chief Justice Charles Evans Hughes, when the Court sustained a controversial Minnesota mortgage moratorium in 1934. Hughes, who had succeeded Taft as Chief Justice in 1930, commented that "the legislation is temporary in operation. It is limited to the exigency which called it forth." See *Home Building & Loan Association v. Blaisdell*, 290 U.S. 398, 447 (1934).

[51] Melvin I. Urofsky, *Louis D. Brandeis: A Life* (New York: Pantheon Books, 2009), 571.

TAFT AND THE LEAGUE

By mid-1918, Taft had emerged as the most prominent and strongest Republican supporter of Wilson's proposed League. Taft's stand placed him at odds not only with TR, and Cabot Lodge, for whom Taft had never possessed great regard, but also with Elihu Root, who, Taft believed, should have known better. Unlike Lodge and TR, whose growing dislike, if not detestation, for Wilson made it impossible for them to separate the League issue from their partisan zeal, Taft had no such difficulty, even as he joined TR in his calls for much more extensive military expansion. He noted that "Wilson is in love with his own style, and he is intoxicated with the commendation of it from the world. He seems never to read one message already delivered, or to consider what he said in it, before writing another." Thus Taft found himself in the difficult position of supporting Wilson's proposal even as he deprecated Wilson's domestic policies. This duality produced some stress for the former president, a strain that grew more pronounced during 1919–1920.

In June 1919, for example, Taft insisted that debate over the League "is not a partisan question. We should be for or against [it] without respect to whether we are Democrats or Republicans...." Such "considerations of this kind are reasons which should have no influence with us in determining an issue so fateful in the world's History[,] and so likely to affect the future welfare of ... all mankind." The real question about the League is, "will it do good for this country or mankind? If it will, let us favor it." Those who oppose the League should base their position "on high and patriotic reasons. But "when we approach the question of the League ... from that standpoint, I do not doubt that the great majority of the people ... and the needed majority of the Senators ... will approve this League."[52]

During much of 1919, Taft crisscrossed the country, rallying all who would listen to support Wilson's League, and at the same time railing against "the narrow partisanship and the brute willingness of these little Americans in the Senate...." His descriptions of some Senate Republicans illustrate his ire: "vicious narrowness," "explosive ignorance," "selfishness, laziness and narrow lawyer-like acuteness," "emptiness and sly partisanship." Indeed, "it is their American selfishness, their American littleness, blinding them to the real interests of this nation, as well as of the world, that rouses me."[53] Such an attitude led Taft to support yet another progressive measure, albeit at a late date, and with a patronizing air.

"I am inclined to think," he wrote, "that modern progress requires that women's influence be allowed to exert itself through the ballot.... Of course it will dilute the electorate by introducing a good deal of ignorance into it in greater proportion than now exists, and the still greater element of

[52] Joseph Tumulty Papers, LOC, June 7, 1919.
[53] Taft to Karger, February 19, 22, 1919, Taft–Karger Correspondence, Folder 48, Cincinnati Museum Center.

inexperience." Since "they are half the people, it would seem that they were entitled to an equal voice in determining the questions of the obligations we ought to assume now in order to prevent war in the future."[54]

By mid-1919, the issue of reservations attached to the Versailles Treaty had arisen. Taft never lost sight of the key goal. If the reservation "does not interfere with the substance of the League, I do not care so long as it means a League."[55] But it soon became very clear that the president, still in Europe, would accept no reservations whatsoever. A confidential telegram wired to Taft on June 24 stated that "the President says that his clear conviction is that adoption of treaty with reservations would put the United States as clearly out of council of nations as rejection; that we ought to either go in or stay out."[56] Yet Taft still hoped for presidential flexibility. "Wilson can carry substantially what he wishes with some reservations[,] if he does not drive the Republicans to blind fury. His appeal will be much more influential with the people if he ... does not attack the opposition."[57]

A few days later, Taft admitted to Karger that "I fear the President's lack of tact. If I could help to bring a compromise from him and the Democrats, I would come to Washington[,] but that is very far along."[58] Committed to the League, and able to perceive what Wilson apparently could not, Taft felt frustrated in his dealings with the Senators. "I ought not to get so wrought up in a cause," he wrote to Nellie. "One should moderate his enthusiasm especially where he is in a situation of helplessness. If I were only a member and could plead with members, intensity of interest producing intensity of activity might help, but not in my present plight."[59]

Taft remained concerned with the apparent use of Article X of the League Covenant as a lightning rod to attract anti-Wilson hostility (much in evidence) rather than anti-League sentiment. Its key provision apparently obligated League members "to respect and preserve as against external aggression the territorial integrity and existing political independence of all members...."[60] Republican proposals to delete the word "preserve" irritated Taft. It "of course would largely destroy the effect of the article as an effective and useful

[54] Ibid.

[55] Ibid., March 1, 1919, Folder 50. Months before the ultimate stalemate between Lodge and Wilson killed the League, Taft had already demonstrated that flexibility so lacking in the president. Moreover, and surprising in one who after all had been trained in law, Wilson "never answers any argument at all. He usually defies his opponent in many different way, and makes a number of taking apothegms [sic] and epigrams, states a few high ideals and lets it goes at that."

[56] Karger to Taft, ibid., June 24, 1919, Folder 52.

[57] Taft to Karger, ibid., June 26, 1919, Folder 52.

[58] Ibid., June 29, 1919, Folder 52.

[59] Ibid. Undated, but mailed to Karger on June 13, 1919. On July 9, Karger wrote to Taft concerning the League that "at the present writing it doesn't seem to have a Chinaman's chance." Ibid., July 9, 1919, Folder 53.

[60] Covenant of the League of Nations, Avalon Project, Yale Law Library, http://avalon.law.yale.edu.

and threatening declaration … and the more you weaken it, the less useful the League becomes."[61] As to what Taft considered the specious claim that would be inappropriately limited by the League, such a view "is domineering, is bullying, is offensive, and is wholly unwarranted by any precedent." I "would not consent at all, and I did not think Wilson would, to elimination of Article X." Reasonable compromise, such as limiting American involvement for an initial five years, was not unreasonable, "but I wish it always to be distinctly understood that I think the Covenant as it is entirely safe for the United St[ates]. and that we might well ratify the treaty without a change…."[62]

Taft even drafted several proposed compromises on his own, and sent them in confidence to several senators, on the assumption that they might serve as a rallying point for those willing to accept reasonable reservations. He hoped that "they can create a group that will grow and will ultimately bring Lodge down to his milk, for Lodge will run like a turkey as soon as he sees the prospect of defeat. He will not wish to appear in the crowd voting against the ratification of a treaty with reasonable interpretations."[63] Increasingly, Taft found himself comparing Lodge with Wilson. While both were arrogant and opinionated individuals, Taft in mid-summer of 1919 still believed that Lodge might yet be brought around to some sort of accommodation concerning the League.

In August, he faulted "the demagogic motives that Lodge has, though he clothes what he does, under the influence of those motives…. One of the features of Lodge's character, however, is that his vanity is usually satisfied by … receiving the plaudits of those who hear him. After that[,] he is usually content to settle down and consent to concessions quite beyond his position in his speech."[64] In the same letter to Karger (June 29, 1919), however, Taft also noted "Wilson's announcement … that he would never consent to textual amendments." Moreover, Wilson's growing tendency to accept no advice or counsel even from his own secretary of state troubled Taft. "[Robert] Lansing is a pathetic figure. A Law Clerk, promoted to be a Secretary of State, finds himself treated like a Law Clerk, because Wilson does not want anything but Law Clerks."[65]

Writing from his vacation home in Canada, Taft now accepted the reality that "the only hope of the treaty is through the mild reservationists, and that they may be strengthened … so they may not be gathered into the group of

---

[61] Taft to Karger, Taft–Karger Correspondence, July 10, 1919, Folder 53, Cincinnati Museum Center.

[62] Ibid.

[63] Ibid., July 27, 1919, Folder 54. Unfortunately for Taft, the letters were somehow released to the press, resulting in what might be called a hardening of the categories on all sides. Taft had tried "to have interpretations and a reservation in view of the situation which Wilson himself had created[,] and thus … made impossible the bringing over of enough Republicans to ratify the treaty as it is." Ibid., July 26, 1919.

[64] Ibid., August 18, 1919, Folder 55.

[65] Ibid., August 15, 1919, Folder 54.

militant obstructionists," a group that included Senate Republicans Lodge, Knox (Taft's former secretary of state), Brandegee, and Borah, "all ... vociferously defying the President and attacking the treaty."[66] Taft believed that these militants risked disassociation from the mainstream of their party. But Taft also understood that "this view may grow out of my earnest desire in the matter and may not reveal a sense of proportion which a fuller and closer intimacy with the situation would give me.[67] Meanwhile, he watched Wilson's ill-fated tour with concern, and observed that the president and his fellow Democrats "have got to recognize that reservations must be made a part of the ratification[,] and that the real fight is as to what the character of the reservations shall be."[68] Taft still believed that if the moderate Republicans, aka "mild reservationists," could join with the Democrats, the treaty might yet gain ratification by isolating the resistance to the proposal as typified by Lodge.[69] But such a hope was based on the assumption that moderate changes would be acceptable to Wilson.

By September 13, 1919, Taft was informed that "by declining to permit the Democrats to dicker with the mild reservations," Wilson "has hog-tied them."[70] He responded that Wilson's "obstinate adherence to a ratification of the treaty without change," had weakened the reservationists.[71] Six days after Wilson's forced return to Washington, Taft indicated that despite the fact that he had been and would always be a Republican, he did not "propose to play an acquiescing part in the destroying of the treaty and the League through the obstinacy and egotism of Woodrow."[72] Indeed, he had little sympathy for Wilson, who remained confined to his bedroom and incommunicado to the Washington establishment. "The truth is that he has [so] insisted on hogging all the authority ... trusting no one, that he has broken himself down."[73] Furthermore, by November, it was clear to Taft that some Democrats "are playing politics as well as a good many Republicans." Possibly with himself in mind, he added that "it makes a man who is seeking earnestly the treaty, sick to find the same spirit on both sides."[74]

---

[66] Ibid., August 24, 1919, Folder 55. So concerned was Taft that he was willing to return to Washington. [I]f it is thought that I can do anything, I would give up every other consideration to help."

[67] Ibid., August 30, 1919, Folder 55. Sadly, Taft was correct.

[68] Ibid., September 8, 1919, Folder 56.

[69] Karger reported that "I found Lodge very emphatic ... 'I mean to kill Article X or kill the treaty,' is the way he put it. By that he meant ... that no Council shall dictate to the United States to go to war." Karger to Taft, Taft–Karger Correspondence, September 10, 1919, Folder 56, Cincinnati Museum Center.

[70] Ibid., September 13, 1919. Writing to Taft, Karger added that "I can find no one in the Senate who believes that Mr. Wilson's tour has helped."

[71] Ibid., undated, but clearly between September 15 and September 30, 1919, Folder 57.

[72] Ibid., September 30, 1919, Folder 57.

[73] Pringle, 948.

[74] Taft to Karger, Taft–Karger Correspondence, November 1, 1919, Folder 58, Cincinnati Museum Center.

Now Taft could see virtually no difference between Lodge and Wilson. "The whole world," he wrote, "has suffered through the bitter personal antagonism, vanity and smallness of two men, Henry Cabot Lodge and Woodrow Wilson."[75] Indeed, "as between Lodge and Wilson there is very little difference." Yet Taft realized that if the "bitter enders" [those Republican Senators who opposed the treaty in any form] joined the Democrats who would follow Wilson's inflexibility, "I presume there will be enough to beat it. We have had a good many instances of blundering, but certainly this is the worst."[76] Unfortunately, "Wilson ... has just as much of vanity and egotism and a disregard of the country's welfare and that of the world as has Lodge or ... Knox, Borah, Brandegee and that gang."[77]

By December 1919, Taft would gladly have accepted the treaty with reservations, if such was the price required for Senate ratification. To be sure, in July, as we have seen, he saw no need to change the treaty at all. But throughout the summer, he had demonstrated a pragmatic flexibility utterly lacking in Wilson, while Lodge – who was fully capable of compromise when he wished to do so – manipulated Wilson's intransigence with a skillful malevolence into a scenario where Wilson's rigidity doomed his League. Taft could only lament "the humiliating spectacle that we are making of ourselves before the world."[78]

The end was anticlimactic, and "of course I don't withhold blame from Lodge ... but it rested on Wilson to save the treaty from death and he declined to do it.... Indeed[,] he could have secured some more concessions had he been willing to compromise at all, but his vanity, his selfishness, his egotism and his mulishness all interfered."[79] Further, "the League is not the important issue Wilson would have it. Wilson by killing it in a deadlock tired the mass of the people[,] and they refuse to get excited in his behalf...."[80] As for the 1920 election, Taft remained very disappointed with his party, and did not hesitate to say so. Although he had worked for a League even before Wilson proposed it, he still would vote for Harding, and if the nominee did not like "my comment and criticism of his attitude," that was unfortunate. "What I have said I believe[,] and I am too old I hope to pervert facts to please the Powers that be."[81]

The former president, understandably disappointed with the League fiasco, wrote that "I am suffering a good deal in my pride of country and hope for better things when I consider the mediocre men we have to vote for this year."

---

[75] Ibid, November 3, 1919, Folder 58.
[76] Ibid., November 11, 1919, Folder 59.
[77] Ibid., December 7, 1919, Folder 59.
[78] Ibid.
[79] Ibid., March 23, 1920, Folder 62. "Wilson butchered the League when he refused reservations." Ibid., July 20, 1920, Folder 64.
[80] Ibid., August 1, 1920, Folder 65. Taft added that Wilson not only killed the league, but killed interest in it also.
[81] Ibid. "I feel it in my bones that Harding is to be elected by a large majority."

As a loyal Republican, of course Taft would vote for Harding, "but [he] falls so far below the standard of Presidents we like to form in our minds that it distresses me. I am much disappointed in his outgivings.... Everything sounds cheap and makes a man of intelligent discrimination ... wince when [he] reads."[82] Moreover, "Harding will be elected wholly without regard to the League issue."[83] Rather, "the minds of the voters are fixed on one thing only[,] and that is to get rid of Wilson."[84] This they did, "and "the overwhelming character of the election exceeded the brightest hopes of any of us, I presume."[85]

AT LAST

Taft watched with some interest as Harding selected several outstanding figures for his cabinet, including Charles Evans Hughes, Herbert Hoover, and Henry Wallace. Responding to a prior invitation, Taft met with the president-elect and his wife on Christmas Eve. Taft later reported to Nellie that his discussions with Harding had been extensive. At one point, the president-elect asked, "Would you accept a position on the Supreme Bench?" Taft replied that "it was and always had been the ambition of my life," and explained why he had turned down TR's earlier offers of such an appointment. But much had changed since 1902, and "having been President, and having appointed three of the present bench and three others ... I could not accept any place but the Chief Justiceship ... " Harding "said nothing more about it."[86]

Taft "was nearly struck dumb when [Harding] asked me if I would go on the Supreme Court." Indeed, he wrote a letter to Harding on Christmas Day stating that what ever Harding decided, "I should still be very grateful for the honor he had done me in making the offer." Taft added "that many times in the past the Chief Justice had said he was holding the office for me[,] and that he would give it back to a Republican Administration."[87] In the meantime, Taft had been informed that Senator Brandegee – in spite of earlier disagreement with Taft concerning the 1912 Republican split – had "spoke[n] to Harding, and said he wished to press me for Chief Justice[,] and that Harding

[82] Ibid., August 22, 1920, Folder 65. Taft's comments bring to mind Wilson's son-in-law William McAdoo's famous remark that Harding's speeches "left the impression of an army of pompous phrases moving over the landscape in search of an idea; sometimes these meandering words would actually capture a straggling thought and bear it triumphantly in their midst, until it died of servitude and overwork." www.wolfscape.com/humour/quotes.htm. H. L. Mencken was more brutal, as well as blunt: Harding "writes the worst English I have ever encountered. It reminds me of a string of wet sponges.... It is so bad that a sort of grandeur creeps into it...." Jack Lynch, *Guide to Grammar and Style* (http://ethnicity.rutgers.edu/~jlynch/writing/n.html).

[83] Taft to Karger, September 15, 1920, Taft–Karger Correspondence, Folder 65, Cincinnati Museum Center.

[84] Ibid., September 24, 1920, Folder 66.

[85] Ibid., November 8, 1920, Folder 67.

[86] Ibid., December 26, 1920, Folder 68.

[87] Ibid. Taft had promoted Justice Edward White to the center seat in 1910.

had said that would be agreeable to him. I don't feel at all confident that it will work out as I would like it, but it is more favorable to my hope and life ambition than I thought possible."[88] So, as the new year dawned, and Harding prepared to take the oath of office, he had already received several indications concerning Taft's interest in the Chief Justiceship.[89] All that was necessary was a vacancy for Harding to fill, and thus far, regardless of any verbal assurances to the contrary, Chief Justice White had shown no inclination to provide it.

Taft grew frustrated as by mid-March he had "heard nothing ... upon which I can assume that [C. J. White] really intends to retire." He realized that "as old men draw near the time[, they] are loth ... to admit that age is affecting their usefulness." Indeed, "they are very reluctant to do so and accept any excuses to delay."[90] With his [White's] well-known deafness, as well as a need for cataract surgery, "there is, therefore, every reason why he should think it reasonable to retire." But Taft sensed that the older members of the Court "have rather resented the frequent references to appointments ... when ... there are no vacancies."[91] Moreover, Harding had repeatedly reiterated his promise to name Taft as Chief Justice.

On March 25, 1921, Taft visited Chief Justice White who "said nothing to me about retiring. He spoke of his illness ... and he complained of the burden of work that he had."[92] Perhaps Taft recalled the famous paraphrase of a Thomas Jefferson observation in 1801 concerning Federalist judges that "few die and none resign."[93] He decided, however, that "I don't think any intervention of mine will hasten matters."[94] By April 1, Taft was informed of a statement by Justice William Day that the Chief "has indicated to no one any intention of resigning, "and in Day's opinion, "no such intention exists." As Karger put it, "the situation seems to rest in the lap of the gods, or in the lap of Mr. White."[95] Taft reconciled himself to continuing uncertainty, noting that "I can get on without further good luck. I have had so much happiness thus far that I have no right to expect exceptional strokes of good fortune."[96]

[88] Ibid.
[89] Indeed, Karger informed Taft on January 14, 1921, that Harding's confidante, campaign manager and soon to be attorney general, Harry M. Daugherty, had made it clear that Harding intended to appoint Taft. Karger to Taft, January 14, 1921, Taft–Karger Correspondence, Folder 69, Cincinnati Museum Center. Apparently Daugherty reiterated the same point on February 4, 1921, Folder 69.
[90] Ibid., March 14, 1921, Folder 70.
[91] Ibid.
[92] Ibid., March 26, 1921, Folder 70.
[93] The actual quotation from a letter is "how are vacancies to be obtained? Those by death are few, by resignation none." See Papers of Thomas Jefferson, vol. 34 (Princeton: Princeton University Press, 1950), 556.
[94] Taft–Karger Correspondence, March 26, 1921, Folder 70.
[95] Karger to Taft, April 1, 1921, Taft–Karger Correspondence, Folder 71, Cincinnati Museum Center.
[96] Taft to Karger, ibid., April 6, 1921.

On May 19, Taft informed Karger that "the unexpected has happened – Chief Justice White is dead. And now the question is 'what is to be done?'"[97] Newspaper opposition to Taft's appointment based on his age had already appeared, and for good reason. It will be recalled how as incoming president, Taft had emphasized the need to rejuvenate the old Court. In fact, he had pledged that he would name no judge over the age of sixty – a rule he had violated with impunity in the case of Horace Lurton and White himself. Now, Taft shamelessly put himself forward despite the fact that he would be sixty-four in September. Thus, as a result of "this attack on me because of my age, it would seem better to make the appointment" before then.[98]

But this proposed timetable apparently did not appeal to President Harding, who was eager to name former Senator George Sutherland to the Court at the same time as he submitted Taft's nomination. A two-term Senator from Utah, Sutherland had been defeated for reelection in 1917. For years he had been a close friend and advisor to Warren Harding. Indeed, he probably had a greater claim on Harding's regard than did Taft. Taft knew and respected Sutherland. But "Sutherland ought to be reasonable. My appointment earlier will not interfere with his."[99] In the meantime, "we must abide events with patience and with a full realization that there is many a slip betwixt the cup and the lip." Taft feared that the long delay would give "those opposed to me an opportunity to emphasize my age...." With a major newspaper printing the ages of the Justices: "Holmes' 80 years, McKenna's 77 and Day's 72 are formidable."[100]

By the end of May, Taft was further perturbed by a rumor that Harding would appoint Justice Day as Chief Justice with the understanding that Day would resign in a few months, thus giving Harding the dual vacancies he sought. Although there was no evidence linking the president to such a scheme, Taft did not hesitate to denounce it. The "idea of appointing Day ... is trifling with a great office, and using it merely as an inducement to retire. It is undignified, and I want nothing to do with it."[101] While Taft had received word of numerous newspaper endorsements, "somehow or other I have a feeling that the appointment is not coming to me. However, we shall see what we shall see."[102] In June, Taft seemed to reflect a sort of pessimistic optimism. The position of Chief Justice "is so great a one that it should not come in an easy way

[97] Ibid., May 19, 1921, folder 72. The complete lack of any sympathetic tone concerning White's death in Taft's letter is striking, although he had already released a tribute to the press, and is indicative of the almost single-minded determination he demonstrated in moving to gain the center seat.

[98] Ibid.

[99] Ibid. Nor ultimately did it. Sutherland would be Harding's second appointment to the High Court, in 1922.

[100] Ibid., May 21, 1921, Folder 73.

[101] Ibid., May 30, 1921, Folder 73.

[102] Ibid. In reply, Karger concluded that the problem lay in Harding's tendency to delay, rather than in any doubt that ultimately Taft would be selected. Ibid., June 3, 1921. Taft had,

... and if it does come, one will be quite willing to have gone through some suspense and some worry before getting it."[103]

Indeed, Taft had done so, as he waited in suspense for some forty days, Finally, on June 30, Harding sent Taft's nomination to the Senate, which did not even bother to refer it to the Judiciary Committee. Taft was confirmed – though not unanimously – on the same day, and eagerly took up the position he had sought for so many years. No other Chief Justice in our history had come to the center seat with such a varied past. "What," wrote Gus Karger, "a wonderful realization of a life-long ambition."[104]

---

however, sounded out "Holmes and Day on the question of their resigning only to learn that neither one had any intention of so doing." Ibid., June 14, 1921, Folder 74. But Karger still believed that the final outcome was certain. Ibid., June 18, 1921.

[103] Ibid., June 21, 1921, Folder 74.
[104] Karger to Taft, June 30, 1921, Taft–Karger Correspondence, Folder 75, Cincinnati Museum Center.

Epilogue

Although not apparently given to deep introspection, Taft was quick to note, as he did soon after Harding's inauguration, that "I would rather have been Chief Justice than President."[1] Almost four years into his tenure as Chief Justice, he recalled that "in my present life I don't remember that I ever was president."[2] Of course, no president ever forgets his term in office, and neither did Taft. One suspects that he was referring to much of the unpleasantness that dogged him – especially after 1911. He wrote no memoir, unlike his wife, but he amassed thousands of letters and documents. Taft had planned to have Gus Karger write his biography, yet that project terminated with Karger's unexpected death in 1924.

In his outstanding biography of Louis Brandeis, Melvin Urofsky asks, "How did a man who throughout his life considered himself a conservative become a liberal icon?"[3] For a study of Taft, the question might be "how did a self-proclaimed progressive-conservative become so widely seen as an old school traditionalist?" In these chapters, I have argued that until Taft went on the High Court, he had indeed been a progressive conservative. Yet Urofsky's query has relevance for this study. It forces us to rethink not only what the hidebound terms "conservative" and "progressive" meant in Taft's era, but also what they have come to mean today. The contemporary historian still confronts, and should resist, the tendency to produce "Whig" history – that is, to look at the past through contemporary values of the present (in this instance, post–New Deal and progressive historiography) rather than through the values and mores of the era that is the subject of historical inquiry. As one examines the themes highlighted in these chapters, one realizes, hopefully, that what Taft meant by the word "conservative" is not necessarily what contemporary historians mean.

[1] Ross, 324.
[2] Pringle, 960.
[3] Urofsky, xii.

In the Preface to this volume, I cite Taft as describing himself in 1916 as "a believer in progressive conservatism." He presumably intended this self-depiction to include his entire career to that date – not just his presidency. One suspects further that Taft saw neither incompatibility nor inconsistency in using the two words together. In this, he was not alone. Preparing to offer himself as a progressive alternative to Taft in 1912, Theodore Roosevelt emphasized that "we are the true conservatives, for in the long run it will be found that the only true conservative is the man who resolutely sets his face towards the future...."[4] Two months before the 1912 election, TR added that "I have always believed that wise progressivism and wise conservatism go hand in hand, and that the wise conservative must be a progressive because otherwise he works only for that species of reaction which inevitably in the end produces an explosion."[5] Taft probably agreed more than he disagreed with TR.

What concerned both men was the ability of the political process to change in all its facets – economic, social, legal. Like most conservatives, Taft believed that the legal order had a primary obligation to protect property rights. But few were the progressives who repudiated outright such a view. They insisted, rather, that protecting property rights had to be interpreted on a much broader basis, and that the role of government in such a process was to be expanded and not limited. Further, they called for a greater role of academic expertise in government. In multiple instances, Taft's actions as president reflected similar values. In 1909, for example, Taft stated that "I am strongly convinced that the Government should make itself as responsible to employees injured in its employ as an interstate-railway corporation is made responsible by federal law to its employees." Here, Taft urged a larger role for the federal government in dealing with workman's compensation for its employees.

More than any other president before him, Taft augmented the scope of commissions during his administration. Mention has been made of his insistence on a tariff commission. But Taft also created a commission on efficiency within the federal government. Among other things, it called for submission of a unified federal budget by the president, and a Defense Department in place of the old War and Navy Departments. Taft strongly supported such an innovation, but it did not come about until after World War II. Similarly, he endorsed the lengthy findings of his efficiency commission, and indeed ordered members of his cabinet to submit their annual budgets directly to him, only to see Congress intervene and block him from such a step, in spite of Taft's insistence that "it was entirely competent for the President to submit a budget."[6] In his emphasis on modernized executive administration, this Chief Executive was well ahead of his time.

A standard measure of TR's success as a progressive is his accomplishments in antitrust enforcement and conservation. It is true that, compared

[4] Roosevelt, Letters, vol. 7, March 1, 1912, 514.
[5] Ibid., August 14, 1912, 597.
[6] Gould, 124.

with previous Chief Executives, Roosevelt was indeed an effective trustbuster, and he, together with his aides James Garfield and Gifford Pinchot, broke new ground in bringing about new federal regulations to preserve the public lands. But in terms of conservation, TR sometimes obtained results by ignoring a statute enacted by Congress. In one instance, Roosevelt took advantage of the time between passage of the bill restricting additions to the public domain, and when he had to sign the statute, to add a vast amount of acreage to it. Pinchot, in particular, had encouraged TR in his conservation efforts, regardless of the law.

Such tactics offended Taft the lawyer and jurist. Pinchot's proclivity for ignoring his "boss," the Secretary of the Interior, and going right to TR was equally unacceptable to Taft, as was TR's conduct concerning Congress. Lost in the hubbub over the Ballinger–Pinchot dispute, one that dogged Taft throughout the remainder of his administration, was the fact that the conservation measure initiated and ultimately signed by Taft placed more lands within the public domain than had been the case with TR. Taft liked to say that his accomplishments would, he hoped, speak for him. But it would have done him no harm to have had someone with the flair that TR demonstrated during his conservation crusades, pointing them out to the public.

So, too, in antitrust policy, Taft enforced the Sherman Act as it had never been enforced before. TR had picked his antitrust suits with some care, newsworthy but few in number. In the four years that Taft was in office, significantly more antitrust prosecutions were launched than in the seven years of TR's administration. Further, Taft rejected the Roosevelt distinction between good trusts and bad trusts. Nor did he accede to TR's insistence that it was impossible to break up large trusts. Rather, he insisted on "the continuous prosecution of all these combinations until they learn better." The issue was power rather than size, and Taft's Attorney General George Wickersham put it well when he noted that "the essence of monopoly is always the power ... to fix prices, control supply and exclude or admit competitors at will."[7] Again, few were the progressives who would disagree.

One should also recall the progressive nature of Taft's service on the National War Labor Board, on which he supported a minimum wage, collective bargaining, and even a temporary ban on "yellow dog contracts." His approach reminds one of a remark by George Bancroft, a famous nineteenth century American historian. In 1834, Bancroft had observed that "the feud between the capitalist and the laborer, the house of Have and the house of Want is as old as social union, and can never be entirely quieted; but he who will act with moderation, prefer facts to theories, and remember that everything in this world is relative and not absolute will see that the violence of the contest may be stilled, if the unreasonable demands of personal interests are subjected to the decisions of even-handed justice."[8] It would be difficult to find

---

[7] Ibid., 165.
[8] Quoted in http://www.digitalhistory.uh.edu/historyonline/us13.cfm

a better description of the progressive approach Taft brought to his work on the NWLB. Further, we can remember Taft's strong support for arbitration agreements, to say nothing of his deep enthusiasm for a League of Nations – a level of support unmatched by other Republicans.

With such evidence in hand, nevertheless one discovers that Taft's progressive innovations have been given short shrift by historians, in part because Taft lacked not only the flair for the dramatic, but also the talent for effective writing and speaking. In truth, he was boring – honest, likeable, but boring. His messages to Congress reflected his style: extensive, thorough, and by 1912, so long that they had to be broken down in separate messages sent up to Congress over several weeks. They did not capture public interest probably because the public did not bother to read them. His single presidential term highlighted administrative reforms within the federal establishment, not in themselves of great public concern. In one way, a fortunate characteristic, in another, less so, the lack of a dramatic incident – such as the great coal strike of 1902 – lessened public attentiveness to his administration.

Another aspect of Taft's tenure diminished his effectiveness. He got out of Washington as often as he could, thus removing himself from the tensions of politics and power. No president before him had traveled and utilized the automobile to the extent he did. All too often, he arranged to be away from the White House when his presence might have been important. One example is the successful internal coup against Speaker Cannon in 1910. Taft's intentional absence from the Capitol left the impression that he was a supporter of the beleaguered speaker's. In fact, Taft was more troubled as he considered the extent to which it was proper or improper for a president to meddle in an internal dispute within the House of Representatives.

In short, for a variety of reasons, segments of the public were not as inspired by Taft as they were by TR, nor – especially in his first term – by Woodrow Wilson. Taft's ineffectiveness as a communicator lessened public awareness, let alone appreciation, of his progressive measures. Taft could never have concluded a speech – whatever the occasion – with the declamation that "we stand at Armageddon and we battle for the Lord!" But he felt committed to ordered change, and it is reflected in the various progressive measures mentioned earlier. While he might (and did) characterize Justice McReynolds as a "reactionary," Taft described himself as a believer in progressive conservatism. He was neither energetic nor dynamic, but when properly channeled, he embraced change.

A final reason for the lack of interest in Taft's progressive conservatism should be noted. The conservatives of today have co-opted progressive forms such as the initiative and referendum, but for their own purposes. Indeed, they have turned progressivism upon itself. Thus, contemporary conservative activists have gone far beyond Taft in their activism against what has become known as the progressive state.[9]

---

[9] See the insightful comments in Milkis, pp. 291–292.

When the former president became Chief Justice, his court confronted problems and challenges different from those he had faced in the White House.[10] Further, his brethren had a very different relationship to him than to his cabinet. Indeed, he saw dissents and judicial disagreements in a very different light.[11] If he became more conservative as Chief Justice than as Chief Executive, such a fact should not detract from his progressive record as president.

Although he could not know it, Taft would serve for barely eight years on the High Court. If he is not remembered for many distinguished opinions, as an able administrator he transformed the Court's procedures and practices. No other Chief Justice in U.S. history has exercised the administrative skills utilized by Taft. The final years of his life were spent in an atmosphere free from the political machinations of the presidency, in which he had been more or less a failure. While the fabled cherry trees in Washington represent a suitable monument to Nellie Taft, there is no memorial to her husband, except perhaps the magnificent home for his Court – one for which he eagerly planned. But he died even before ground was broken for the structure. As he reacted to his overwhelming defeat for reelection in 1912, Taft had written that "I must wait for years if I would be vindicated by the people.... I am content to wait."[12] Perhaps he has waited long enough.

---

[10] This epilogue comments only peripherally on Taft's term as Chief Justice, as I am preparing a separate volume on his tenure from 1921 to 1929.

[11] See Jonathan Lurie, "Chief Justice Taft and Dissents: Down with the Brandeis Briefs," 32 *Journal of Supreme Court History* (2007), 178–189.

[12] Pringle, 842

Bibliographical Note

This bibliographical note is brief because all the sources utilized and/or cited in these chapters have been listed in the notes. Further, Lewis Gould in his recent book, *The Taft Presidency (2009)*, has included an excellent and extensive bibliographical essay. Readers who wish to go further on the Taft era should refer to Gould. Rather than repeating the entries found therein, I have listed and briefly commented on some of the sources that were especially valuable in preparing this study.

Manuscripts (all in the Library of Congress) include the Mabel Boardman Papers; the James Garfield Jr. Papers, especially the diaries; the Gifford Pinchot Papers; the Elihu Root Papers; and copies of various documents from the Taft Papers, prepared by Henry Pringle and later deposited in the Library of Congress as part of the Pringle Papers.

The most significant collection of printed manuscripts is the eight-volume *Roosevelt Letters*, edited by Elting Morison and John Blum (1950–1954). Volumes 4–8 contain a great deal of material about Taft of three different types: the letters to him from TR; TR's comments concerning Taft in other correspondence, which become increasingly numerous especially after 1910, and the editorial annotations in the Morison–Blum volumes, which are as significant as the letters themselves.

Portions of my earlier chapters relied on Professor Paul Kramer's analysis of American policy in the Philippines, *The Blood of Government (2006)*, and William Wiecek's classic account of *the Lost World of Classical Legal Thought (1998)*. Although this volume focuses on William Howard Taft, TR of necessity represents an inescapable counterpart to Taft's career after 1900. While there is a vast collection of works about TR, sustained scholarly interest in Taft has been minimal, with the important exception of Lewis Gould. Within the expanded output on TR, the three volumes by Edmund Morris concerning TR reflect this trend. See *The Rise of Theodore Roosevelt (1979)*, *Theodore Rex (2001)*, and *Colonel Roosevelt (2010)*. Unfortunately, Morris's books offer few additional insights into the complex relationship between TR and Taft. I found two works on TR more helpful: Kathleen Dalton's book,

Theodore Roosevelt: A Strenuous Life (2002), and Patricia O'Toole's study, *When Trumpets Call: TR after the White House*, (2005).

Similarly, works on progressivism have focused on TR and Wilson, while omitting Taft. Two recent studies, however, have pointed to a changing interpretation. Although perhaps I go further than Morton Keller in attempting to link Taft to a progressive context, I found Keller's recent volume, *America's Three Regimes* (2007), persuasive and perceptive concerning his comments on Taft. Although concluding that Taft was "a pallid second act after TR's star turn," Keller claims that "Taft in his way was a Progressive president" (p. 182). See also Sidney Milkis, *Theodore Roosevelt, the Progressive Party, and the Transformation of American Democracy (2009)*. While Miklis's title does not so imply, he has a number of insights in his study concerning Taft's take on progressivism. Miklis implies that the Taft emphasis on traditional institutions and values might be preferable "to a modern form of conservatism apparently at war against the progressive state" (p. 292). No serious student of the Taft era can study it without benefiting from the extensive published scholarship of Lewis Gould. His *Four Hats in the Ring* (2009) and the *Taft Presidency (2010)* are very significant, and if my own view of Taft varies slightly from Gould's, it is more in nuance than in disagreement.

Index

CPSIA information can be obtained at www.ICGtesting.com
Printed in the USA
LVOW080615150812

294362LV00003B/5/P